D0222923

Slaves, Masters, and the Art of Authority in Plautine Comedy

Slaves, Masters, and the Art of Authority in Plautine Comedy

Kathleen McCarthy

PRINCETON UNIVERSITY PRESS

PRINCETON AND OXFORD

Copyright © 2000 by Princeton University Press
Published by Princeton University Press, 41 William Street,
Princeton, New Jersey 08540
In the United Kingdom: Princeton University Press,
3 Market Place, Woodstock, Oxfordshire OX20 1SY

All Rights Reserved

Second printing, and first paperback printing, 2004
Paperback ISBN 0-691-11785-3

The Library of Congress has cataloged the cloth edition of this book as follows

McCarthy, Kathleen, 1962–
Slaves, masters, and the art of authority in Plautine comedy /
Kathleen McCarthy.
p.   cm.
Includes bibliographical references (p.) and index.
ISBN 0-691-04888-6 (cl. : alk. paper)
1. Plautus, Titus Maccius—Criticism and interpretation.
2. Master and servant in literature.
3. Literature and society—Rome.   4. Authority in literature.
5. Slavery in literature.   6. Comedy.   I. Title.
PA6585 .M38 2000
872'.01—dc21   00-022418

British Library Cataloging-in-Publication Data is available

This book has been composed in Janson

Printed on acid-free paper. ∞

www.pupress.princeton.edu

Printed in the United States of America

3   5   7   9   10   8   6   4   2

In Memoriam

D. McC.
iucundum lumen ademptum

CONTENTS

Preface	ix
Abbreviations and Conventions	xiii
CHAPTER I	
The Crowded House	3
Double Vision	7
Powerful Pleasures	17
The Art of Authority	29
CHAPTER II	
The Ties That Bind: *Menaechmi*	35
Rebellion Meets Reconciliation	40
The Cast of Characters	61
CHAPTER III	
Love's Labour's Lost: *Casina*	77
A Rake's (Lack of) Progress	84
Comic Husbands and Wives	115
CHAPTER IV	
A Kind of Wild Justice: *Persa*	122
The Three Faces of Toxilus	127
The Limits of Farce	158
CHAPTER V	
Truth Is the Best Disguise: *Captivi*	167
The Theater of Truth	180
In Dialogue with Farce	201
CONCLUSION	
The Slave's Image in the Master's Mind	211
Works Cited	215
Index of Plautine Passages	221
General Index	227

PREFACE

THIS BOOK grew out of an attempt to understand the figure of the clever slave in Plautus. The two prevailing views, though often not explicitly articulated by the scholars who hold them, have been that the clever slave in comedy is the product either of masters' patronizing tolerance (letting the slaves have a certain kind of inconsequential heroism, one that affords them no dignity) or of a half-acknowledged sympathy with the downtrodden (the revenge of the witty on the powerful, so to speak). What I find striking about both of these views is that they assume that the beneficiaries of any pleasures the clever slave brings are the less powerful members of society (the emphasis is usually on slaves and sons in the power of their fathers). But everything we know about the production conditions of comedy suggests that it was by no means a marginalized activity: it was the centerpiece of important festivals of Roman civic religion, and the audience was made up overwhelmingly of citizens. Therefore, I consider it more likely that Plautus' comedy was part of what the political theorist James Scott calls "the public transcript": the language and actions that make up the communal life of the Romans and display the dominant's own naturalized view of their domination (i.e., the public transcript is a performance of the dominant ideology). Although we might assume that the purpose of such a performance is to indoctrinate subordinates, in doing so we are in danger of making the mistake of the gullible spectator at a magic show: we are training our gaze where the white-gloved hand directs us, instead of focusing our attention on what the magician is trying to distract us from. Scott raises the possibility that the public transcript might function as "a kind of self-hypnosis within ruling groups to buck up their courage, improve their cohesion, display their power . . ." (1990: 67). My project in this book is to describe the investment socially dominant Romans had in Plautine comedy.

But my path toward this goal is a rather crooked one. My argument at its most fundamental level has to do with the messiness and complexity of both Plautine comedy itself and its social effects. I believe that the most effective way to free ourselves from the hegemonic persuasion of the public transcript is to question the very categories it uses to divvy up experience. Therefore, far from accepting either "Plautine comedy" or "socially dominant Romans" as transparent, objective facts in the world, my argument is concerned with exposing the processes by which each of these concepts comes to have the appearance of cohesion, in the face of the multiplicity and ambiguity that characterize them. At the literary level of the plays themselves, I will argue for understanding Plautine comedy as the dialogic interaction of two very different modes of comedy, a naturalistic mode and a farcical mode. Not only does each of these modes operate with a distinctive set of plot devices, character types, and stylistic preferences, but each also has a distinctive way of envisioning the functioning of authority in the world. The naturalistic mode sees the hierarchies that order society as grounded in universal and transcendent moral certainties, while the farcical mode sees these hierarchies as merely arbitrary. At the social historical level of the audience, I will argue that each member of the audience cannot be assigned unambiguously to a single, stable niche in Roman society but occupies a number of different (and shifting) positions in relation to domination in his or her daily life. The implication of this more complex view of the status of individual audience members is that they cannot then be assumed to have any simple and enduring investment in either the maintainence or subversion of hegemonic claims; each audience member has a stake in both the clever slave's rebellion and the master's reassertion of control in the finale. Thus, the doubleness of the literary modes of Plautine comedy serves the bifurcated interests of the audience.

After an introductory chapter, in which the arguments outlined here will be more fully explained and supported, the bulk of this book consists of readings of four plays, *Menaechmi*, *Casina*, *Persa*, and *Captivi*. It may be surprising that, although I said the original impulse of this investigation was the desire to understand the clever slave, I am not focusing on the plays most obviously organized around this figure, plays such as the *Pseudolus* or *Mostellaria*. Instead, I have chosen to focus on plays where the dynamic processes of Plautine comedy can be seen in action most clearly, plays in which the desire of each audience member to inhabit simultaneously the positions of rebel and authority figure comes closest to being expressed explicitly on stage. In these four plays, the hero is an illogical and tenuously balanced combination of dominant and subordinate; by charting the trials and triumphs of such heroes, their attempts to negotiate the contradictory bases of their heroism, I will describe the joint effect of the literary dialogue between naturalism and farce and the ideological dialogue between dominant and subordinate. In all four cases, slavery provides the language and imagery through which the broader principles of domination are explored. Although the specific practices, values, and ideas that clustered around slavery in ancient Rome will form an important element of my overall argument, I believe that slavery functions in Plautus as a medium for the fantasies and anxieties of the mostly citizen audience, much as slaves themselves functioned as instruments through which masters achieved their desires. In resisting the temptation to read the clever slave as "about slavery," I am again trying to counter the text's sleight-of-hand, trying to look where it is not pointing.

I would like to take this opportunity to acknowledge the many teachers, students, colleagues and friends who have helped me over the course of writing this book. This project started life as a dissertation at Princeton, where the advice and support of my advisor, Elaine Fantham, and readers, Jim Luce and Alessandro Schiesaro, were invaluable. I would also like to thank others at Princeton who helped to shape the perspective from which I write, especially Richard Martin, Froma Zeitlin, Brent Shaw, Nancy Worman, Hilary Mackie, and Andre Lardinois. The next stage of development took place in Chicago, where I owe debt of gratitude for support to John Wright, Dan Garrison, Ahuvia Kahane, Maggie La Barbera, Deborah Weiss, Fred Whiting, and, above all, Michael Dickinson. The final and perhaps most important period in the life of this project has been its West Coast maturation, when it had the good fortune to be read and critiqued by Mark Griffith, Leslie Kurke, Erich Gruen, W. S. Anderson, Maurizio Bettini, William Fitzgerald, Carole Newlands, Sander Goldberg, and the students of my seminar on Plautus (Julie Anderson, Pattie Wareh, Chris Geissman, Laura Gibbs, Bill Jennings, Jed Parsons, Dylan Sailor, Joe Shepter, Haley Way, and Alan Zeitlin). Thanks also to Pat Larash for her editorial assistance. This book is dedicated to the memory of my brother, Daniel McCarthy, who taught me lessons he had not learned himself.

ABBREVIATIONS AND CONVENTIONS

PLAUTUS' PLAYS will be abbreviated as follows: *Amphitruo* (*Am*), *Asinaria* (*As*), *Aulularia* (*Aul*), *Bacchides* (*Bac*), *Captivi* (*Capt*), *Casina* (*Cas*), *Cistellaria* (*Cist*), *Curculio* (*Cur*), *Epidicus* (*Epid*), *Menaechmi* (*Men*), *Mercator* (*Mer*), *Miles Gloriosus* (*Mil*), *Mostellaria* (*Mos*), *Persa* (*Per*), *Poenulus* (*Poen*), *Pseudolus* (*Ps*), *Rudens* (*Rud*), *Stichus* (*St*), *Trinummus* (*Trin*), *Truculentus* (*Truc*), *Vidularia* (*Vid*).

The text of Plautus quoted and referred to throughout is Lindsay's Oxford Classical Text of 1904–1905. Scene and act divisions were not part of the original texts but introduced by later critics; however, sometimes these divisions can conveniently designate a discrete section of the play's action, and in these cases I will use them in addition to or instead of line numbers in my discussions.

Although I have translated or paraphrased all Latin that appears in the main text, I have chosen to use the Latin labels for stock characters, in part because each of these labels carries a very specific set of associations with it, as I will discuss in the chapters that follow. (The one exception to this is that I use the Anglicized "parasite" for *parasitus*.) The following is a list of all these labels as they will appear, with an English translation.

uxor (pl. *uxores*) — wife (also *matrona* [pl. *matronae*] for a wife, specifically in her role as the manager of the household)
uxor dotata (pl. *uxores dotatae*) — wife with a dowry
senex (pl. *senes*) — lit. old man, but age is less important than the fact of being a head of household
senex amator (pl. *senes amatores*) — such an old man as above, in love
adulescens (pl. *adulescentes*) — young man
meretrix (pl. *meretrices*) — prostitute
pseudomeretrix (pl. *pseudomeretrices*) — a young girl who has been raised as a prostitute, but is the daughter of a citizen family
leno (pl. *lenones*) — pimp
lena (pl. *lenae*) — madam, bawd
servus (pl. *servi*) — slave
servus callidus (pl. *servi callidi*) — clever slave
virgo (pl. *virgines*) — an unmarried girl (implicitly from a citizen family)

Slaves, Masters, and the Art of Authority
in Plautine Comedy

Chapter I

THE CROWDED HOUSE

The purpose of poetry is to remind us
how difficult it is to remain just one person,
for our house is open, there are no keys in the doors,
and invisible guests come in and out at will.
—Czeslaw Milosz, "Ars Poetica?"

PLAUTUS is a poet whose house is open to a bewildering variety of guests. Earnest ingénues and cynical tricksters make themselves at home there; both masters and slaves proclaim themselves to be honored inmates. The plots that focus on reweaving familial bonds and the triumph of love are often almost derailed by the emphasis on deception tricks and gags through which these plots are brought on stage; likewise, the socially conservative values of such familial plots, the ways that they support existing hierarchies, must coexist with the charmingly subversive intelligence of the clever slave. Conversely, the amoral genius that motivates these clever slaves is never really allowed to embrace its logical conclusion, that is, the revelation that the master's authority is merely arbitrary, and so this liberatory potential goes unrealized as well. In these plays neither the humane mode of naturalistic comedy nor the cynical mode of farcical comedy ever completely frees itself from the other; the two are engaged in an ongoing dialogue. This book is an attempt to interpret the literary and the social effects of Plautus' comedy by analyzing the complex instability that these two contradictory modes of comedy produce.

Let me make clearer what I mean by the difference between these two modes with an example from a familiar play. Early on, Plautus' *Mostellaria* advertises that its theme is the undoing of a young man in love. Through a famous monody in which he compares himself to a dilapidated house, the young lover reveals an intriguingly clear vision about what his amours have cost him, financially and morally (84–156). This monody prepares the audience for a play that will explore the psychological and social tensions between self-indulgence and self-respect. In other words, this young lover's speech fits perfectly with what we have learned to expect in New Comedy,

Epigraph translated by Lillian Valle, with the author.

a conflict of social paradigms that pits the erotic satisfactions of the individual against the moral norms of the community, a conflict that will be resolved in the end by a fortuitous twist that obviates the need for any real choice between the two alternative paradigms. But the *Mostellaria*, in important ways, is not a play that explores these psychological and social tensions. This monody is preceded by a farcical slapstick battle between two slaves, in which the slave who is advocating immorality clearly has the upper hand (1–83). Even more puzzling, after the first act, the *Mostellaria* completely abandons the young lover and develops instead the role of the fiendishly clever slave, a role that has no edifying moral or psychological lessons for us. Indeed, this style of comedy too, even though it is fundamentally different in tone and moral outlook from the tender troubles of the soul-searching young lover, is utterly familiar. In this farcical style of comedy, we are used to seeing downtrodden slaves and sons kick over the traces; they have no remorse for their misdeeds, and moreover they bring to rebellion the attitude that could be summed up in the Latin word *malitia*, a not-too-distant cousin of English "malice." Like the more sentimental mode of comedy, this mode too will sidestep the need for any radical changes in the household, but where naturalistic comedy avoids changes be "revealing" the conflict of values to have been illusory all along, farce acknowledges that conflict is permanent and unchanging: the master forgives the slave for tricking him, but neither does he change his policies of mastery nor does the slave learn the lesson of obedience. The end leaves them coexisting in their opposition just as they began:

> TRANIO: Quid gravaris? quasi non cras iam commeream aliam noxiam:
> ibi utrumque, et hoc et illud, poteris ulcisci probe.
>
> (*Mos* 1178–79)

> TRANIO: Why are you being so difficult? Don't you think I'll commit another wrong tomorrow? Then you can punish me properly for both of them, today's and tomorrow's.

Although it is possible to develop an interpretation of this play that involves explaining away the presence of one or the other of these comic modes, or subordinating one to the other, to do so would inevitably distort the reader's and spectator's experience of the play, which is that each of these modes is presented on its own merits, not as a strawman for the other.[1]

---

[1] Leach (1969c) argues that, anchored by the imagery contrasting the two houses, the play has a serious point to make about the conflict between generations, even though we never see on stage the father and son together, only the slave and master. Although her reading is filled with well-observed points, it still requires that we privilege Frye's notional template of comedy (i.e., that it is about the conflict of generations) over the evidence before our eyes.

One of the major themes of Plautine scholarship has been the attempt to assert a reasoned basis for deciding what is really Plautine in Plautus, for separating out the signal from the noise.

Because Plautus adapted his comedies from Greek plays, and because the fragments we have from these Greek authors seem to fit cleanly the pattern of naturalistic comedy, the problem of inconsistency in Plautus has often been solved by invoking the scripts' foreign origins. If, as many earlier critics argued, Plautus was a semicompetent adapter of Greek New Comedy, then the silly antics of clever slaves in his plays could be seen simply as intrusions into the plots of familial crisis, as (at best) comic relief for the drama of humane values.[2] If, on the other hand, as many more recent critics believe, Plautus was a sly parodist, who used his Greek models merely as a foil for his own carnivalesque wit, then the plots of young love and lost children serve only to provide grist for his mill, and a narrative framework for trickery and rebellion.[3] But even this quick sketch of the *Mostellaria* shows that neither of these two views can account completely for the overall effect of this play, in which both comic modes perform positive functions. Furthermore, these explanations assume a neat boundary between naturalistic Greek comedy and farcical Roman Comedy, an assumption that relies heavily on the meager evidence for Greek New Comedy (of which we have many fragments but only one complete play, Menander's *Dyskolos*, and only one passage of about one hundred lines where a Greek original can be compared with its Latin adaption, Menander's *Dis Exapaton* with Plautus' *Bacchides*). If we explain the presence of naturalistic comedy in Plautus by appealing to reconstructions of Greek New Comedy, we reduce the complexity of both the Greek and the Roman texts, by ignoring the possible variation within the Greek corpus, and by assuming that naturalism has only a negative function in Plautus. What is needed is not a finer gauge for separating the genuine Plautus from the distracting accretions but a way of theorizing the text as we have it, as an irreducibly complex structuring of these varied elements.

I am suggesting two ways of thinking about the coexistence of these modes that will help us give a truer description of the Plautine genre. First, rather than seeing this genre as one of these two modes with the (welcome or unwelcome) intrusion of the other, I propose that the genre consists precisely of the combination of them. It is not that Plautus is trying to

---

On the other hand, Segal's (1974) treatment of this play takes no account at all of the striking monody and its dramatic effect.

[2] E.g., Norwood (1932), Webster (1953).

[3] E.g., Anderson (1993), Halporn (1993).

write Menandrian comedy and somehow his farcical style keeps intruding, nor that he wants to write Atellan farces but unaccountably bases them on Greek plots. The knitting together of the two modes is exactly what defines the pied beauty of this genre. The second proposal is to see the coexistence of these two modes as dynamic and self-conscious, a relationship that could be characterized by Bakhtin's concept of dialogism. That is, each mode represents itself in response to the other, with what Bakhtin calls "a sideways glance" (1981: 61). The essence of dialogism is not a polemical argument but rather the self-consciousness of discovering how one's own language and worldview sound and look to another language and worldview.[4]

What function could such a ragtag dramatic form have played in the civic life of the Romans, who gave these frivolous plays a place in some of their most important religious festivals?[5] Especially since the two modes of comedy that constitute this corpus offer two very different attitudes towards authority, we must wonder what was the investment of socially and politically dominant Romans in having such plays performed. I hope to demonstrate here that the combination of the two modes allowed Plautine comedy to fulfill multiple and mutually contradictory fantasies for its audience. What this genre sacrifices in coherence and dramatic unity, it more than compensates for in the powerfully protean dreams it offers, dreams that are at once liberatory and deeply grounded in traditional authority. Thus my view of Plautus' audience also stresses an unresolved multiplicity: just as the plays do not present a unified dramatic mode, neither the audience as a whole nor each individual member of the audience can be assigned to a fixed point in the social network, an assignment that would allow us to label their interests as either in favor of or against maintaining social hierarchies. Because, as I will argue below, masters have a need for rebellion in their own lives, as well as anxiety about the possible rebellion of slaves, this form of comedy both promotes and undermines rebellious fantasies. What I am advocating in the following pages is a way of grappling with the question of elite investment in popular literature by finding a middle path between augmenting the ideological power of the elite (by accepting their own naturalized view of their domination) and giving way to a romantic impulse to see subversion where none existed.

---

[4] Morson and Emerson (1990: 132): "Bakhtin cautions that it is a crude understanding of dialogue to picture it as 'disagreement'. . . ." Unlike the novel (Bakhtin's model system), Roman comedy does not attach each worldview to a specific, highly developed character but retains a greater degree of authorial control in orchestrating the interactions of the two worldviews.

[5] L. R. Taylor (1937) on frequency and organization of these festivals; see also Gruen (1990: 124–57; 1992: 183–222).

Double Vision

It may seem that the description I am giving of Plautine comedy—the free dialogic interaction between two comic modes, without an overarching organizing structure—would make it impossible to think of these plays as literary texts at all. In this section, I will argue for a way of thinking about Plautus' literary activity that will explain how such texts could come to be and how they can be recognizable as dramatic comedy. I will also give a more detailed picture of the stylistic, thematic, and dramatic traits that characterize each mode.

The foundation of my argument is that the literary aesthetic that shaped Plautus' plays was in the strictest sense, "traditional." The fullest exploration of Plautine comedy as the product of a traditional dramatic style is John Wright's *Dancing in Chains: The Stylistic Unity of the* Comoedia Palliata, in which a thorough analysis of the extant fragments demonstrates that the style we think of as characteristically Plautine was in fact the common property of all the authors of this genre, the so-called "comedy in Greek dress." If we accept Wright's argument, we can see that Plautus' theatrical instincts allowed him to combine and recombine a relatively small vocabulary of comic forms into plays that were satisfying dramatic experiences; but this argument in favor of Plautus' traditional aesthetic also means that we should not assume that he wrote with the goal of self-expression. Plautus made his artistic decisions based on a subtle knowledge of the comic forms at his disposal. This is not to say that he knew or cared about the meanings of these forms, but he understood with precision how the audience wanted them to be used, combined, and modified. If the aesthetic that governed Plautus' work was traditional, shared by all the authors of the *comoedia palliata*, it might seem that this kind of tradition precludes the literary self-consciousness we are used to attributing to individual authors (e.g., Ovid). But it is possible that this traditional aesthetic was centered on a distinctively self-conscious stance towards language and literature.[6]

This self-conscious aesthetic can be seen especially in three characteristics of Plautine comedy I will discuss here: stylization (using language for its formal properties as much as for the content it conveys), secondariness

---

[6] Thus, although I agree with many of the observations of Sharrock (1996), particularly the emphasis on literary self-consciousness, I would disagree that this is necessarily the product of a sly individual author pretending to be at a loss for working out a complicated plot. Rather, the evidence for Plautus' traditionality should make us reconsider exactly how sophisticated a tradition can be. Further, Sharrock's argument implies that we can take Plautine comedy seriously as an object for literary study only if we first prove that it is informed by the same aesthetic rules that inform later texts. I think that the plot of *Pseudolus* really is weak in the way that its detractors have noticed but that the specific kind of weakness that Plautus tolerates and why he tolerates it should become the objects of our analysis.

(embracing Latin literature's epigonal relation to Greek literature), and dialogism (juxtaposing comic modes to highlight the incommensurability of languages and worldviews). This description of Plautus' aesthetic has implications for the literary analysis of his corpus, but I will also use it to lay the foundation for a methodology that will allow us to discuss the social effects of these plays without positing (directly or indirectly) the desire of an individual author to make a coherent statement. My thesis is that we can derive from these plays an understanding of the internal logic that governed Plautus' use of these comic forms, a logic that is itself shaped by his audience's broadly held assumptions about social relationships. In fact, because these plays are both traditional and popular, one could argue that they provide a clearer insight into Roman society than those dramas that are the product of an individual playwright who stamps them with his own mark.[7]

Stylization, secondariness, and dialogism are all products of a specific attitude towards language that subtends the peculiarities of early Latin literature as a whole and Plautus in particular. Although it has not been phrased in exactly these terms before, scholars have long recognized the influence that the material aspects of language, especially sound patterns, had on the style of early Latin literature.[8] We can push these observations a little further by positing that this privileging of sound patterns is itself a manifestation of a deeper principle, the consciousness of language as a separate system that is never exactly coextensive with its function as a means of communication.[9] Thus, form (language) and content (meaning) in Plautus and other early Roman authors are juxtaposed rather than unified. The familiar description of Plautus as stylized and secondary (in relation to Greek literature) can be understood in these terms, and these qualities can in turn help us to understand dialogism in Plautine comedy.

[7] To risk a comparison that may seem irrelevant to some readers, I might point to the American TV situation comedy. Like the domestic comedies of Plautus, sit-coms strive to work a given formula in a way that is both utterly familiar and yet satisfyingly different every time; furthermore, the social biases that shape sit-coms (assumptions about class, race, gender, sexuality) almost by definition agree with the biases of the audience since sit-coms "give the people what they want." Examples of scholarly analysis of sit-coms include E. Taylor (1989), Jones (1992); for similar analyses of soap operas, see Mumford (1995).

[8] E.g., Conte (1994: 19–22), Williams (1982: 53–55).

[9] We should consider the possibility that the multilingual atmosphere of archaic Italy created this ability to think outside any individual language, the kind of atmosphere that Bakhtin posits as a necessary condition for the development of the novel: "The new cultural and creative consciousness lives in an actively polyglot world. . . . Languages throw light on each other: one language can, after all, see itself only in the light of another language. . . . In this actively polyglot world, completely new relationships are established between language and its object (that is, the real world) . . ." (1981: 12). See also specifically on Latin's relationship to Greek (1981: 62).

Stylization is Roman comedy's most striking characteristic, as Wright puts it, a "concentration on language as an object of interest in itself . . . " (1974: 36). Again and again in Plautine plays, we have the sense that the stream of words (dappled as it is with alliteration, homoioteleuton, *figurae etymologicae*, etc.) exists for its own sake, not for the expression of any thought but just because it sounds right. Throughout Wright's study of the fragments of the *comoedia palliata*, he repeatedly points to the patterning of language, rather than the content conveyed, as a guiding force in the work of all the authors, not just Plautus.[10] Fraenkel's detailed study of Plautus comes to a similar conclusion. Comparing the opening of Menander's *Heros* and the opening of Plautus' *Curculio*, he writes, "Plautus' dialogue doesn't settle for being a medium; it is, to an extreme degree, an end in itself" (1922: 413 = 1960: 391 [my translation]). Fraenkel explicitly associates this emphasis on language with the centrality that archaic Latin literature grants to the perception of the senses and the experience of the moment.[11] Stylization and the emphasis on sense perception differentiate these texts from those organized around abstract thematic principles and intended to convey ideas, not just dazzle the ear and eye of the beholder.

Like stylization, what I am calling secondariness (the choice to write in reaction to an existing text rather than to start fresh) has long been seen as a definitive quality of Plautus and other early Latin authors.[12] I would argue that this quality, too, grows out of an attitude towards language that acknowledges the gap between form and content. Fraenkel makes only a negative connection between the richness of Plautus' linguistic resources

[10] All the authors, except Terence, that is (1974: 127–51). For stylization in other authors, see (1974: 18, 32, 119–20). Bettini (1985) suggests yet another way in which stylization is constitutive of archaic Roman literature. He argues that it exerted a force by organizing language and marking it as specifically poetic, i.e., that stylization performed for archaic poetry the functions that meter performed in the classical period. This explains why the highly stylized literature of this period exhibits a metrical system that seems to us to be curiously loose or ridden with exceptions.

[11] Fraenkel (1922: 418 = 1960: 395): "Ungemein stark entwickelt aber ist bei ihm [sc. Plautus] die auf der Intensität des sinnlichen Wahrnehmens ruhende Fähigkeit das Charakteristische eines äußeren Vorgangs, einer Bewegung, eines Geräusches oder dergleichen bis in die leisesten Nuancen hinein aufzunehmen, das Aufgenommene in der Phantasie jederzeit zu reproduzieren und dann dafür reiche und erstaunlich präzise sprachliche Ausdrucksmittel von suggestiver Kraft zu finden."

[12] Rather than finding a new, more positive term than "secondariness" to describe Latin literature's relation to Greek literature (a move that would, I fear, imply that my object is the aesthetic recuperation of early Latin literature), I am asking the reader to think of secondariness as a value-neutral term that merely describes a literary process. Although he chooses to reject the term "secondary" to describe this quality of Roman literature and myth, Feeney's recent comments on the process of Roman appropriation of Greek cultural forms comes close to my own; he proposes "the Romans as founders of an active and dynamic trans-cultural sensibility" (1998: 75).

and his use of Greek New Comedy as a model. He believes that Plautus'
skills did not include the ability to create a plot line from scratch; in order
to make up for this deficit, the Roman playwright turned to the well-made
plots of Hellenistic Greek comedy (1922: 405 = 1960: 383). But we can
also imagine a positive reason for his use of Greek models. The view of
language and literature attributed to Plautus here is exactly the kind of
perspective that would lead to an interest in translation, reworkings, parody, adaptation. All these forms of literature depend on the fact that language and the content it expresses are not coextensive: on one hand, content does not exist only in language, since it can be translated or expressed
in different words; on the other hand, these new, secondary texts never just
repeat the primary text but in reexpressing the content inevitably introduce
new tones and emphases. These secondary texts derive their power from
the difference between two kinds of meaning: the meaning that is expressed
through form and the meaning that exists in form. The latter kind of meaning is, by definition, untranslatable. This literary perspective that exploits
the gap between form and content differs profoundly from one that asserts
the unity of form and content.[13]

This attitude towards form and content in language defines the genre in
which Plautus works, creating a body of plays written in stylized Latin but
based on Greek texts, which were originally composed with a very different
attitude towards language; thus the dialogism I am positing for Plautus is
a congener of the more familiar Plautine characteristics of stylization and
secondariness. But even after the archaic Roman penchant for form, sepa-
rable from content, has operated by using a foreign (in every sense) play
as a model, its presence can be felt in the comedies themselves. The plays
highlight the separability of form and content by exaggerating, rather than
minimizing, the contradictions between the attitudes toward language embodied in Greek New Comedy and in its Roman adaptations.[14] These two

---

[13] Fraenkel (1922: 410 = 1960: 387–88) figures the contrast between the two attitudes as
the contrast between a tree (a growing organism in which the bark and the interior of the
tree are united in an organic relation) and a vase (a plastic object, the surface of which can be
elaborated and that has no essential connection to the content with which it is filled). Wiles
(1991: 213) puts these observations in the context of the modern critical concerns: "[In Plau-
tus] the audience can relish the fact that the word is a sign rather than a meaning. There is a
dissociation between signifier and signified, the word and the thought behind the word. . . .
[In Menander] the audience is not aware of the words but of the 'chosen content,' the thought
behind the words. . . . There is no sense of a dissociation between word and thought, signifier
and signified."

[14] This is different from the position often expressed (e.g., Gratwick [1982], Slater [1985:
166–67], Wiles [1991: 7], Anderson [1993: 3–29]), that the Greek elements in Plautus serve
as a foil to be subverted. I am suggesting that their presence has a fundamental positive function, not just the negative function of providing contrast. Further, I would differentiate between my approach and what we might call a "bricolage" approach, which argues that the

attitudes produce two very different modes of comedy, modes that differ in diction, meter, and characterization but also in their fundamental literary and moral orientation. Because the incommensurability of the two modes is the driving force behind this use of Greek models in the first place, the modes are left unsynthesized and allowed to coexist and interrogate each other. Plautus' text becomes a crowded house, populated by guests who do not necessarily agree either with each other or with their host.[15]

Although both these modes are present in each of Plautus' plays, there is a range across his corpus from plays that are almost entirely in one mode to those almost entirely in the other. To help clarify what I mean by each of these modes, for the moment I will be describing each as it would look if it were on its own.[16] The literary mode of idealizing naturalism represents the familiar world of the spectators, but with all the rough edges smoothed away, and keeps this represented world seamless in itself.[17] This is not to say that this mode is realistic; the occurrences and coincidences that move

---

presence of contradictory attitudes in the text is intended to add up to one meta-meaning and to reveal the untenability of a specific moral position (see, e.g., the moral interpretations of the *Casina* by Forehand [1973] and Slater [1985: 91–93] and of the *Persa* by Chiarini [1979: 219–29]). This approach is unsatisfactory for reasons similar to those I noted for Sharrock's argument (above, note 6), namely, these arguments assume that a text we recognize as literary must be characterized by some kind of underlying coherence, no matter what chaos exists at the surface. Furthermore, consistent with the unwillingness to accept a "broken" or inconsistent text is the unwillingness to accept a poet who may be encumbered by the same kind of moral/political baggage as his contemporaries; thus, it is no coincidence that the readings produced by the bricolage approach save for us the convergence of carnivalesque wit and humane sensibilities.

[15] I find an interesting parallel to this dialogism of modes in Lott's discussion of the mixed musical modes of blackface minstrelsy (1995: 171–86). Relying on the work of Richard Middleton (1983, 1986), Lott distinguishes between "musematic" repetition in music (roughly equivalent to a stylized, nonrepresentational literary style) and "discursive" repetition, which lends itself more to the expression of narrative (roughly equivalent to a representational literary mode). Lott emphasizes, as I do in the Plautine case, that there is no essential connection of slave culture with one kind of style (the musematic in his example, the farcical in mine). What is important in both Plautine comedy and early nineteenth-century blackface minstrelsy is that the mixture of styles allows a member of the audience to see two possible sites for identification, without having to decide finally which represents the self and which the other.

[16] Examples of the most extreme naturalistic plays are *Captivi*, *Rudens*, *Aulularia*, and *Trinummus*. Examples of the most extreme farcical plays are *Pseudolus*, *Casina*, *Bacchides*, and *Miles Gloriosus*.

[17] Wiles' (1991) analysis of Menander serves as an excellent reminder of the subtlety and complexity of naturalism. Wiles characterizes Menandrian theater as the use of idealized, conventional character types (masks) to express ethical and philosophical principles. It is not that Menander is blind to the artificiality of his creations but that the dichotomy between reality and artifice is so useful to him that he strengthens it rather than challenges it, as Plautus does. See esp. 1991: 225.

the plot forward are often extremely improbable. But these improbabilities are clothed in the garb of everyday life. This mode presents itself as somehow "truer" than real life, as if we are seeing the workings of both social life and divine will, without the distracting minutiae of life as lived. The plot device of recognition (*anagnorisis*) is virtually constitutive of this kind of comedy and perfectly expresses its worldview: in these comedies we find out in the end that the identities we took seriously were merely optical illusions, caused by the flux of appearances, and the real identities remained all the time hidden beneath this veneer. Resolutions in this mode have a profound and permanent effect on the characters' lives: families are reunited and marriages contracted. The language and dramatic style of this mode further emphasize this possibility of stripping away the distracting details of life that prevent us from perceiving the truth. The style of naturalistic comedy calls attention to the content of the plays rather than to the play itself, again with the sense that this elegant and self-effacing language is truer to the fundamental truths of life, even though it is, in the narrow sense, "unrealistic."[18] The overall effect of this mode is to make the dramatic illusion as powerful as possible, as if we are spying on the characters through a one-way mirror, rather than watching a play scripted by an author and performed by actors.

The second mode, which I will call the farcical mode, both in its stylized language and in its frequent rupture of the dramatic illusion, draws attention to the theatrical artifice itself, undermining any attempt to focus on a transcendent meaning of the play.[19] In this mode, form triumphs over content: the reader and the spectator are regaled by a stream of patterned language, slapstick bits, and stereotyped characters—all leading exactly nowhere, in dramatic terms. Just as the recognition scene revealed the idealizing mode's attitude toward truth, in the farcical mode trickery is given pride of place. This plot device presumes that the confusions of life are neither created nor dispelled by divine workings but by the tendentious and half-baked schemes of individuals. In sharp contrast to the resolutions of the naturalistic mode, those of the farcical mode never change anything fundamental to the characters' situation: the trick is revealed, but the clever

---

[18] Wiles (1991: 223–24) on Menander: "The actual words efface themselves, throwing attention on the *legomena*, the 'what-is-said.' Every trace of the actor's body is effaced, beneath mask, cloak and tights. Body-language is never remarkable in itself, but draws attention to the situation represented. Concealed behind the figures physically represented on stage is deemed to be an *ethos*." Cf. again Fraenkel (1922: 413 = 1960: 390–91).

[19] Wiles (1991: 225). Grimal (1975b: 151): "Plaute est parfaitement conscient des limites de cette prétendue vérité dont se souciant les poètes comiques grecs. Il préfère, pour lui, le *ludus* barbare, qui pénètre plus avant dans le réel, en surmontant, même si pour cela, il est nécessaire de bousculer les conventions de la pseudo-vérité." This is true, but it ignores such Plautine plays as the *Captivi* and *Trinummus* that not only show a preference for "pseudo-vérité" but also manage to overturn the nonteleological conventions of farce.

slave remains a slave, looking forward to another round of trickery without consequences. This literary mode is obviously more fantastic than the other, relying on elaborate language and disguise tricks, and yet in its willingness to leave loose ends untied, it could be seen as more realistic; or at least, it is more faithful to a vision of reality that sees the details of life as the real thing, not as static that is clouding the picture of the real, underlying pattern. And yet, this mode continually reminds us of the play's status as an artifact, created by an author and embedded in a system of literary conventions, both through the emphasis on "artificial" language and dramatic construction and through the sometimes explicit identification of the playwright with the clever trickster.

The difference between these two literary modes is partially obscured in the plays because they share a common impulse toward rebellion. Both forms of comedy tend to privilege youth over age and freedom over constraint, a property of comedy that Northrop Frye (1957) elevated to its defining characteristic. But this similarity masks a much more important difference. In the naturalistic form of comedy, whether instantiated in the romantic plot type or the plot type of the misanthrope (comedy of humors), this rebellion is in the service of a more humane, more flexible, happier society. The young lovers overcome the narrow-mindedness of their parents, or the miser is taught the value of generosity to point the way towards a better life, what Frye calls "paradigmatic freedom" (1957: 169). In the farcical mode, on the other hand, the rebellion is its own justification. Far from being justified by humane values, farcical trickery is a mockery of these values. Many of the fathers who are hoodwinked in Plautine comedy are not oppressive tyrants, and most of the young lovers are almost anonymous in their lack of a distinctive personality. The interest in the deception comedies falls primarily on the scheming slave, who is motivated neither by love nor by a desire to correct the flaws of the misanthrope but by a sheer desire for fun. Thus even in their common impulse to overturn the authority of the *paterfamilias*, the two modes of comedy clearly differentiate themselves.

The difference in the two kinds of rebellion gives us a way to characterize the differing moral/ideological stances of the two modes. The moral perspective associated with naturalistic comedy affirms the real contemporary social code by exalting those who exhibit the virtues of nobility, generosity, piety. This perspective constructs a form of authority based on these virtues and on behavior that is self-assured, honest, and proof of an inborn nobility.[20] As with this mode's attitude towards plot and style, its moral perspective is a better version of real life (a version in which people really observe

---

[20] Whether this nobility of character coincides with nobility of birth is a charged issue that is usually avoided by a plot twist. For an extensive discussion of this problem, see below, chap. 5, on the *Captivi*.

the moral laws they claim to value) but does not replace the values of real
life with a new and different set of values. Because this mode presents itself
as a disinterested mirror of reality rather than merely the poet's idiosyn-
cratic view, the moral values it champions take on the status of transcendent, uncreated truth. To take the example of *anagnorisis*, this mode's defining plot device: we are left at the end of recognition plays believing that
wrongs have been righted, mistakes corrected, by a divine force that will
always prevail; these plays draw our attention away from the long time
when everyone was living in error, treating a freeborn girl as a slave and
focus instead on the moment of realignment with the underlying, persistent truth. Therefore, it would not be too much to say that these plays
perform the function of hegemonic discourse: they make the world around
us seem to be the one that is destined by divine (or superhuman, at least)
will. There is a benevolent Providence, these plays say, that operates reli-
ably to correct human error, and if that is so, then the way things are must
be the way they ought to be.

Opposed to this moral perspective is that of farce, which reverses normal
hierarchies through the fantasy of the slave as hero. This perspective reverses the identities of those in power and even exalts virtues exactly opposed to those exalted by the idealizing perspective. Duplicity, aggressiveness, and boldness win the day.[21] This inverted authority is fundamentally
linked to the fictive world of poetry. First, the cleverness of the hero, and
his pride in the power of his bare-faced lies, is explicitly compared by Plautus to the inventiveness of the poet.[22] Furthermore, just as the first type of
authority is sanctioned by the audience's everyday experience, the second
type is sanctioned by the familiar fictive world presented in this conventional body of comedy.[23] Even more telling, these plots undermine the nat-
uralness or inevitableness of contemporary social structures by showing
everything to be contingent, the result of accumulated choices and actions.
Although the subversiveness is limited by the slave hero's ultimate failure
to challenge his status, this mode does contain the germ of a genuinely
subversive idea, as if the trickery plots are written from the perspective of
a sharp-eyed and unsentimental subordinate who sees the claims of hege-
mony for what they are: the attempt on the part of the dominant to pretend

---

[21] Chiarini (1979: 54, 61, *passim*), Petrone (1977: 19–20), and Anderson (1993: 88–106)
have very good analyses of the concept of *malitia* as the ruling principle of Plautine antimoralism.

[22] Slater (1985) gives ample evidence and a thorough description of this pattern.

[23] Wright (1974: 47–48, 105–6) on the existence of clever slaves in other authors of Roman
comedy; Fraenkel (1922: 231–50 = 1960: 223–41) on the clever slave as the distinctively
Roman contribution. Contra: Spranger (1984). Slater's (1985) emphasis on the concept of
comic heroism and its use of the theater (rather than real life) as the implicit referent of "life"
in Plautus is the best analysis of this phenomenon.

that their domination is the nature of things, not an edifice that has been constructed and is always in need of maintenance.

I have described these modes as each would be if it alone controlled any given play; but in order to read Plautine comedy as we have it, we have to understand the way the two modes work in a dialogic interaction. Although the relation is not always polemical, each mode does consistently present itself in response to the other, highlighting the differences in dramatic style and worldview that separate them. An aesthetic that seeks rather than avoids inconsistency in tone, style, characterization, and plot, and that organizes plays by reference more to language than to content, calls for a new kind of interpretive methodology. The principles of literary interpretation usually employed to describe and analyze Roman literature, especially when we assume the primacy of content and the author's desire to convey a transcribable meaning, will not alone suffice for a full treatment of Plautine comedy. These principles will take us most of the way towards an understanding of those plays in which the naturalistic mode predominates. But even in these cases they must be augmented by principles derived from a dialogic aesthetic. For the most farcical plays, which are close to being incomprehensible if we use only the values of naturalistic theater, the principles of a criticism based on a division of style from content will offer a more effective point of departure.

First, the division of style from content means that individual elements of Plautine comedy—everything from characterization to a way of phrasing a question—are influenced more powerfully by the system of comic convention than by any content-based meaning of the play itself. Precisely because, as Wright demonstrates, the genre of *comoedia palliata* is so stylistically uniform, we must see stylistic choices as growing out of a relationship to other texts rather than out of a relationship to the thematic content of the play itself. The conventionality of Plautine comedy continually reminds the audience of the artificiality of the play they are watching by emphasizing that the play is a text reflecting other texts. This stance rejects any attempt to pretend that the characters are real or that their words have any indissoluble link to their essences. It emphasizes the artifice of the characters (by reminding the audience of other plays) and the manipulability of their language (by divorcing their words from any attempt to express an individual essence).

As a result, while each play has its own constellation of motifs (both substantive and stylistic), an individual play cannot be fully understood without reference to the corpus as a whole. The practical consequence for methodology requires the reader to read "horizontally" across the corpus, in addition to reading each play as a unit. Only by cataloging the repeated instances of a particular plot situation, character type, or speech pattern can we recover the artistic context within which each of Plautus' literary decisions was made. Bettini's comprehensive study of Plautine plots has shown the truth of this assertion at the level of the action in the plays and in the distribution of functions among the character types.[24]

Of these "horizontal" aspects in each play, perhaps the most important are the plot types, patterns of situations that help the audience orient itself with reference to the characters and expected outcomes of each play. Usually the very first scene of each play offers enough clues to the spectator or reader familiar with the genre to define the heroes, the villains, the major lines of the action, and the outcome. If this is so, it is equally obvious that suspense is not among the pleasures that Plautus offers his audience. In place of suspense, we get the pleasure of experiencing an extremely subtle teasing, as the author capriciously alternates between fulfilling and disappointing our expectations. The clarity of the system of conventions and the obviousness with which these conventions are invoked allow Plautus the capability of joining two seemingly incompatible plot lines (plot lines, for example, that identify opposed characters as the heroes).[25]

Further, because these plays adhere so strictly to a limited set of conventions, the audience gains a deep and precise knowlede of the fictive world represented in Plautine comedy. Since the interaction between the two types of authority depends in part on the normalcy of the slave's power in farce, the stronger the audience's impression of the workings of this world, the more effective the slave's authority. Again and again we see the same pattern of actions that create and support the clever slave in his power. Thus, this body of comedy makes the audience automatically use a set of assumptions about what is likely and what is unlikely that is the exact opposite of the set of assumptions they would use in everyday life.

The second methodological implication of this aesthetic is that it requires us to explore the text's social meaning in ways that do not rely on authorial argument or opinion. If Plautus constructs plays on the basis of the opportunities they offer for the juxtaposition of contradictory literary and moral outlooks, we cannot expect that these plays will offer consistent judgments or opinions. But just because these plays were not intended as social commentary does not mean that we should ignore the evidence they

---

[24] Bettini (1982). These functions in turn have great effect on the surface details of the particular play. For example, a plot aimed at the tricking of a rival or a pimp will always stress a linear trajectory, in which the trickery is not rescinded at the end but is permanent. Plots that involve tricking a father, on the other hand, stress a conciliatory conclusion in which the trick is forgiven and order restored.

[25] Konstan (1983) provides the best example of how rich an analysis can come from perceiving the interaction of two (or more) traditional plot lines. See esp. his readings of *Asinaria Cistellaria*. The only way I would disagree with these readings is to argue that these shifts need not add up to one meaningful whole but might result in plays that have no center. See below my treatment of the *Casina*, chap. 3.

give us of social life. The view of Plautine comedy as a crowded house may seem to imply that it has a liberating effect, since it allows a point of view that critiques naturalized social structures to take a place beside the point of view that performs that naturalizing. I suggest that this dialogue does chip away at authority's claim to be natural and uncreated, but, in part because the dominant themselves are among the beneficiaries of this effect, it does not really undermine authority in any substantial way.[26] In the next section I will describe more fully how the specifically Roman form of authority works, especially what use it makes of comedy and what use comedy makes of it. What I offer here is not a social historian's reading of Plautus; it is a literary reading that analyzes the effect of social forces in this system of comic forms and, I hope, opens up new ways for Roman historians and historians of slavery to make use of these texts.

Powerful Pleasures

> It is not always the case that pleasure . . . entirely
> coincides with ideological intention; it has an
> underestimated ability to take its captives in wayward
> political directions . . .
> —Eric Lott, *Love and Theft*

The link between the literary dialogue of comic modes that I have described above and the social effects of comedy can be seen most clearly if we focus on understanding the pleasures that Plautine comedy offered its audience. First we should define to whose desires these pleasures catered. Because these plays were performed at publicly funded religious festivals, it is difficult to categorize them as the self-expression of those who were normally without a voice in Roman public life.[27] It is much more likely that

---

[26] This shows, contrary to Bakhtin's own sense, that dialogism is compatible with the maintainence of authority, what Lott (1995: 146) calls the "less than liberatory effects" of grotesque realism. I will show here that Plautine comedy gives an example of dialogic openness as part of an ongoing successful domination and therefore that dialogism is not necessarily connected to a more humane social practice. In view of Bakhtin's overall optimism/denial (Morson and Emerson [1990: 470]), it should not surprise us that he did not emphasize this possibility.

[27] Since Plautine comedy was both traditional and public entertainment, and since it was funded by the aediles, I think it improbable that it expressed viewpoints at odds with those accepted as mainstream. As for the possibility that it voiced the viewpoint of slaves in some allegorical way, we must ask whether these servile viewpoints were intended to be understood by the nonservile members of the audience or not. In the first case, if masters are intended to feel the sting of these barbs, then we have to ask, again, why the free population as a whole would continue to fund and attend such performances (and clamor for more) if they were insulted by them. If the airing of slaves' viewpoints is not intended to be understood by anyone other then slaves, why would slaves choose a public performance, where the majority of the audience is made up of nonslaves, for their literary expression of solidarity? The com-

they formed part of what the political theorist James Scott has called "the public transcript" (1990), those actions and words that dominant and subordinate groups use when they are together. By definition, this public transcript expresses the dominant's view of their own domination; the contribution of subordinates to this transcript is circumscribed by the imperative that the transcript as a whole preserve a view of the existing social order as both natural and just. The theatrical metaphor that Scott uses is helpful (though, for our purposes we need to keep it separate from what is actually going on in dramatic comedy): "The dominant never control the stage absolutely, but their wishes normally prevail. In the short run, it is in the interest of the subordinate to produce a more or less credible performance, speaking the lines and making the gestures he knows are expected of him. The result is that the public transcript is—barring a crisis—systematically skewed in the direction of the libretto, the discourse, represented by the dominant" (1990: 4). I am emphasizing the logic for thinking of Plautine comedy as part of the public transcript because it gives a firm basis for arguing that it is the desires of the dominant in Roman society, rather than those of subordinates, that exert the primary force shaping these plays.

The next step is to ask in what did the pleasures of Plautine comedy consist. Following Eric Lott's (1995) arguments about the pleasures that blackface minstrelsy offered to white, Northern, working-class audiences, we should be wary of explanations that imagine masterly audiences to be completely in control of the comic fantasies that entertained them. Lott's argument about minstrelsy situates the forces militating against ideological control in tensions surrounding race, class, and sexuality. For the nineteenth-century Northern urban audiences he is studying, these axes of hierarchized difference are embedded within a culture that placed great value on the egalitarian and individualistic principles of democracy and capitalism. For the Plautine audience, on the other hand, such axes are embedded within a fundamentally hierarchical and authoritarian culture, a culture that never shrank from explicitly ranking people and assigning unequal rights and responsibilities. Roman society is fractured by divisions within divisions within divisions, each one marking out difference as well as marking out a hierarchical relation. These mutually complicating divisions include gender, juridical status, census rank, geographical provenance,

---

parison with fables, for which this kind of argument has been made (Bradley [1987: 150–53], Hopkins [1993]) only strengthens my point with respect to Plautine comedy, because fables are the ideal literary form to be passed around within the slave community without ever having to be performed before a mixed audience. Also, for all these arguments, we must ask how not just Plautus but all the authors of this traditional form of comedy (since both Wright and Fraenkel argue that the clever slave is endemic to the tradition) came to be so familiar with the viewpoints of slaves and so sympathetic to it. Did Naevius and Caecilius also take a turn at that mill?

wealth, and cultural/intellectual achievement.[28] Furthermore, each of these bases of assigning social value does not divide the Romans into "haves" and "have nots" but establishes a finely calibrated scale on which each person is placed above some and below others. The result was that the ranking of each person in Rome was extremely open and unapologetic but could never be fixed in anything more than a relative and ad hoc way, since the multiple scales on which value was measured could very well be in conflict.[29] Just as important as this complex pattern of hierarchy is the dynamic quality of it. Because status could be defined in so many different ways and because status was so important in the functioning of Roman society, the contesting of status, the continual battle to define and assert oneself in preference to others, was a defining feature of Roman life. In such a society (almost) no one is permanently and universally subordinated and (almost) no one is permanently and universally dominant.[30] Thus the audience of a Plautine comedy is not made up of "masters" per se but of spectators, each of whom enjoys and struggles against a contradictory cluster of privileges and obligations made concrete in a variety of relationships defined both upwards and downwards. When analyzing what such spectators might want from comedy, we should take account of their fears and vulnerabilities as much as of their powers and self-confidence.

The clever slave in comedy serves as a talisman against anxieties having to do specifically with slavery but also, more broadly, against the anxieties

---

[28] The prologue to the *Poenulus* (esp. 17–35) has been seen as particularly rich evidence for the range of social statuses represented in the Plautine audience (Slater [1992], Moore [1995: 114–17]), but even the kinds of labels this prologue encourages us to use (e.g., slave, matron) are oversimplifying, because each individual audience member occupied a variety of different positions in relation to domination in his or her daily life. See now Fitzgerald (2000) for a reading of this prologue that pays close attention to the ways it expresses an implicit decorum of appetites that separates the free from slaves and that connects this decorum to the paradox of repression and freedom that is key to the use of slaves in comedy.

[29] Nicolet (1980: 343–44): "The whole structure of Roman civic life was pervaded and organized by the differential system. Citizens were classified in terms of a civic hierarchy which did not precisely coincide with the spontaneous social hierarchies, nor was it wholly distinct from them." See also Nicolet's insightful description of the census as the backbone of this system, since it assures those ranked that they are full Roman citizens and at the same time enforces clear-cut distinctions among the citizens (1980: 49–50, 57–60).

[30] This raises the possibility that we should compare Roman slavery not only to the slave systems of the New World but also to other slave systems that, like the Roman, are embedded in more generalized systems of hierarchy rather than within a capitalist democracy. Cooper's (1977) study makes explicit the differences between the East African plantation system and those in the New World. In particular, he emphasizes the personalization of power and the fact that the allowances and prohibitions that structured slaves' everyday lives were fundamentally shaped by the surrounding social context (1977: 241–42). Cooper's astute treatment of this topic frees him from the dichotomy of generosity/harsh treatment in assessing the actions of the slave owners in such a personalized society, a dichotomy that is singularly unproductive.

that arose from the constant need to jockey for position in the many mi-
nutely gradated hierarchies that ordered Roman society. The clever slave
presents a character who is specifically marked with the attributes of slavery
and yet stands in for all those who are actually or potentially subordinated
to others (in other words, the whole audience). This heroic character, then,
slides back and forth between being a figure of difference for the majority
of the audience and a figure of sameness, a site for sympathetic identification. It should be clear that my understanding of this social effect stands
in stark contrast to the widely accepted "safety-valve" theory of comic rebellion,[31] that is, that fictive rebellion is permitted by the dominant as a
way of bleeding off the pressure of resentment among the subordinated
(especially slaves and sons). I am arguing that since everyone is subordinated in some sense, the desire to participate imaginatively in staged rebellion does not divide the audience (say, between masters and slaves or between fathers and sons) but unifies it. Furthermore, the doubleness of the
comic slave himself, his ability to be seen as both "different" and "same,"
allows this figure to allay each audience member's anxieties about his/her
relations downward in hierarchical scales (distancing oneself from the
clever slave as different, as a charming but ultimately infantile trickster)
and upward (identifying with the clever slave as same, as a smart subordinate who sees through the pretensions of those who claim superiority).

Nor is the use of the slave to effect the conjoining of these two audience
responses coincidental. Since comedy is part of Rome's "public transcript,"
it makes sense that the citizen population used this opportunity both to
reassert their difference from slaves (and, in doing so, reaffirm the essential
meaninglessness of slave resistance) and to enjoy under the cover of this
very difference the pleasures of liberatory release (without ever having to
admit that they, not just their slaves, were in need of such release). In order
to see masters taking pleasure in the clever slaves' antics, of course, we

---

[31] For Plautus, see esp. Segal (1987). Parker (1989) provides a variant on the safety-valve
theory that brings his argument close to mine here, by positing that the son's improper desires
to rebel against the father go unpunished because they are are routed through the anarchic
clever slave: "The audience can identify with the young man, who is allowed to step outside
of the power of his father, even to make the Oedipal wish for his father's death, yet incurs no
guilt and is reunited in the proper order of family and property. That guilt is displaced onto
the slave, who satisfies the son's anarchic and libidinous desires, yet is always controlled by
the threat of punishment, but remains unpunished. Power is mocked but mollified. Desire is
satisfied, but without cost. The wish for rebellion is indulged, but the fear of rebellion is
pacified." Two primary differences between my argument and Parker's are that I want to
stress the potential to be subordinated that everyone in the audience feels (including even a
paterfamilias) and that I see no reason to posit the *adulescens* (always the least interesting character in any Plautine play) as the site of identification (we can easily do without this bland
middleman and see that it is the slave himself with whom the audience identifies).

must believe that it is possible for them to identify across the boundary of status with slaves rather than assume that they will always identify with the fictive masters onstage. Although this kind of cross-identification might seem counterintuitive, perhaps we tend to dismiss this possibility precisely because our intuition has been shaped by Roman masters' own loudly voiced denials. It is an important element of the accepted self-presentation of masters that they would never identify with slaves and that they themselves have no need of the liberatory release that comic rebellion provides. Thus the clever slave allows masters to mask, from themselves and others, their investment in fictive rebellion, since this figure also so clearly fulfills the requirements of a comic safety valve operated at the will of the authoritative to placate the powerless.[32]

Slavery, although it represents just part of the continuum of domination, offers an attractive choice for the dramatic presentation of the audience's broader anxieties about subordination for several reasons. First, the slave's social role as an instrument of the master's will makes him or her the perfect choice for a dramatic embodiment of the fantasies of the free population as a whole. The objectification that is fundamental to the use of a person as an instrument easily extends itself into the use of a fictional character as a screen onto which fantasies are projected.[33] Thus the success of the comic slave as a talisman both depends on and, in turn, supports the social practice of treating slaves as instruments and objects.

But the slave's status as a subject is just as important for the dramatic uses of slavery as his or her status as an object. One of the most powerful reasons for putting the relationship between master and slave on center stage to stand in for all relationships of domination is that slavery poses in an extreme form the problem that competing subjectivities create for the effective practice of domination. The crux of slavery is that slaves become useful only when they can combine two contradictory attributes: being as much as possible as extension of the master's persona and yet exercising judgment and skills of their own.[34] In other words, a slave who can merely

---

[32] Scott (1990: 67, *passim*) on elite as consumers of their own fictions of authority. See also Clover (1987) for an argument about identification across gender lines in slasher films, where the femaleness of the person endangered on the screen allows the male spectator to experience this vulnerability but also to shield from himself his investment in it.

[33] See now Fitzgerald's (2000) suggestive readings and analyses of slavery in Latin literature, in which he explores a wide range of functions performed by literary slaves, including this kind of imaginative projection.

[34] This idea finds somewhat different expression in Finley's concept of the "ambiguity of slavery" (1980: 93–122), i.e., that the slave was a human being and yet was denied recognition as such. He writes (1980: 99–100): "I cannot discover that, apart from individual exceptions (and they are extremely rare in the available documentation) awareness of this ambiguity produced doubts or guilt-feelings in the master-class. . . . No guilt-feelings were called for,

carry out explicit orders is useless, and a slave who goes his or her own way is useless. This paradox of slavery finds concise expression in Varro's formulation of the slave as an *instrumentum vocale*, a speaking tool,[35] a formulation that expresses both the slave's instrumentality and his or her persistent subjectivity. But this subjectivity that is so useful also provides a platform from which the slave can perceive his or her own interests to be different from the master's interest. It is the unresolved subjectivity of the slave, and the difficulties it poses for the practice of domination, that provides the impetus behind the audience's desire for this particular vision of freedom and the substance of that freedom.

In order to analyze the ways that comedy and mastery support each other, we need to start by looking more closely at the practice of mastery at Rome. Just as slavery is only part of a continuum of domination, mastery itself fits into a continuum of practices of authority or, in Latin, *auctoritas*. Karl Galinsky, writing about a later period, has called *auctoritas* "a quintessentially Roman and therefore untranslatable term . . ." (1996: 12) and has described it in language that emphasizes its intersubjective, noninstitutional and dynamic attributes: "*Auctoritas* is something that is not granted by statute but by the esteem of one's fellow citizens. It is acquired less by inheritance, although belonging to an influential family or group is accompanied by some degree of *auctoritas*, than by an individual's superior record of judgment and achievement. Again, *auctoritas* is not static but keeps increasing . . . by continual activity of the kind that merits and validates one's *auctoritas*" (1996: 14). In other words, the socially and politically dominant Romans may be born into a presumption of authority, but they must each as individuals realize this authority by constructing and maintaining it in action every day.

This personalized form of power fundamentally differentiates Rome from those societies (such as modern Western capitalist democracies) in which power is routed through more abstract institutions such as bureaucracy and wage labor. Galinsky is right in differentiating Roman *auctoritas* from a sheer exercise of coercive power, since *auctoritas* consists above all in the idea that the subordinate's will is in compliance, not just his or her actions. But even if this kind of authority bases itself on subordinates' acceptance/acquiescence, it does so not out of any egalitarian impulse but

---

only the endless complexities and refinements of juristic analysis arising from the ambiguity of the institution." I would just add that these "endless complexities and refinements" were not confined to juristic analysis but were required in every area of the master's life.

[35] Varro, *de Re Rustica* I.17.1; cf. Aristotle, *Politics* 1253b, who elaborates further on the intertwining of subjectivity and intrumentality by imagining slaves as intermediaries between the master and the physical tools by which work gets done; in fact, he writes, if tools could do the work themselves (as Daedalus' and Hephaistos' robots could), then slaves would be unnecessary.

because this view of power recognizes the subjectivity of subordinates and so sees that true authority consists in the subordinate's assent to the power of the dominant.[36] For this reason, it is important that we acknowledge the fundamental ways that this kind of authority is different and resist the temptation to grade it as more or less humane, more or less cruel than the impersonal kind of authority that is familiar to later Western societies.[37] In a regime of this kind of personalized power, mastery is made up of a series of specific, concrete events in which subordinates express their acceptance of the master's will. The master must be always on the lookout for ways to impose his or her subjective viewpoint on the slave and to protect his or her subjectivity from the contrary imposition.[38] Although this struggle to impose one's view on another without being imposed upon is fundamental to all domination, Roman culture, with its constitutive emphases on hierarchy and personalized power, made this kind of impermeable sovereign self both more desirable and more obviously unattainable.

Slavery holds a central place in such a system of personalized power, since in the abstract at least, it can be seen as the exercise of almost pure authority: the slave must carry out the master's orders, put the master's interest before his or her own, without compensation or consideration, just because the slave is a slave. Furthermore, one of the central tenets of mastery is that the slave should not just obey the individual commands of the master but should have accepted the master's point of view so fully that the slave can anticipate the master's wishes and make the master's will

---

[36] Cicero, *Pro Caecina* 51–52: "What law, what decree of the senate, what edict of the magistrates, what pact or agreement or even, if I may speak of civil law, what will, what judgments or stipulations or formulae of agreement and contract could not be weakened and pulled apart, if we wanted to twist the substance to suit the words and leave unaccounted for the intentions, reasoning and *auctoritas* of those who wrote the document? By god, everyday household language will make nonsense, if we try to pounce on each other's words (*si verba inter nos aucupabimur*); ultimately there would be no household authority (*imperium domesticum*) if we allowed our slaves to obey us in accordance with our words, and not comply with what can be understood from the words."

[37] Bourdieu (1990: 122–34) on the modes of domination in precapitalist societies where economic relations are carried out not through objectified institutions but through euphemized social intercourse (1990: 126): "Because the pre-capitalist economy cannot count on the implacable, hidden violence of objective mechanisms which enable the dominant to limit themselves to reproduction strategies (often purely negative ones), it resorts to forms of domination which may strike the modern observer as more brutal, more primitive, more barbarous, and at the same time as gentler, more humane, more respectful of persons." Cf. Cooper's historical analysis of East African slavery (see above, note 30).

[38] Scott (1990: 10–11) uses Orwell's essay "Shooting an Elephant" as an example of how subordinates' subjectivity might be imposed on the dominant. Orwell writes: "A sahib has got to act like a sahib; he has got to appear resolute, to know his own mind and do definite things. . . . And my whole life, every white man's life in the East, was one long struggle not to be laughed at."

effective in the world in ways that the master might not even have consciously desired.[39]

Thus successful mastery would confer on the master a mark of unquestionable prestige, the mark of someone who was constantly up to the difficult task of making others conform to his or her will and whose power in the world was multiplied by being able to act through others. Conversely, however, the very difficulty of constantly imposing one's will and getting others to accept it means that, in practice, slavery was conducted not by exercising pure authority but by offering slaves a variety of overt and covert forms of compensation in return for good service and obedient behavior. It should be obvious that although slaves can make mastery labor intensive, by obeying the letter but not the spirit of the master's injunctions and thus forcing the master to offer compensation in return for more enthusiastic participation, this small pressure that slaves can exert will nearly disappear in the face of the overwhelming social and economic advantages of slaveholding. The key word in the previous sentence is "nearly": this form of resistance will never break down the institution of slavery, will never even make an individual slaveholder give up on the system that offers to him or her so many satisfactions, but it does constitute a thorn in the master's side, by undermining the absoluteness of masterly authority. This kind of resistance can do no more than unremittingly demonstrate the separate, unresolved, unassimilable subjectivity of the slave, but even that tiny defiance troubles the master precisely because the slave's separate subjectivity is both the reason for slavery and the chink in its armor.

A concrete example will clarify this important point. Scholars of slavery at Rome and in other cultures have recognized the importance of manumission and other rewards as instruments by which the master could motivate and control a slave. A prominent and strongly stated version of this argument in regard to Roman slavery has been made by Keith Bradley (see esp. [1987: 81–112], [1994: 154–65]). He argues that Roman masters held out the promise of eventual manumission and other rewards in exchange for loyal, obedient, and trouble-free service. Certainly this must be right. But even when masters could get slaves to accept the deal, they opened themselves to the possible interpretation that the slaves' obligations were owed only in exchange for these rewards, thus undermining the essential point of slavery that differentiates it from wage labor: the absoluteness of the slave's obligation. For this reason, the promise of manumission, or even

---

[39] See Cicero quotation, above, note 36; also the importance of slaves as agents in Roman law rests on exactly this kind of understanding of slavery, that the master need not supervise every decision a slave business agent makes as long as the slave is trusted to act in ways that are consistent with the master's wishes. The corollary of this is that trusted slaves were granted an enormous amount of responsibility and "freedom."

the actual giving of other smaller rewards, is not an end to the master's problems but always opens a new round of negotiations, starting with new offers and counter-offers that each party will in turn try to redefine in its own favor.[40] This is not to overstate the slave's power in this situation by imagining that he or she is an equal partner and can make demands that must be met. On the contrary, the atmosphere of these negotiations is always conditioned by the master's ultimate authority; the master can re-fuse to agree or can even renege on previous commitments. But we should recall that if the master's power were as absolute as these last alternatives imply, he or she would not need to make the original promises of rewards in the first place. And, while it is true that masters always have the threat of (sanctioned) physical punishment to back them up, so do slaves have the threat of (unsanctioned) physical retaliation. Even in the Republic, when masters did not have before their eyes such enlightening examples as Peda-nius Secundus and Larcius Macedo,[41] the implications of angering their slaves cannot have been lost on them.

Thus the Roman form of personalized authority produces a form of domination that can be extremely effective in its repressive aims but is also very labor intensive for the dominant. Although slavery embodies this kind of authority in an extreme way, we can also see it in operation in all the many hierarchical relations of Roman life. It would not be surprising, then, that the audience of a Plautine comedy looked for release from the labor of mastering those below them, especially slaves, but also others in various hierarchical relations. Further, when we recall that each member of this audience is not simply either "dominant" or "subordinate" but stands on both sides of domination in various relationships to others, it also makes sense that they would enjoy a release from the labor of fending off the impositions of those above them. With this in mind, we can ask again the question with which I started this section: What pleasures does Plautine comedy offer to such an audience?

Each of the two comic modes offers something to each audience mem-ber, and the interaction of the two maximizes these enjoyments while lim-iting the liabilities. Farcical comedy offers the chance to identify with someone whose low juridical status does not prevent him from controlling

---

[40] Scott (1990: 70–107) examines the role of hegemonic discourse in encouraging the com-pliance of subordinates and in (against the intention of the dominant) offering subordinates concessions with which to stake a claim. He writes, "The plasticity of any would-be hege-monic ideology which must, by definition, make a claim to serve the real interests of subordi-nate groups, provides antagonists with political resources in the form of political claims that are legitimized by the ideology" (1990: 95).

[41] Two senators killed by their slaves; on Pedanius Secundus, see Tacitus, *Annales* XIV.42–45; on Larcius Macedo, see Pliny, *Letters* III.14. On these and other possible cases of masters killed by slaves, see Bradley (1994: 112–13).

those around him and, more important, who can see through all the pretensions and high-minded claims of justice and right. But this fantasy is always
limited by the fact that the social order reasserts itself in the end: the master
regains control, even if he demonstrates that control by pardoning the
slave. Conversely, the naturalistic mode reassures the audience members
that their control over others is as it should be and is safe from any irre-
sponsible challenges. But this mode itself is often enlivened by the cynicism
and rebellion that trickery can offer. This understanding of the coexistence
of two very different modes of comedy can explain the popularity of Plautus
and the role that his comedies played in Roman dramatic festivals. This
doubled form of comedy presented a mixed form of heroism with which
people in very different social positions could identify while at the same
time ensuring that the potentially subversive element of farce was leavened
by the more conservative element of naturalistic comedy.

This description of Plautus can also explain the centrality of the clever
slave as the canonical hero, a figure who provided a wellspring of subversive
energy. The defining characteristic of slaves in Plautus is their attitude
toward the meaningfulness of masterly rhetoric. Most readers would agree
that there are two easily distinguished types of slave in Plautus.[42] The first
is "the good slave," a slave who accepts the masterly structure of rewards
and punishments; that is, he believes that the master will adhere to the
structure as set out and even that these rewards and punishments are mean-
ingfully related to, and anchored by, an abstract moral scheme of good
and bad.[43] Obvious examples of this type of slave include Messenio in the
Menaechmi, Grumio in the *Mostellaria*, and Sceledrus in the *Miles Gloriosus*.
The second type of slave is, of course, the *servus callidus*, the "clever slave,"
who is defined not just by disobedience but, more accurately, by his disbe-
lief in the master's rhetoric. Slaves like Pseudolus, Tranio (in the *Mostellaria*), and Epidicus seem to believe that the master might actually punish
them (or reward them if they could choose to be good), so the important
point is not that they dismiss the reality of the rewards and punishments in

---

[42] Spranger (1984: 22–26, 39, 115, *passim*) distinguishes between good slaves and clever
slaves and believes that both, while exaggerated in comedy, reflect real slaves. Stace (1968:
72–73) unquestioningly accepts the masters' point of view when he asserts that the good slaves
were more realistic. Although Bradley argues more carefully, he ends up agreeing with the
idea that rebellious comic slaves are a fantasy, and good slaves are realistic. He takes the view
that the clever slaves in Plautus reflect the master-class assumption that slaves are deceptive,
lazy, greedy, etc. (1987: 28–30). In reference to good slaves' loyalty and fear of punishment,
he writes, "Once all allowance is made for comic exaggeration and irony in the plays which
provide the material, it seems inconceivable that they are not grounded on true servile fear
of slave-owners . . ." (1987: 136; see also 1987: 38–39).

[43] Spranger (1984: 26): "Dieser [sc. the good slave] betrachtet sich selbst mit den Augen
seines Herrn und mißt seine Tugenden mit den Wertmaßstäben des Freien, die er unbedenk-
lich als die richtigen Normen anerkennt."

themselves but that they refuse to take these as meaningful in the master's structure of meaning. For example, physical pain is only part of the effect of whipping intended by the master; what whipping is supposed to accomplish is branding the slave with marks of shame and dishonor that go far deeper than the scars on the skin. Indeed, much modern scholarship about slavery has focused precisely on this kind of consistent degradation as the ultimate source of masterly control.[44] But when we think of the clever slave's attitude towards whipping, it is exactly this degradation that is missing. The clever slave may not relish the actual pain involved in whipping but refuses to see this physical act as depriving him of honor. In fact, the most consistent attitude expressed towards whipping by clever slaves is to talk about their scars as a mark of honor.[45]

If the primary characteristic defining comic slaves is the degree to which they accept the master's view of mastery, this is the point where we should look for the source of comic pleasures. It is the ability to be free from another's subjectivity that is embodied in the clever slave and other heroes of Plautine comedy. The clever slaves of comedy are unburdened by the master's view of the world in a way that real masters hope to be but can never be, unburdened by the slave's view of the world, since in practice masters must always act in the knowledge of potential slave resistance. This freedom from another's viewpoint inside our own heads is the miraculous freedom with which the clever slave is endowed. What makes this freedom so powerful and so attractive is that it goes far beyond the juridical freedom that we might think of as the opposite of slavery. It embodies rather the illusion that anyone can be free from others' subjectivity (in Bakhtin's terms, that anyone can be truly monologic). This kind of freedom is desired and unattainable in almost any society. But Roman society, in which both hierarchy and personalized authority were at an extreme, would recognize even more acutely the desire and the impossibility of locking our doors against others and "being just one person."[46]

Thus we can explain the slave-master relations in Plautine comedy as the conjunction of two pictures: the good slave embodies the view that masters would like slaves to have of slavery, and the clever slave embodies the view that masters themselves would like to have of their own lives. But

---

[44] E.g., Patterson (1982). For this argument in the context of the Roman household, see Saller (1944: 133–53).

[45] E.g., *As* 545–77; *Bac* 1055–57; *Per* 20–23 (this example specifically makes use of the language of civic and military honors to describe slaving at the mill), 264, 268–71; *Ps* 1325; for more examples of this phenomenon, see Segal (1987: 143–54).

[46] My explanation of the clever slave makes him a complementary opposite to the gladiator, as that figure has been explicated by Barton (1993: 12–25, *passim*). The clever slave offers his audience the illusion of an absolutely unencumbered subjectivity through rebellion, while the gladiator similarly elevates his subjectivity, but through submission.

although comedy provides these two complementary pictures, it cannot prevent them from complicating each other. First, the hero of the play, the person we can most easily identify with, is also the person against whom masters—if they were only or even primarily masters—would have to identify themselves. The clever slave is not only ideologically defined against the worldview of mastery, but he is much more obviously dramatically defined against the master in each individual play, especially the canonical clever slave comedies, like *Pseudolus*, *Mostellaria*, or *Miles Gloriosus*. Plautine comedy's moral/ideological discontinuity offers to the audience the pleasures gained from identifying with two contradictory forces. It is not an illusion that these plays seem to both exalt and undermine rebellion, to both deify and infantilize the clever slave. Nor must we choose one of the impulses (either the exaltation or the dismissiveness) as primary, defining the other as a negligible side effect. The conjunction of these two contrary impulses is the source of Plautine comic pleasure.[47]

But there is even a further complication. In many of the plays, including the four I will be examining in detail, the hero is not literally a clever slave but a master who invades the territory of the trickster and steals all the best lines.[48] These plays, then, push to an extreme the logic implicit in the other plays; in these plays, the master not only notionally identifies with the clever slave but becomes a clever slave himself. It is fundamental to this logic that when the master usurps the power of the clever slave, the uses to which he puts this power are the uses of domination. That is, when the master fantasizes about locking out the meanings others have given to social actions, the fantasy is one of effortless domination.

And yet there is another attribute of this miraculous power that has decisive importance for the ways that the plots of actual plays are organized. Although the emphasis in Plautine comedy is on the clever slave as a site of liberatory release, this emphasis does not exclude its counterpoint: the pleasures that the dominant might take in temporarily experiencing the

---

[47] Lott (1995: 153) describes the violence in minstrelsy perpetrated against black women by black men in similar terms: "The violence against black women vicariously experienced but also summarily performed; the spectacle of black male power hugely portrayed, but also ridiculed and finally appropriated. Just as the attacker and the victim are expressions of the same psyche in nightmares, so were they expressions of the same spectator in minstrelsy." Lott cites the work of Carol Clover (1987) as fundamental to this analysis.

[48] This is not so clearly the case in the *Persa* as in the other three. In the *Persa* there is a double switch: the usual clever slave who offers a site for masterly identification has been made into a master who retains all the qualities of a clever slave. The presence of the two contrary identifications in a single character is enough to show how clearly this play is related to the scheme I outline here, but the ways that this somewhat unusual instance gets worked out will become clear in the full analysis offered in chap. 4.

demeaning life of the subordinate.[49] The point of audience identification with the clever slave, then, depends on both his lowliness and his triumph over that lowliness. When a master takes on the role of hero in these comedies, he must define himself as, in some way, subordinated or at least constrained "normally," that is, outside the fictive frame of the play. This is particularly challenging when the hero is a *paterfamilias* "rebelling" against his own dependents, but even there it is possible.

THE ART OF AUTHORITY

The art of authority in Plautine comedy is the skill that allows a hero to negotiate the tightrope between dominating and being dominated, between the degradation of slavery and the wearying labor of mastery. It is the art of managing two incompatible literary styles in order to possess the authority that masters have in real life and the authority that slaves have in comedy. Further, we can see Plautine comedy itself, with its ability to both disarm rebellion and appropriate it for masters, as an art of authority, though it will never be so successful in soothing masters' anxieties that it does away with the need for its services.

The explanation I have given above of the sources of comic pleasure for masters should make it clear that both the literary mode that replicates the authoritative structures of real life, and the literary mode that reverses those structures, have pleasures to offer masters. We can see the good slave as the product of the naturalistic mode and the clever slave as the product of the farcical mode. Although these two modes envision the relation between comedy and real life very differently, together they create a complementarity that allows for the kind of dual identification for which I have argued above. There is no essential or necessary connection between the naturalistic mode and the master's voice or between the farcical mode and the slave's voice. If we assumed such connections, we would be back in the trap of believing that masters are so completely defined by their mastery that they

---

[49] Clover (1987: 220) argues, for the slasher film, that the identification of male viewers with females on the screen is fueled by "the willingness and even eagerness . . . of the male viewer to throw in his emotional lot, if only temporarily, with not only a woman but a woman in fear and pain. . . ." Barton (1993) places great emphasis on the cultural and psychological operations of inversion, and the paradoxical disruption and proliferation of the categories in which these operations are grounded, as a way of understanding the "sorrows of the ancient Romans." Stallybrass and White (1986: 191) in reference to later European manifestations of the carnivalesque: "But disgust always bears the imprint of desire. These low domains, apparently expelled as 'Other', return as the object of nostalgia, longing, fascination." However, unlike the high literature (Jonson, Pope and others) that Stallybrass and White are analyzing, Plautine comedy is not written from a vantage point outside the popular cultural forms that it uses.

can have no imaginative stake in rebellion, or believing that when we see slaves in comedy rebel, we are witnessing the *cri de coeur* of an oppressed population. Both the literary perspective that accepts contemporary social structures as natural and the literary perspective that allows us to see the world upside down are useful to masters, but both also attest the masters' need to bolster their own morale.

The four readings offered in this study aim at an explication of the related literary and sociological aspects of each play. Such literary and social dialogues pervade the entire corpus of Plautus, but we can obtain a precise grasp of how this dialogue works only in the close study of specific plays. I have chosen these plays, the *Menaechmi*, *Casina*, *Persa*, and *Captivi*, for three reasons. First of all, they are spread out over the spectrum that Plautine comedy offers. These four plays differ from each other in ways that are illustrative of the variety of the corpus as a whole. For example, the *Menaechmi* and *Casina* illustrate Plautus' comic vision of the household and the tensions that pervade it, while the *Persa* and *Captivi* are more civic, bringing to the fore the differences between citizens and outsiders. On the other hand, in treatment, the naturalistic mode of comedy dominates the *Menaechmi* and *Captivi*, while the other pair (*Casina* and *Persa*) gives two extreme examples of the farcical mode. Precisely because I am arguing that the divergent comedies of Plautus can be seen as products of a single aesthetic, I have not favored any single type of play but have attempted to engage with the full range of the corpus.

The second reason for choosing these particular plays is that each of them makes use of the plot devices that express the perspectives of the two comic modes: the trickery, which is central to the farcical mode, and the recognition of (previously mistaken) identity, which is central to the naturalistic mode. In particular, the hero in each of these plays offers a variation on the standard slave trickster. In the *Menaechmi*, the Syracusan twin inadvertently plays the part; in the *Casina*, this function is shared between a freeborn husband and wife, with the help of their own slaves; in the *Persa*, Toxilus, unlike all other clever slaves, schemes in his own interest; and in the *Captivi*, two *adulescentes* act the part of comic slaves in order to assert their true liberality. Each of these plays also contains either a real recognition scene or a parodic reflex of one. An analysis of how the canonical elements of each mode are combined in these plays will offer a way of making concrete the dialogue between modes.

My third reason for choosing these plays is a corollary of the second: because of the particular way that the two comic modes interact in these plays and the particular oddities of the tricksters, these plays offer insight into the ways that characters other than slaves try to lay claim to the subversive energy of rebellion. We will see embodied in the heroes of these plays the audience's own contradictory desire to be a clever, cynical subordinate while remaining an authority figure whose power is morally justified. None of these heroes remains completely in one camp or the other, unambiguously identified as either rebellious or authoritative; it is the very blurriness of their relations to the kinds of authority constructed by the naturalistic and farcical modes that makes these figures both powerful dramatic presences and useful test cases for my theory of comic pleasures.

Further, the methodology of my analysis has also influenced the organization of the chapters that follow. Because it is the ongoing dialogue between the two modes that endows these heroes with their particular powers, not a teleological dramatic structure where we can read the play's literary and ideological orientation from its outcome, it will be especially important in the following chapters to chart the progress of the play from scene to scene, to pay attention to the false starts, wrong turns, and dead ends that characterize Plautus' loose plotting. Therefore, a major part of each chapter will be a linear analysis that describes the effect of the play as it unfolds in time, like music; this analysis will describe the language and dramatic structures at each point in the play, in reference both to the specific forces at work in the individual play and to the broader horizon of expectations created by the system of comic convention. Each chapter will then be rounded out by a concluding section in which the particular thematic structures of the play are summed up and considered against the backdrop of Plautine comedy as a whole, especially focusing on the operation of the character types in articulating these themes.

The *Menaechmi* lies squarely in the familiar tradition of comedies of mistaken identity. Twin brothers, one who is a native to the town in which the play is set and one who is a visitor, spend the day unintentionally living each other's lives. But this play also engages the plot device of trickery by having the visiting brother (without malice) trick his twin out of money and a girl. In other words, the twin motif is a way of naturalizing and softening the plot device of trickery, since in this case the trickster did not set out to create a deceptive appearance but was born with it and only partially realizes its power.

This play shows most clearly the links between the tiring labor of mastery and the master's desire to become a clever slave. Epidamnian Menaechmus, the native brother, is depicted as a weak-willed and beleaguered man just looking to escape from the strictures of his life, while his brother, Syracusan Menaechmus, proves to be clear headed and secure in his identity as master. The weaker brother has a style of mastery that requires him to bribe his dependents for their loyalty and inevitably opens him to the dangers of such mastery. As I argued above, this way of rewarding and punishing dependents can never settle the question of mastery but only opens a new round of negotiations. The Syracusan brother, on the other hand, shows a masterful control of his slave, who obeys him not for rewards but simply because he is master. Furthermore, as he helps himself to the good things his brother has arranged for his own delectation and as he manages to avoid the consequences, the Syracusan twin makes use of the techniques and language that, in other plays, constitute the resources of the clever slave. As hero of this play, he combines within himself the highest degree of masterly authority and of "slavish" cleverness. Through his skillful use of the art of authority, and through the final recognition scene, even his bumbling brother gets to take part in this triumphant release from the burdens of mastery.

In the *Casina*, the element of farce becomes so prominent that the continuity and transcribable meaning of the play are greatly diminished. The inroads that the farcical aesthetic has made into romantic comedy are demonstrated explicitly in the prologue, where Plautus makes a point of telling us that he has written out of this play of young love and *anagnorisis* the young lovers and the recognition scene, leaving only the buffoonery of an old man in love. Because of this violent restructuring, the *Casina* shows very clearly the differences between the two modes that make up Plautine comedy. One of the most important effects of the shift from a naturalistic paradigm, ending in marriage, to a farcical one, ending only in the revelation of the trick, is that it brings to our attention the differing temporal structures of these two types of comedy. When a son rebels, this rebellion is implicitly understood to mark the inevitable succession of generations; that is, the son must eventually resist his father's authority in order to grow up and become a father himself. So plays that make central the rebellion of the son, rather than that of the slave, end with a glance toward the future, usually represented through the marriage of the young lovers. On the other hand, because a slave will never grow out of slavery, slaves' rebellion cannot lead anywhere. So plays that emphasize the slave's rebellion will end with a scene that restores us to the situation at the beginning of the play. The peculiarities of the *Casina*, especially its story line that encompasses young love, recognition, and marriage without any of these being represented onstage, derive from its telling a romantic, idealizing story through the means of a farcical plot.

This play, like the *Menaechmi*, ends with a hero who can claim to be both the master and the clever slave. The *paterfamilias* who rebels here mistakenly crosses over the border allowed by comedy, when he uses his real-life household authority to bring about his subversive release from such authority. Rather than relying on the authority he gains from being a rebel, he forces his wife and slaves still to treat him with deference. The result is that he (temporarily) loses his identification as hero, and his wife becomes the clever trickster for the central part of the play. But in the final scene the *senex amator*, who has been beaten, ridiculed, and hoodwinked, reasserts his priority not by asserting his rights as master but by assimilating himself to the clever slave. His ingenious wife, who has devised and carried out a plot worthy of Pseudolus, is thus implicitly put into the position of master, as she pardons her husband's wrongs and accepts his promise not to act up again. Again, a master has shaken off the burdens of his mastery by taking on the clever slave's ability to ignore the degradation others see in his actions.

In the final two plays, the *Persa* and *Captivi*, the relation between the two modes is more polemical, and each play exhibits an extreme form of one mode's dominance. These two plays are also more extreme examples of the Plautine aesthetic in that each uses the separability of content from form to undermine the credibility of the opposing mode. The *Persa* pulls off a nasty, subversive trick with the language and plot elements of civic-minded romantic comedy, and the *Captivi* asserts the ethical values of the naturalistic mode through a disguise trick performed by a clever slave. These two plays also complement each other in terms of the strategies by which they turn fictive slaves to the desires of the audience. The *Persa* reveals what fictions result from an extreme view of the slave as an instrument, and the *Captivi* reveals what fictions result from an extreme view of the slave as a subject.

In the *Persa*, even more than in the *Casina*, the domination of the farcical mode engenders a discontinuity of tone and action. This discontinuity in turn destroys any attempt to derive a transcribable meaning from what is essentially a series of almost vaudevillian tableaux. The prominence of the farcical mode in the *Persa* is signaled early in the play, when we realize that the clever slave is also the lover and that characters of the demimonde constitute the entire cast. But it is important for the dialogism of this genre that this is not merely a farcical play without any elements of naturalism or morality. The elements of the opposing mode are parodied in a brilliant twist. The trickery of this play, superficially aimed at tricking a *leno* so that the clever lover does not have to pay for his girlfriend, involves a play within a play that manipulates the most revered aspects of the naturalistic mode, including the recognition of a freeborn girl unjustly enslaved, the defense of civic virtue, and the bonds of gratitude that unite true *amici*.

Of the two aspects of slavery that motivate the invention of the clever slave, instrumentality and subjectivity, the logic of this play is emphatically based on the former. Since the slave is defined as an extension of the master's personality, in the fantasies of comedy, he or she can accomplish not only the liberating work of rebellion for the master but also the authoritative work of shoring up civic and domestic hierarchies. The view of the slave as an instrument creates the strategy that most readers find so striking in this play: that the main character is both a clever slave and a young lover. This conflation of the comic types of *servus callidus* and *adulescens* serves instrumentally as an avenger against the pimp who violates civic values (values that a slave *qua* slave could have no stake in) and as a stand-in master against whom the resistance of slaves can be portrayed more explicitly than usual. In keeping with the fact that Toxilus' slave is bolder in his back talk than other fictive slaves, Toxilus is also harsher and more explicit in his domination than other fictive masters. The *Persa*, then, shows a somewhat different side of the clever slave, emphasizing his ability to help maintain hierarchies rather than his ability to offer release from social constraints.

The fourth and final play to be analyzed here is the antithesis of the *Persa* not only in theatrical style but also in the idea of the slave as a subject, not as an instrument. The *Captivi* makes use of the confusion of identities between two *adulescentes*, one who knows himself to be free (though temporarily enslaved) and the other who thinks he is a slave by birth, to comment on the natural and cultural sources of virtue. The character Tyndarus, stolen at age three and raised as a slave, represents the elusive harmony of honor and obedience, of loyalty and self-assurance that defines masters' dreams of the perfect slave. He is disobedient, but only in saving the life of his master; he has a sense of honor, but it requires him to die for his master rather than to escape slavery. Tyndarus, then, gets to enjoy all the naughty pleasures of trickery (and thereby the pleasures of unencumbered subjectivity); but his trickery also defends in the strongest terms the possibility (indeed, necessity) of good, obedient slaves.

But even this most high minded of Plautine plays does not excuse itself from the dialogic struggle of naturalistic theater and farce. By structuring its main character as a rehabilitated version of a clever slave, the *Captivi* defines both its difference from these amoral tricksters and its superiority to them. Without indulging in the kind of explicit metatheatrical exhibition characteristic of the *Pseudolus*, for example, this play discredits the rambling antics of slave farce that go round and round only to end up back at the beginning. It does this in two ways, by transforming the paradigm of slave trickery into one that leads to an important result (instead of falling into the void) and by showing the typically comic stereotype of the parasite as not just greedy but in fact a bumbler. The *Captivi*'s ethical message about the nature of virtue, its ideological imagery of slavery and freedom, and its literary polemic against the emptiness of farce reinforce each other and illustrate the complex relations between literary values and moral values in this dialogic form of comedy.

Chapter II

THE TIES THAT BIND: *MENAECHMI*

A MAN, harried and harrassed by the strictures of his domestic life, rebels against his domineering wife and declares for himself a day of freedom. Through a series of coincidences, this declaration of independence ends up benefiting not him but his twin, who has come to this town in the course of a years-long search for his brother. But in the final scene, where the long-lost brothers are reunited, the visiting twin suggests that they both go back to their native home; thus, even though the harried man's rebellion against his wife did not free him in the way that he had hoped it would, through a twist of fate, he is freed from his domestic bonds finally and forever.[1]

The *Menaechmi* ("*The Menaechmus Brothers*") illustrates two of the principles that will be central to this study. First, even plays that focus on familial reconciliation may be structured around rebellion. In this case the two elements of reconciliation and rebellion are so well balanced that this play has been interpreted both (by Segal) as a paradigm of farcical wish fulfillment and (by Leach) as a parable of humanistic self-awareness.[2] Second, this play shows us that "rebellion" is an extremely flexible concept; it may apply to the temporary exaltation of the downtrodden but can also be appropriated by more powerful members of the society for the permanent release from irritating domestic constraints. In the *Menaechmi*, we see that the *paterfamilias* (the master, husband, patron) can appropriate for himself the experience of liberation notionally reserved for those who are powerless in real life. This concept of the *paterfamilias* as comic hero is possible only if we agree to see him as "normally" (i.e., in the imagined comic life that goes on before and after the script of the play) downtrodden, and the dependent members of the household (in this case his wife, parasite, and prostitute) as "normally" in power over him.

---

[1] Leach (1969a: 33) on this resolution: "Through the agency of his brother, Menaechmus of Epidamnus comes to realize not only that his domestic life is intolerable, but also that it is dispensible. As the wandering brother turns his thoughts homeward to Syracuse and Messenio promises to convert the troublesome worldly possessions [n.b. including the Matrona!] into welcome cash, we see the liberation of the protagonist from a humor-ridden society and his escape into a new world."

[2] Segal (1987: 43–53, *passim*); Leach (1969a).

To some degree, this image of the *paterfamilias* overmastered by his own subordinates is a rhetorical ploy, aimed at getting for him the sympathetic response owed to comic heroes. But this is not only a rhetorical construction: the master's feeling of being beleaguered by his mastery is also a recognition that subordinates do resist, they do manage to make life difficult for the dominant by attempting continually to renegotiate the relationship by exploiting any and every loophole in the master's justificatory logic. When the master rebels against his own dependents, he is rebelling against the frustrating ability of dependents to find the loopholes that allow them to turn the master's promises/threats against him. In the service of this rebellion, he uses exactly the tactics that dependents use against him, though at the same time maintaining his own authoritative power.

The release that this play offers to masters, a release from the burdens of mastery, explains the very substance of the plot. This play uses the characters of the twin brothers, who share the name Menaechmus and have been separated since one was kidnapped and taken to Epidamnus as a child, to frame the central dramatic tension as a contrast between two styles of mastery. Each brother has a distinctive way of handling the problem that inheres in relations of domination: to motivate subordinates to cooperate even passably, the dominant must both promise rewards and threaten punishment. The brother who makes his home in Epidamnus and who will play the part of the rebellious *paterfamilias* has relied on promises of rewards to such an extent that his dependents now see these rewards as due payment, not as largesse at Menaechmus' discretion. The brother visiting from Syracuse, on the other hand, has impressed his slave, Messenio, with the absoluteness of a slave's obligation; Messenio is energetic in his service, even when the master's pockets are empty.

But these two styles of mastery are not just offered as two possible ways of managing dependents: the Syracusan form of mastery "solves" the problems created by the Epidamnian form of mastery. The resolution of the play depends on Syracusan Menaechmus' intimidation of the wife of the Epidamian brother and her father; Messenio's loyalty is even more central, since in the end it is he who rescues Epidamnian Menaechmus (mistaking him for his own master) and then reveals the two brothers' identities through questioning. This solution, though, works by implicitly judging nonslave dependents on the same standards as slaves. In other words, Syracusan Menaechmus' more sure-handed authority, the fact that he resists the temptation to bribe Messenio for his loyalty, is at least partly explained by Messenio's status as a slave, and thus his obligations are less negotiable than those of a wife, a parasite, or a prostitute.

Epidamnian Menaechmus' dependents fall into two categories: his wife, to whom his relation should be ordered by legal, social, and personal bonds as well as by economic bonds, and the parasite Peniculus and the prostitute

Erotium, to whom his relation should be purely economic without the complex entanglements of emotion and decorum. As my description of these relationships implies, Epidamnian Menaechmus has conflated these two categories by defining his marriage economically and his employment of a parasite and prostitute in terms of loyalty. His distorted view of these relationships explains why and how his brother's authoritative treatment of his own slave can be an antidote for this domestic confusion: slavery is exactly the point where loyalty meets economics, because it is a fundamentally economic relation in which the master is considered justified in expecting a moral, legal, and social committment. In fact, we could say that buying a slave is an economic act envisioned as putting an end to the need for economic acts; one buys a slave to free oneself from the need to pay someone to perform each separate service.

This play, then, follows the logic of the slaveholder in optimistically believing that slavery can be a solution to the complex problems presented by the inevitable confusion of social and economic relations. Slavery, itself founded on the illusion that pure unbought loyalty can somehow arise from an economic act (an act that works, in fact, by denying the human status of the merchandise), in the *Menaechmi* offers this illusion to solve the difficulties of other social relations. And yet, slavery itself is by no means secure in this illusion. Mastery is difficult precisely because the problem of loyalty cannot be solved by reducing it to a commodity that can be bought. Thus this play, by a sleight-of-hand, glosses over the problems inherent in slavery itself by making slavery seem like a clear and straightforward relation that implicitly offers a way out of the messiness of other economic and social relations.

The twin brothers are distinguished not only by their styles of mastery but also by their relation to the two modes of comedy. The Epidamnian brother opens the play on a farcical note: his rebellion, like those of *senes amatores*, is defined in contrast to his "usual" subordination to his wealthy wife, who is labeled in the play only as "the Matrona"; we suspect from the start that she will reassert her power over him in the end. Reinforcing the prominence of the farcical mode at the beginning of the play is that this rebellion is not based on any moral principle but merely on his desire to enjoy himself away from the watchful eye of his wife. But if we assume from the opening act that we are watching a typical *senex amator* farce, then the second act forces us to reorient our expectations for this play. The second act introduces the traveling brother and, with him, the themes of mistaken identity and the desire to heal familial bonds that have been breached, themes central to the naturalistic mode. Instead of a play of aggressive rebellion, the second act prepares us for a play of redemption: through the agency of Tyche (Chance deified), Epidamnian Menaechmus' real identity will be discovered, and he will be rescued from the social nightmare in which his ignorance of this true identity has forced him to live. In the perspective of the naturalistic mode, Epidamnian Menaechmus looks not like a *senex amator* but like a *pseudomeretrix* (a freeborn girl enslaved to a pimp).[3] In the remainder of the play, after these first two acts, the two modes continue to be associated with the two brothers respectively: the farcical mode comes on stage when the Epidamnian brother does, and the naturalistic mode with the Syracusan brother. But in the resolution of the play, which I described above as informed by the Syracusan brother's worldview, the naturalistic mode eventually absorbs the farcical mode in this play and uses the farcical mode to its own ends.

Just as the Syracusan brother's self-assured style of mastery solves the problems of his brother's beleaguered domestic authority, the naturalistic mode, with its emphasis on revealing the true order that lies hidden beneath apparent chaos, solves the problems of the farcical rebellion with which the play began. The farcical beginning of this play accomplishes something that a play completely in the naturalistic mode never could: it garners for the Epidamnian brother the admiration owed to comic tricksters, those who rebel aggressively (not in the service of some higher principle but merely out of *malitia*).[4] But precisely because farcical rebellion is grounded in principles opposed to those ratified by real morality, it never challenges the legitimacy of the authority figures it rebels against. (For example, the clever slave is content to smirk at his master's authority and to remain a slave.) This abdication from the struggle to have one's authority justified would be unacceptable in the case where the rebel is a *paterfamilias*, because it implies that the rebel is actually (i.e., not just because of another's act of injustice or a twist of fate) a subordinate outside the time covered by the script. In this case, this would imply that Epidamnian Menaechmus' wife is justified in her control over him. Furthermore, the lack of moral principle implies that farcical rebellion is merely temporary, that beyond the fictive time of the play, the hierarchies will revert to what they were before; in this case, the Matrona will regain her ascendancy. If the whole play were framed in the farcical mode, Epidamnian Menaechmus would come unacceptably close to the figure of the clever slave whose subordination is socially justified and whose rebellion is merely a personal desire to act out/up, not a defense of overarching moral values.

---

[3] Cf. Tyndarus in the *Captivi*; these plays show that, although people of both genders may play the role of "damsel in distress" (the person who is alienated from his/her proper social place and who is rescued from that alienation in the course of the play), the female is the notional template for this role; when men play it, it is always layered with other themes. This question will be discussed more fully below in chap. 5.

[4] On *malitia*, see Chiarini (1979: 54, 61, *passim*), Petrone (1977: 19–20) and Anderson (1993: 88–106).

If we look at other *senex amator* comedies, in which the *senex* does maintain the role of farcical rebel throughout and is in the end reduced to a subordinate position to his wife, we can see that the degradation of the father is balanced by the triumph of the son, who gains his love object when the father is punished and whose rebellion embodies humanistic values.[5] In the beginning of the *Menaechmi*, we have no son who carries the banner of true love, just a philanderer who merely wants to escape his marital bonds. The balance is preserved, however by introducing an identical twin and, through him, the naturalistic mode. The Syracusan brother, although he is not in love, still represents a commitment to real moral principles, in this case, the reintegration of the family. Because of the physical resemblance of the two brothers, and because of the value given to family relationships in the naturalistic mode, the visiting twin not only enjoys the kind of privileges that the Epidamnian brother desires but also frees the Epidamnian brother from the subordination to which his farcical rebellion would have led.

Although these two modes of comedy may seem to be working at cross-purposes, they are united in identifying the Menaechmus brothers as the comic heroes and the wife, prostitute, and parasite as the figures who stand in the way of the heroes' happiness, the so-called blocking characters. Making a wife, especially a rich one, a blocking character is so common in all eras of Western comedy that we lose sight of the way that this device quite radically inverts the liberatory logic of comedy. The need for the socially dominant to rebel is central to the traditions of Western comedy and yet constitutes a persistent blind spot in our cultural perception of comedy; by generalizing as "human" the dominant man's need to rebel against the potential resistance of his subordinates, we grant to him the power to be a sympathetic rebel without laying down his real authority.[6] Erich Segal has offered perhaps the best description of the farcical aspect of Plautine comedy, with its emphasis on rebellion. His central argument is that Plautine comedy allows the audience to escape the requirements of *pietas* and decorum that keep their own desires in check on a day-to-day basis. Yet he never confronts the problem of what it means for men to rebel against their wives in the way that slaves rebel against masters or sons against fathers. He explicitly compares the piety a son owes his father to the piety a wife owes her husband (1987: 21), but when it comes to describing the actual plays,

---

[5] This is the pattern in the *Asinaria* and *Mercator*. Like the *Menaechmi*, the *Casina* also removes the sympathetic node represented by the son and his committment to "true love"; the peculiar negotiations by which that play handles the interaction of the farcical and idealizing modes will be discussed fully in the next chapter.

[6] E.g., Segal (1987: 43): "Wife and mistress dwell at the antipodes of *human* experience" (emphasis added).

he accepts that it is husbands who rebel against their wives and never notes that, according to his own logic, it should be the wives who rebel.[7]

The *Menaechmi* goes even further and turns into blocking characters those usually associated with comic liberation: a prostitute and a parasite. Both of these characters have strong associations with the sensual pleasures that are so clearly opposed to the drudgery of everyday life, and thus they are emblematic of festivity. Yet both also have a somewhat ambiguous relation to comic release because of the greed and self-interest at the heart of their relation to sensual pleasures. The prostitute when figured as an object can join the list of pleasures enjoyed by the male comic hero; but when she is seen as a grasping, deceitful subject, she gets aligned with the wife as another one who wants to control the man through his lusts and resists the control he would exert over her. The parasite, likewise, can be emblematic of the festive focus on satisfaction of appetites, as long as we do not see how he schemes to provide that satisfaction and that this scheming implies a bid to control his patron.

In each case (the wife, the prostitute, the parasite) we have a blocking character constituted not by a socially defined position of power, as is the case for *senes*, those canonical blocking characters, but by resistance to Menaechmus' power. He holds the upper position in the hierarchical relation that binds him to each of these characters, yet the "back story" of this play is that each of the dependent characters has used Menaechmus' own mechanisms of mastery against him (the wife with her dowry, the prostitute with her sexuality, and the parasite with his knowledge of Menaechmus' indiscretions from "friendly" participation in his habitual revels). Thus the potentially subversive energy that notionally is reserved for those who assert an ideal of humanistic freedom and dignity in the face of pharisaical small-mindedness is here put into service to reassert an elite man's "proper" control over others.

Rebellion Meets Reconciliation

As the play unfolds, we can discern four phases or movements, each of which presents the actions and characters from a particular perspective. Each of the first two movements presents one of the brothers, along with the thematic elements that define him. The first movement (Act I) introduces the Epidamnian brother and his ambiguous authority over wife, parasite, and prostitute. This movement emphasizes farcical themes, especially rebellion and sensual pleasure, as we see Epidamnian Menaechmus resisting his wife's attempts to control him and planning an extraordinary

---

[7] See esp. (1987: 27): "On the Plautine stage, the attitude of sons to fathers as well as *husbands to their wives*, is the exact opposite of the exemplary behavior of *pius* Aeneas. . . . The departure of *father or wife* is always the occasion for a Plautine party" (emphasis added).

feast with the parasite Peniculus and the prostitute Erotium. But before he can enjoy this feast, he must take care of some business in the forum. The second movement (Act II) introduces the visitor, Syracusan Menaechmus, and shows him first asserting his command over his own slave and then being mistaken for his brother by Erotium and her cook. That this brother breathes the air of idealizing naturalism is evident in, among other things, the strong emphasis on misunderstanding in this movement, an emphasis that prepares us for a play about the limited degree to which humans understand the "reality" that exists beneath unreliable appearances. The third movement (Acts III, IV, V.1–5) is characterized by a hectic merry-go-round of mistaken identities and indignant recriminations, as the two dramatic modes (farcical and naturalistic) and the two styles of mastery become entangled with one another. In this pivotal third movement, the Syracusan brother becomes predominant, as he uses his resemblance to his brother to appropriate pleasures and wield authority in exactly the way his brother would have liked to do. Meanwhile, for his less lucky twin the shared appearance of the two brothers has only negative effects: he gets harangued by his wife for the party his brother has enjoyed and ultimately is almost carried off as a madman, because the Syracusan brother has pretended a mad rage to escape the clutches of the Matrona. In keeping with Syracusan Menaechmus' ascendancy, the naturalistic mode of comedy and the self-assured mode of mastery also begin to predominate over farce and mastery-by-payment. As the silliness and sensuality of Epidamnian Menaechmus' rebellion are overshadowed by his brother's more substantive assertion of control, the play as a whole shifts away from the farcical perspective and toward a perspective that will reveal the order concealed beneath chaos.[8] This shift, begun in the third movement, is worked out fully in the fourth movement (Act V.6–9). This final movement brings to a logical conclusion the possibility presented by the third movement: that the type of authority represented by the Syracusan brother and the naturalistic perspective could solve the problems against which Epidamnian Menaechmus is struggling. By standing in for his harried brother, reasserting authority over the troublesome subordinates, and pointing the way toward a life back in Syracuse that will erase all their problems, the Syracusan brother finally fulfills the wish for liberation with which this play began.

Life in Epidamnus

The very first scene of the opening movement (= Act I) provides a potent statement of the themes that will shape the play. The monologue of the

---

[8] Frye (1957: 166, 169) defines the resolution of comedy as the emergence of "reality," which throughout the play is clouded by various characters' impositions of their illusions.

parasite Peniculus (I.1) presents both a problem and a solution. The problem is how best to keep slaves from trying to run away or rebel, and the solution is to feed them as well and as plentifully as possible (79–95). In fact, the argument here opposes two possible methods of maintaining control over slaves, chains and seduction by food, and shows the latter to be superior. The monologue performs several dramatic functions. First, it establishes Peniculus as a parasite according to the conventions of comic theater,[9] by presenting him as preoccupied by food and heedless of his own honor or respectability (he would just as soon be slave as free so long as he is well fed; see 97). This characterization diminishes the importance of the other feature usually associated with parasites, their use of their wit for sustenance. In doing so, it emphasizes by contrast the dependency of the parasite's situation and his desperateness.[10] Second, this aspect of the parasite's character prefigures the vindictiveness that will drive the plot, namely, that Peniculus will betray Menaechmus to his wife, out of anger for missing the promised feast.[11] Third, this monologue reveals a thematic connection between the generosity of those in power and the loyalty of their dependents. Food is figured here as the bond that keeps slaves from running away. This image expresses one of the central issues in the play, the role of food and wealth in mediating between the subordinates' desire for freedom and the master's desire for maintenance of his authority.

Although Peniculus presents the control of subordinates as a problem, the irony is that the advice he gives to masters is in the interest of subordinates, and so this speech is an example of just the kind of cynical manipulation of the appearances of loyalty that a master must fear. Peniculus' groveling obedience (e.g., 156–57) in return for abundant feasts reveals the tenuousness of a loyalty based on material satisfaction. His argument, which makes bribing by food the central prop of masterly power, can be interpreted in two ways, each of which implies a particular conception of the relationship between master and slave. It can be seen to imply a con-

---

[9] These self-descriptive monologues addressed to the audience are the province of parasites and, less often, of clever slaves; cf. *Capt* 69–109, 461–97; *St* 155–233; *Per* 53–79; see Wilner (1938: esp. 25–27, 31). In reference to Saturio's self-description in the *Persa*, Slater (1985: 41) adapts to the *Persa* Halporn's argument (1980 APA paper) for the *Captivi*, that the parasite's blunt introduction of comic stereotypes serves to place an otherwise unfamiliar situation clearly in the realm of comic convention.

[10] Lowe (1989a) notes two trends that separate Plautus' parasites from those of Terence and Greek New Comedy: a decreased emphasis on wit as a means of making a living and an increased emphasis on food itself (1989a: 163–64). He further speculates that this could be the influence of Atellan farce on Plautus (1989a: 168). The reduced aspect of joking appears in the aptly named Gelasimus of the *Stichus* (esp. 221–25) and, vestigially, in Saturio's offer of jokes as a dowry for his daughter (*Per* 392–96), but in both places it is subordinated to the search for food.

[11] Leach (1969a: 36).

tract in which loyalty and obedience are not absolute values but are only the return for material satiety. By contrast, it can be seen as a debasement of the slave to the level of an animal;[12] the master can be sure that slaves have no desire for freedom as long as they are kept in comfort. The doubleness of this idea, its containment of radically different notions of the subordinate, is precisely what makes it so powerful as a dramatic and thematic hub. The subordinates see themselves as owing obedience only when the conditions of the contract are met. Menaechmus, on the other hand, believes that he is still master even when he steals his wife's clothes, takes back gifts from his mistress, and causes his parasite to miss a meal. His actions show that he is buying his dependents' loyalty, but he continues to believe that his mastery is derived from himself and not from his openhandedness.

After Peniculus' monologue has prepared us for domestic conflict, we see Menaechmus as a young married man exulting over his wife in the military language we expect to hear from the clever slave. Having delivered a long tirade (110–24), spoken over his shoulder as he leaves the house, Menaechmus exhorts all philanderers to congratulate him for boldly fighting a battle against his over-bearing wife (*quia pugnavi fortiter*, 129). Even more telling, he refers to the cloak he has stolen from his wife as booty (*praeda*, 134), to his wife as the enemy, and to Erotium as his ally. Because this language is conventionally associated with slave tricksters, Menaechmus' use of military language establishes that the Matrona is the blocking character to be deceived and punished. Identifying the wife as blocking character implies that she is the one "normally" in power, and only the comic day of inversion can topple her.[13] Furthermore, this language establishes the preliminary expectation that Menaechmus is a clever trickster who will succeed, the hero of comedy and the focus of the audience's sympathy in opposition to the Matrona.[14]

Yet the spectator familiar with the forms of comedy sees a further displacement. While the master plays the part of the clever slave, the play is beginning where it should end, with the trickster triumphantly celebrating

---

[12] Note *rostrum* (snout) at line 89; cf. the bird simile in *Capt* 116–18.

[13] Segal (1969: 81) on *hodie* as a marker of the comic, by emphasizing the specialness of the day of reversal; see also Segal (1987: 42–43, 52–53, 164–69). Leach (1969a: 35) perceives the pyrrhic nature of this victory by noting the social dimension of subjection to his wife but does not mention the literary dimension of her identity as blocking figure implying Menaechmus' powerlessness.

[14] Elements here characteristic of the clever slave: military imagery for defeat of blocking character (129, 134–36, 184–88, 191–92); exulting in his deception by invoking "comic decorum" (i.e., *decet* used in a metatheatrical sense to refer to the difference between comic and social convention; see 131); the nature of the acts he is exulting (theft, deception). See Leach (1969a: 35), Fraenkel (1922: 238–39 = 1960: 230).

the defeat of the blocking character.[15] This anomaly undermines our confidence in Menaechmus as the comic hero, since we expect to see the hero at first beset by impossible difficulties, which will be overcome in the course of the play only by his dominating ingenuity.[16] This shift places emphasis not on the brilliance of the scheming but on the benefits of the outcome, exactly the opposite from the emphasis in slaves' trickery.

Before looking more closely at Menaechmus' festive plans, it will be useful to characterize just what it is he is rebelling against. His complaint against his wife is that she questions him about his life outside the house and tries to keep watch over him, as if she were a customs inspector rather than a wife (117).[17] Even more important than her watchfulness is Menaechmus' reasoning as to why she should be more indulgent of his escapades.

> quando ego tibi ancillas, penum,
> lanam, aurum, vestem, purpuram bene praebeo nec
>   quicquam eges,
> malo cavebis si sapis, virum opservare desines.
>
>   (120–22)

Since I generously supply you with slave-women, food, wool, gold, clothes, and dyed fabric and since you don't go without anything, if you know what's good for you, you'll keep an eye out for trouble, and you'll stop keeping watch over your husband.

Two striking features of this marriage shape Menaechmus' complaint: that he treats his wife like an employee (by paying her for her services) and that she rejects his understanding of how luxury goods operate in this relationship, by accepting the goods but continuing to believe that she has other claims on him as well. In fact, Menaechmus himself undercuts the validity of his "contract" with his wife: we find out in line 130 that he has stolen from her a *palla* (cloak) in order to give it to Erotium. This theft shows that he does not even hold up his end of the bargain (although the bargain itself exists only in his mind); it also shows how closely Menaechmus' relationships to the two women echo each other. This theme will be picked up

---

[15] Konstan (1983: 49) notes that the *Asinaria* too plays with this temporal dimension of convention by beginning with the *senex iratus*, the denouement of many other plays. See also Slater (1985: 57) and Ketterer (1986b: 54).

[16] Segal (1987: 116): "The slave is not completely in charge at the beginning of the play. . . . This active campaign, the outsmarting of a presumably smarter master, is the subject of the most characteristic and most successful Plautine plots."

[17] Segal (1987: 43–45) stresses this element of the play and has a good description of the wife's characteristic *industria*.

and expanded later, but for now we can see the first hint that he treats his wife like a prostitute and expects a prostitute to act like a wife.

Menaechmus' possible heroism is further drawn into question by Peniculus' cynical outlook. We have seen in Peniculus' monologue how confident he is that he can manipulate Menaechmus' generosity for his own ends. His first scene with his patron makes us believe even more strongly that Peniculus is a sharp operator and that Menaechmus is naive enough to think that the parasite's attachment to him is motivated by loyalty rather than the profit motive. Before Peniculus begins flattering his patron, in an aside to the audience he reveals that although he seems to be enlisted in Menaechmus' rebellious cause, his interest lies in keeping Menaechmus in an ambiguous position, where he neither completely submits to his wife nor completely throws over his domestic life.[18]

> illic homo se uxori simulat male loqui, loquitur mihi;
> nam si foris cenat, profecto me, haud uxorem, ulciscitur.
>
> (125–26)

> That guy pretends it's his wife he's cursing, but really it's me;
> If he dines away from home, he's taking his vengeance not against his
>   wife but against me.

In Menaechmus' interaction with Peniculus (135–78), the imagery of a military alliance, united for the purposes of rebellion, continues to be the controlling metaphor. However, as noted above, Peniculus' relation to the audience frames this rebellion in such a way that Menaechmus' status as comic hero is qualified. In addition to our seeing him as a naive victim of Peniculus' show of deference, he is also throughout this scene depicted in ways that bring him closer to the type of *adulescens* than *senex amator*. Peniculus' first words to him are an address as *adulescens* (135). His insistence in the following lines (137–39) that Peniculus has come just in the nick of time remind us of the young lover's helplessness and dependence on his clever slave. Even his captured booty (his wife's cloak) contributes to the impression that, like *adulescentes*, Menaechmus has been almost enslaved to a *meretrix*, a relationship symbolized in the expensive gifts he must constantly supply for her. Menaechmus tries on the cloak he has stolen from his wife, and this bit of dramatic spectacle is heightened in the text by reference to the painting of mythological subjects (143–44). Although the mythological references to Ganymede and Adonis expresses Menaechmus'

---

[18] It is important that Peniculus' manipulative wiles have been expressed in direct address to the audience, in his monologue (I.1), and in this aside. Peniculus' choice to confide in the audience allows us to see that his flattery of Menaechmus is cynical and, significantly, puts the audience in a position of knowledge exterior to that of Menaechmus.

heroism, the two examples he gives are of the capture of a young male *eromenos* (beloved) by an *erastes* (lover) and the capture of a man by a goddess; both undercut the male heterosexual authority that he claims.[19] At the end of this scene is another very explicit use of the language we expect from young lovers: when Erotium comes out of her house, Menaechmus' ecstatic praise of her beauty (and blindness to her rapaciousness) put him in the same category as those sacrificial lambs.

The next scene (I.3) introduces Erotium. The rivalry between the prostitute and the parasite serves to highlight their cynicism and Menaechmus' naivete. Although Erotium does not reveal her cynical designs to the audience as Peniculus did, still her hostility to the parasite as a rival for Menaechmus' generosity (182) and her obvious imitation of wifely decorum (in her willingness to devote herself solely to fulfilling her patron's desires; 186, 192, 203, 207, 213, 215) show that she is just as skillful as Peniculus in playing Menaechmus for all he is worth. In case we might have missed that Erotium is merely playing a part and is not truly devoted to Menaechmus, Peniculus interprets her actions for the audience in a series of asides (193–95, 204, 206).

It seems, then, that Menaechmus' claim to heroism is not like that of the clever slave but closer to that of the *senex amator*. Unlike clever slaves, whose heroism is defined by their acknowledgment that it is not real and cannot last, *senes amatores* are marked by self-delusion. They are intoxicated with the sense of rebellion but deceive themselves as to the essential quality of such a rebellion: that it is predicated on subordination in the time outside the play and therefore can never last beyond the play's boundaries.

To sum up the principal ideas of the first movement: we have seen that Menaechmus' normal life consists of using money, food and luxury goods to get for himself the flattery of Peniculus and the amorous attentions of Erotium, and to pay off his wife's claims on him. However, it is not Menaechmus himself who is in control of this system but his three subordinates. They take what he gives them and only go along with his demands insofar as this compliance will produce more payments in the future. This cynicism is clear in the cases of Erotium and Peniculus; because the Matrona is in the opposite position (she has a moral and legal foundation for her relationship with Menaechmus, a foundation that his gift giving tries to ignore; the others pretend to such a noneconomic basis in return for economic payments), she has less control over the system and can only signal her will

---

[19] Note also that at 513-15, transvestism is equated with pathic sexuality, which Lilja (1982) shows is in itself a marker of slave status in comedy. See also Leach (1969a: 42) and Ketterer (1986b: 53). This transvestism (by my reading, he seems to keep the cloak on until at least line 199 [*si non saltas, exue igitur*]) is later recalled in the Senex's claim that the power the Matrona desires would reduce her husband to a slave girl (795–97). See Leach (1969a: 34–35, 37) on the theme of Hercules subordinated to Omphale.

by accepting the material goods without relinquishing her other claims. This first movement sets up a farcical context in which we expect rebellion to be privileged over reconciliation and in which the power lies with those who can see the situation from the audience's point of view. In this movement Menaechmus is set up as a rebel (and therefore, in the farcical mode, hero), but we also see his naivete.

The Visitor's Perspective

Into this world of rebellion and cynicism walks a man who neither pays off his subordinates to do what they should do anyway nor grouses about the power over him that such payments would give. Just as the first movement focuses on establishing the character of Epidamnian Menaechmus and his relation to his dependents, the second movement does exactly the same for Syracusan Menaechmus, thus establishing the differences between the two brothers.[20] In a particularly pointed contrast to Epidamnian Menaechmus' ambiguous power and lavish gifts (or promises of gifts) to his dependents, Syracusan Menaechmus is restrained and wary and demands absolute obedience rather than obedience in exchange for goods from his slave Messenio. His encounters with Cylindrus the cook and with Erotium clarify his differences from his brother and lay the groundwork for the themes of insanity and trickery that will be developed in the critical third movement.

The opening scene of the second act immediately establishes a contrast with the preceding act in tone and theme. In the first act, the brother native to Epidamnus came onstage from his own house, shouting back over his shoulder at his wife. Here in the second act, the visiting brother comes onstage from the port, and his first exchange with his slave is about the hardships of travel. This contrast highlights the difference in the brothers' situations: one who is all-too-snugly surrounded by hearth and home, while the other wanders in search of familial bonds. Even more fundamentally, the contrast between the two brothers is also a contrast between the two modes of comedy. The first movement foregrounds the farcical mode by shaping the tension of the play as a rebellion against constraint and by emphasizing the more aggressive (rather than positive, reconciliatory) aspects of such rebellion. This second movement, on the other hand, starts out with the Syracusan brother's desire to heal up the breach in his family.

---

[20] Ketterer (1986b: 54) observes that each brother's identity is revealed through the use of a prop: the cloak for Epidamnian Menaechmus and the empty moneybag for Syracusan Menaechmus. It should be clear from my discussion so far that these two props are not just chance objects, but each is an emblem of a style of authority: the Epidamnian's use of luxury goods that "unman" him, and the Syracusan's ability to control his slave without offering rewards.

Far from trying to escape from the demands of social life, this brother is trying to bind himself more tightly to his blood relations.[21]

As the play shifts from rebellion to reconciliation, it also reorders our understanding of the dramatic situation and introduces a new explanation for why people might not be able to interpret events correctly: because human knowledge and understanding are limited. Erotium, deceived by Syracusan Menaechmus' appearance, offers to him for free the services that she plans to charge to his brother's account. But, unlike the first act, where Menaechmus' naivete was contrasted with the cynicism of Peniculus and Erotium (if Menaechmus failed to see that he was being manipulated, the audience certainly did not), here the focus is on sheer misunderstanding. In other words, if Erotium does not see that she is being taken, and Syracusan Menaechmus does not see why she should be so "generous" (notice that his suspicion of her when he is getting everything he wants from her is the opposite of his brother's naivete in believing her even when he is not getting what he wants), this confusion is explained not by cynicism on the one side or naivete on the other but because each is operating with incorrect information.

This shift away from cynical self-interest and towards misunderstanding as an explanation of human motivation is extremely important because it is part of a general shift away from the farcical mode and towards the naturalistic mode. Furthermore, the emphasis on misunderstanding creates, in Syracusan Menaechmus, a trickster who is free from cynicism; when he enjoys pleasures without paying for them, his actions mirror the swindles of the most ambitious tricksters, yet he never consciously plots to deceive anyone. In most Plautine plays that center on trickery, the malice that motivates the trickster is defused by the trickster's status as slave, whose child-like attitude towards the trick ensures that he is looking for no permanent reversal of power. In other plays where, like the *Menaechmi*, the ending does envision a permanent change, the trick that the good guys had planned to use against the bad guys is usually trumped by a twist of fate.[22] The decorum of naturalistic comedy has no place for malicious trickery. Malice itself is contrary to the tone of this type of comedy, and this mode is also

---

[21] Segal's interpretation of this play focuses on rebellion to set the tone of the play; Leach's interpretation focuses on this desire to reestablish identity. Leach (1969a: 33): "Each brother is a personality manqué; the two need not be regarded as separate identities, but rather as separated halves of one complete self. As these two unknowing halves approach the discovery of one another, the plot may be considered as the completion of a whole personality through the interaction of its parts. The play itself becomes symbolic of man's seeking for a fully realized self."

[22] The tricks are trumped in *Captivi*, *Trinummus*; *Poenulus*, *Epidicus*, and *Curculio* represent intermediate cases, where the trick has its effect, but a broader and more complete resolution comes through a twist of fate.

rather uncomfortable with the emphasis that trickery plots place on human action as the decisive factor in events. One of the fundamental concepts of the naturalistic mode, after all, is that humans are mere playthings in a world ruled by deeper, invisible principles. The *Menaechmi* shows, however, how even this mode that privileges superhuman control can accommodate the pleasures and practical benefits of trickery. Syracusan Menaechmus plays the role of the trickster here, by "stealing" luxury goods, food, and Erotium's attentions. But the disguise that makes his trickery work is given him by nature rather than made up by him, and he is not even aware of its power. The twin motif can be seen as a naturalized version of a disguise trick.

Scene II.1 introduces the master and slave entering Epidamnus for the first time. The dominant issue in this scene is whether or not to continue the search for the lost twin. How Syracusan Menaechmus and Messenio react to this question reveals their relationship to each other. Syracusan Menaechmus insists that the search will be ended only by the certainty, not the probability, of his brother's death,[23] while Messenio argues on practical grounds that this search is bankrupting his master. Menaechmus' absolutism in the face of practical difficulties is paralleled by his absolute sense of himself as master, even when his purse is empty. Messenio's reaction shows concern for his master, and, coupled with his warning against the wiles of the denizens of Epidamnus, it establishes that he promotes his master's interest better than the master himself does, a quality that will be highlighted in the final scene where he recognizes the two brothers before they recognize each other. Messenio throughout the play is distinguished by his ability to see everything from his master's point of view rather than his own. The complementarity between the characteristics of absolutism in the master and empathy in the slave is summed up here:

> MEN: dictum facessas, datum edis, caveas malo.
> molestus ne sis, non tuo hoc fiet modo. MES: em!
> illoc enim verbo esse me servom scio.
> non potuit paucis plura plane proloquei.

> (249–52)

MEN: Do what you're told, eat what you're given, keep an eye out for trouble.
Don't be difficult, this won't be done to suit you.
MES: Well! That's the way to tell me I'm a slave.
He couldn't have clarified it more clearly and concisely.

---

[23] The death/rebirth theme, of much greater importance in the *Captivi*, remains vestigial in this play; see also the metaphor of cremating the day at 152–55, 492. Leach (1969a: 33–34, *passim*) grants this theme greater importance.

Menaechmus expresses his impatience with Messenio's suggestions by reminding him that this search will be carried out to the master's pleasure, not the slave's.[24] Messenio immediately translates these dicta into their global meaning: you're the slave and I'm the master.[25]

Another speech of Messenio's closes the action of Act II. In this, his last speech before the important monologue of V.6, he sums up his own position in language that reveals the strong contrast between himself and the dependents of Epidamnian Menaechmus.

> sed ego inscitus qui domino me postulem moderarier:
> dicto me emit audientem, haud imperatorem sibi.
>
> (443–44)

But what a fool I am to demand that I govern my master:
He bought me to to do his bidding, not to lord it over him.

This, the clearest possible statement that his own relation with his master is the exact opposite of the Epidamnian brother's model of authority, solidifies the contrast between the two kinds of mastery. It is followed immediately by the second entrance monologue of Peniculus, who exemplifies the dependent who wants to be *imperator*.

While Messenio's relationship to his master demonstrates the Syracusan's principles of authority, at the same time, his suspicions of the Epidamnians serve to reorient the audience's understanding of the previous act. In the first act, we were treated to two contradictory impressions of Epidamnian Menaechmus: as a sympathetic rebel kicking over the traces and as a naive dupe of the wily Erotium and Peniculus. Messenio's characterization of this city in scene II.1 constitutes a warning to his master:

> nam ita est haec hominum natio: in Epidamnieis
> voluptarii atque potatores maxumei;
> tum sycophantae et palpatores plurumei
> in urbe hac habitant; tum meretrices mulieres
> nusquam perhibentur blandiores gentium.
> propterea huic urbei nomen Epidamno inditumst,
> quia nemo ferme huc sine damno devortitur.
>
> (258–64)

---

[24] The implicit use of slavery as a standard against which to measure all relationships of hierarchy is evident in the fact that the Epidamnian brother tells his wife to watch out for trouble in almost exactly the same language as the Syracusan brother tells his slave (*malo cavebis* [122], *caveas malo* [249]).

[25] See also lines 265–71 where Syracusan Menaechmus further exhibits his authoritative style by mistrusting even so good a slave as Messenio and not giving in to the temptation to make use of slaves as trusted extensions of the self.

I'll tell you what this bunch is like: among the Epidamnians are pleasure seek-
ers and drinkers without rival; second, a great many sycophants and flatterers
live here; and finally, nowhere else in the world will you find such sweet-talking
prostitutes. That's how Epidamnus got its name: because practically no one
takes this place in without getting damn well taken.[26]

Messenio's description of the people to be found in Epidamnus perfectly
matches with the inhabitants we saw in the first act: Peniculus (*sycophantae
et palpatores*) and Erotium (*meretrices mulieres [blandissimae]*). Our experience of the first act, then, establishes Messenio to be an extremely wise
advisor, able to predict exactly the characteristics of a population we have
just seen at first hand. But Messenio's astute warning does more than
just identify him as astute: by warning his master against people like Peniculus and Erotium, he also reinforces the possibility that the brother who
lives in Epidamnus is not in control and is a dupe of these wily inhabitants.
Like the Syracusan brother, Epidamnian Menaechmus is also "really" a
visitor, not someone who ever belonged among such hucksters. (In the
naturalistic mode, birth—not experience—defines identity.) Unlike the
brother who is just getting his first look at this perilous city, the brother
who lives in Epidamnus has already discovered to his cost the rapacious
habits of Epidamnians.

Scenes II.2 and II.3 continue to demonstrate the differences between the
two brothers, while they also introduce two new motifs that will take on
greater importance as the differences between the brothers get played out
dramatically. The scene with the cook Cylindrus is the first where misunderstanding leads to hostility, expressed in imputations of insanity.[27] Here,
as he will do later in Act V, Syracusan Menaechmus refuses to back down
when confronted by people who claim to know him and wields his knowledge of religious ritual (288–93) as a weapon. The confrontation with Erotium presages later developments even more closely. It continues the par-
rying of accusations of insanity, but from line 417 on it shows Menaechmus
cleverly taking advantage of others' misperceptions to put himself in control.[28] As in V.2, where he will use the show of religious ecstasy to pretend
to marginalize himself while really taking control, here he imitates the
lovesick *adulescens*' submission (*impera quid vis modo* ["just tell me what you
want"], 425) to conceal his masterful appropriation of his brother's feast.

---

[26] In Latin, the pun relates the name Epidamnus to the word *damnum* (cost).

[27] Leach (1969a: 38).

[28] Hough (1942) identifies lines 391 and 403 (both responses of Syracusan Menaechmus
to Erotium) as examples of a "reverse comic foil"; i.e., where a freeborn, high-status character
uses a person of lower status as a straight man. In the context of the interpretation here, it
will be obvious that this reversal is evidence of Menaechmus' ability to usurp the linguistic
habits of clever slaves.

At lines 428–29 his cleverness is repeated and symbolized in his assumption that Erotium sends the cloak to the embroiderer for deceptive, not aesthetic, purposes. Together, the imputations of insanity (which call to our attention the characters' mutual misunderstanding) and Syracusan Menaechmus' ability to use his resemblance to his brother to gain entrance to Erotium's house lay the foundation for his naturalized and nonmalicious trickery, an element extremely important to the ways that this play negotiates the competing assumptions of the two modes of comedy, using rebellion to the ends of reconciliation.

The Visitor Takes Control

The play's third movement (= Acts III, IV, and Act V.1–5) contains the central scenes of confusion and disorder caused by the brothers' being mistaken for one another. This disorder emphasizes the contrasts between the brothers' styles of mastery and the literary modes associated with them, as it charts the visiting twin's increasing dominance over those around him. In the first two movements the brothers' difference was shown in terms of their attitudes towards saving and spending[29] and the assurance with which they assume roles of authority. In the scenes of confusion that constitute the third movement, the difference is emphasized by the open rebellion of dependent characters against Epidamnian Menaechmus, who is penned in and beleaguered by this revolt, while Syracusan Menaechmus consistently either escapes or shouts down those who accuse him. The scenes of questioning that make up most of this third movement will show that the brothers' strategies of dealing with confusion and confrontation play out the contrast between the two types of mastery and the two literary modes that were introduced in the first two acts.

This movement opens with a monologue of Peniculus, again, as with his first monologue, setting the tone for what follows.[30] He defines participating in an assembly (*contio*) as a crime (*facinus*) then suggests that "idle" men, that is, nonparasites, should be the ones to spend their time in political debate.[31] The strongly moralizing language (*decuit* at 453, *oportet* at 459) further sharpens the point of this incongruous proposal, which reverses the Roman social norm on its most important axes: civic duty versus private pleasure, *negotium* versus *otium*. As in his first monologue, Peniculus here

[29] Leach (1969a: 36), Ketterer (1986b: 54).

[30] This thematic internal prologue is, like the self-descriptive monologues noted above in note 9, often given by parasites or figures like them. Cf. *Capt* 461–97, 768–80; *Bac* 573–83; in the *Amphitruo* the numerous "internal prologues" are shared by Mercury and Jupiter, who perform many of the usual functions of parasite and clever slave, respectively; see *Am* 463–98, 861–81, 984–1008. See also Slater (1985: 102, note 11).

[31] Cf. the parasite's legislative proposal at *Per* 62–74.

parodically takes on the values of the elite and, again, only for his own advantage. When he places looking for a dinner invitation above engaging in public life, we know that for Peniculus, as for other comic parasites, food has crowded out every other value, both public and private.

Between this monologue and the important monologue of Epidamnian Menaechmus (IV.2) are three short scenes that highlight by repetition the differences between the two brothers in their handling of authority.[32] In scene III.2, Peniculus confronts Syracusan Menaechmus, who is able effortlessly to brush off the parasite's complaints and threatened blackmail, thus making explicit that his style of mastery fundamentally undermines the assumptions on which Epidamnian Menaechmus' household authority was based.

The Syracusan's style of dealing with dependents is again pointedly opposed to his brother's when we see him taking from Erotium the valuable cloak just given to her by Epidamnian Menaechmus, under the guise of taking it to the embroiderer for improvements. His over-the-shoulder address to Erotium, followed by his gloating over his *praeda* (booty) should be compared to the first entrance of Epidamnian Menaechmus, where that brother is haggling with his wife. Epidamnian Menaechmus heatedly reproached his wife and rejoiced in his triumph of having stolen the cloak; Syracusan Menaechmus is superficially calm, reassuring, and conciliatory but is equally proud of having stolen the cloak. Unlike his brother, who made the theft a bold military maneuver (cf. 128–34), Syracusan Menaechmus explains this feat as the result of his trickiness and the manipulation of perceptions rather than the use of brute force.[33]

> quoniam sentio
> errare, extemplo, quasi res cum ea esset mihi,
> coepi adsentari: mulier quidquid dixerat,
> idem ego dicebam. quid multis verbis <opust>?
> minore nusquam bene fui dispendio.
>
> (481–85)

As soon as I realized that she had the wrong idea, immediately, as if I really had some connection with her, I began to agree: whatever that woman said, I

---

[32] Wilner (1930: 68).

[33] Slater (1985: 16–17, note 29) defines the clever slave's heroism as his ability both to manipulate his own dramatic identity (by taking on one of the other stock roles) and to use the traditional features of other stock characters against them. "Pseudolus, Chrysalus and the others base their power on the ability to manipulate others as *artistic* constructs" (emphasis in the original). What Syracusan Menaechmus is doing here is manipulating Erotium more as a character than a character type, since gullibility and generosity are not canonical features of the comic *meretrix*. In general, this fits with my contention that the difference between this trickster and a clever slave is that his trickery is naturalized and made less cynical.

said the same. To make a long story short, nowhere have I enjoyed myself at less expense.

In scene III.3 the imagery and language of the trickster even more prominently coalesce around Syracusan Menaechmus. He succeeds in tricking Erotium's maid out of a gold bracelet, in much the same way that he acquired the cloak: using deceptive speech (note especially the ironic double entendre at 539–40, the stock in trade of the clever slave). At the end of this scene, he engages in more slavish linguistic behavior when he meditates on how he can get away safely with his loot. His self-apostrophe at line 554 can be paralleled by his confrères in other plays, Pseudolus, Epidicus, Gelasimus, and Tranio.[34] Finally, the next scene emphasizes and makes explicit his successful scheming when he is able to misdirect Peniculus and the Matrona by leaving behind a party-goer's garland as a misleading clue to his whereabouts (565–6).[35]

Just as Peniculus' joking introduction of his own selfish view of food and loyalty at I.1 influenced our view of Epidamnian Menaechmus (by allowing us to see the patron's self-deceiving naivete), his monologue at the beginning of Act III gives a framework within which the audience will interpret Epidamnian Menaechmus' monologue at lines 571–601. This latter monologue purports to be a diatribe against contemporary manners, somewhat less ridiculous than Peniculus' diatribe; its target is the nouveaux riches clients who make their way through litigation with little help from truthfulness. Epidamnian Menaechmus' complaint squares with traditional values rather than reverses them, as Peniculus' does. But this sermon is made ironic in two ways. First, in the context of comic convention, Fraenkel has shown that this monody fits a pattern of a lover (especially a *senex amator*) complaining about missing his personal pleasures because of public business.[36] The closest parallel in the surviving corpus is that of Lysidamus at *Casina* 563–73.[37] But here in the *Menaechmi*, the contrast between business and pleasure is heightened and made more ironic by Menaechmus' stern moralizing on the perfidy of clients, as if he would not have minded missing his tryst in order to serve honest clients![38] Second, in the context of the

---

[34] For self-apostrophe by name, see *Ps* 394, 453; *Epid* 82, 96, 161, 194; *Mos* 1068; *St* 632. See also Slater (1985: 21–24, 126–27) for a metatheatrical interpretation of self-address in *Epidicus* and *Pseudolus*.

[35] Ketterer (1986b: 58).

[36] Fraenkel (1922: 159–61 = 1960: 152–53). Segal (1987), chap. 2, "From Forum to Festival," is predicated on the opposition between business and pleasure; see esp. 50–52.

[37] But see also *As* 871–72, where this theme appears reflected. Artemona, on finding her husband with the *meretrix*, now doubts all his previous alibis: *eum etiam hominem <aut> in senatu dare operam aut cluentibus, / ibi labore delassatum noctem totam stertere!*

[38] This convention also implies another joke in Peniculus' monologue, i.e., rather than mourning the lost opportunity for sex, the parasite mourns a lost meal. This expands on

play itself, this upstanding diatribe is immediately followed by a long scene in which Epidamnian Menaechmus tries to escape his wife's wrath through blandishments, lies, and—most pointedly—false oaths (616–17, 655–56).[39] His behavior in this scene undercuts any moral authority Menaechmus might have claimed, as it assimilates him to the clients he has spoken of, thus again implying his wife's ascendancy over him.

In the repeated scenes of questioning that begin to dominate this movement, Syracusan Menaechmus uses others' irrational beliefs to consolidate his claim to authority, while his Epidamnian brother loses even that precarious hold on his mastery that he held in the first act. (The end of this movement shows the Epidamnian at his lowest ebb, about to be tied up and carried off by a doctor to be treated for insanity.) The most important effect of these scenes of questioning is that they shift the prevailing tone of the play so that rebellion is no longer associated with self-interest on the part of those who are normally downtrodden but is transformed into an instrument for freeing the two brothers from the greedy and vulgar townspeople of Epidamnus.

It is significant for the relation of the farcical and naturalistic modes in this play that the first of these questioning scenes, IV.2, is the only one in which all the participants are basing their behavior on a correct knowledge of the facts: they all know that Epidamnian Menaechmus has stolen the cloak and given it to Erotium, and they correctly assume the identities of the people to whom they are talking. By contrast, in V.2 and V.5, the humor and dramatic impact turn on mistaken identity: the wrong Menaechmus at the wrong time does not understand what he is being accused of (theft and adultery in V.2, insanity in V.5), and the others mistakenly assume the identity of the person they are accusing. This difference between scene IV.2 and the latter scenes (V.2 and V.5) marks the spot in the play where the farcical worldview finally gives way to the naturalistic, where the theme of rebellion gives way to the theme of mistaken identity, where aggression gives way to a humanistic emphasis on freedom.

In scene IV.2, where Peniculus and the Matrona confront Epidamnian Menaechmus, in keeping with the farcical understanding of rebellion as real aggression, the conflict centers on control of knowledge and speech. Peniculus' tactic is obviously that of the frustrated blackmailer: he reveals his knowledge of Epidamnian Menaechmus' theft and adultery to get a reward from the Matrona when he realizes that concealment will no longer

---

the pattern of equating a high-status man's lust with another's gluttony, a pattern especially prominent in the *Casina*.

[39] Note that the word (*manufestum*, 594) Menaechmus uses indignantly when his clients deny deeds in which they have been caught red-handed is the same word that Peniculus uses in promising to prove his guilt to the Matrona (562).

bring a reward from her husband. Because his power lies in the revelation of facts, his interest throughout the scene is in promoting that revelation. This general strategy is echoed at a smaller level in the byplay when he tattles on Menaechmus for attempting to silence him through winks and nods.[40] This strategy is in tension with that of the Matrona, who prefers to express her power not by revealing her knowledge but by forcing Menaechmus to confess. For most of this scene (604–40) she speaks only in questions, oblique exclamations, and declarations that Menaechmus himself knows more than he pretends. The Matrona's general strategy is repeated on a smaller scale in the silliness of the game of "you're getting warmer/colder" at lines 621–25.[41] At lines 642–44 she explicitly admits that her goal has been to elicit a sense of shame from Menaechmus, and, since she has failed, she will be straightforward from this point on. Exactly at this point Menaechmus begins a series of evasive questions, aimed at representing innocent ignorance where the Matrona's questions were aimed at demonstrating a powerful knowledge. By assuming that she must be angry with the slaves, he tries to both displace his own guilt and subtly reinforce the idea that the household is the Matrona's sphere of power. In the context of what the audience has already seen of the relations of power in this household and the assimilation of Menaechmus to a (nonclever) slave, this attempt only strengthens his identification with a household slave. When this strategy fails to fend off the Matrona's anger and knowledge (655–56), he retreats again to the false oath (cf. 616–17) and verbal quibbles (657).[42] The Matrona exits, disappointing both Peniculus' hope of a reward and Menaechmus' hope of forgiveness. Peniculus leaves immediately after, ending his role in this play. Just as Erotium will later equate husband and wife in her final dismissal of Menaechmus, so does Peniculus here, emphasizing their similarity as patrons who never quite deliver on their part of the bargain.

The second scene of questioning (V.2) features the Syracusan brother and, with him, an emphasis on misunderstanding. This scene also intro-

---

[40] Note also at line 626 that Peniculus shows the transfer of his allegiance to the Matrona by "decoding" an attempt at deception, just as he did for Menaechmus at line 193, but in both cases this service is clearly to his own advantage. His language also betrays his increasing association with the blocking characters: often *malus* is used approvingly by those in on the scheme of deception. Peniculus' negative use of it here shows him to be outside the circle of comic heroes.

[41] This whole scene is paralleled by that of Dorippa and Lysimachus in the *Mercator* (714–40). Points of contact between these two scenes include the wife's strategy of trying to get her husband to confess rather than of accusing him, the theme of *pudicitia*, the husband guessing that it is the slaves who are at fault, and the prominence of legal language. Fantham (1968: 177, 178) notes parallels also to *As* V.2.

[42] There is a nice ambiguity about the falseness of both oaths: the first would depend on a producer's choice of whether to emphasize Menaechmus' cowardliness or Peniculus' tattling, the second is up to a semantic quibble. Segal (1987: 181, note 19) notes the sexual pun in *dedisse* at 656.

duces the Matrona's father, the Senex, supposedly as a mediator, but it quickly becomes apparent that he endorses Menaechmus' point of view against that of the Matrona.[43] Only later is he himself cowed by Syracusan Menaechmus' impressive performance as madman. Here we see a theme common in idealizing comedy. As Frye (1965: 73–74) has shown for Shakespearean comedy, the forensic way of thinking externalizes the characteristics of rigidity and small-mindedness associated with the society of the blocking characters.[44] The language of the first discussion between the Senex and the Matrona is the language of the courtroom. The father consistently uses the language of a judge (see esp. *postulo* at 794, 796 bis; cf. *insimulo* at 806), while his daughter makes it clear that she brought him not to judge but to plead her case (798–99). Although they disagree as to the role of the father and as to the points of "law" in the "case," they are united in their understanding and expression of the couple's marital problems in legal terms.

In opposition to this legal worldview is that of Syracusan Menaechmus, who makes use of two types of authority. In addition to the humane authority, which in the naturalistic mode of comedy is on the side of the righteous against the wicked (expressed here in his religious language), Syracusan Menaechmus also shows himself to be vested with the authority that farcical comedy grants to the clever slave (expressed here in his theatrical abilities). From his very first line (811–12) his language has religious overtones. Even when he decides to fake madness to avoid his accusers, the madness he chooses to pretend is that of religious ecstasy. Although his use of religious imagery may seem cynical, there is also moral content throughout. First, at lines 811–14, his true oath stands in stark contrast to the false oaths offered by his brother in IV.2.[45] Second, his madness is a portrayal of obedi-

---

[43] A side note: the humor of the Senex's two monologues stressing his slowness because of his age (753–60) and the long time he has spent waiting for the doctor (882–88) results at least in part from their contradictory relation to the movement of the play. In both cases, he comes on much sooner than any realistic theater could reasonably hope to cover for. Plautine theater, rather than trying to gloss over this improbability, exaggerates it by inserting what must have been canonical "covering speeches" to explain away necessary lapses in dramatic time, e.g., after a choral interlude. Thus we have a good example of how even maintaining comic conventions without any manipulation at all can metatheatrically wink at these conventions and the illusionistic expectations they imply.

[44] See also Frye (1957: 166): "The action of comedy in moving from one social center to another is not unlike the action of a lawsuit, in which plaintiff and defendant construct different versions of the same situation, one finally being judged as real and the other as illusory." (169): "Thus the movement from *pistis* to *gnosis*, from a society controlled by habit, ritual bondage, arbitrary law and the older characters to a society controlled by youth and paradigmatic freedom is fundamentally, as the Greek words suggest, a movement from illusion to reality."

[45] This oath is emphasized by the interruptions, esp. *deierat?* ("is he swearing?"), which calls attention to his oath taking.

ence to Apollo in punishing a wrongdoer (see esp. 838–39); note that the offense is that of *falsum testimonium*. At the same time, he draws on the farcical mode, in which the hero is that character with more theatrical skill, better able to act his way out of a difficulty.[46] Syracusan Menaechmus' use of the amoral wiles of clever slaves and righteous moral principles in this struggle shows him to be in control of both of these modes and the authority each implies.[47]

The third scene of questioning (V.5) closes what I have called the third movement of the play, and in several ways, the relation of this scene to those preceding it sums up the tensions of the play here, at the brink of its resolution. This scene restates the differences between the two brothers, but it also points toward the final scene of reconciliation. Where Syracusan Menaechmus was able to escape the attempts of the Matrona and her father to contain him through a cleverly thought-out ruse that embodied the authoritative power of religion, Epidamnian Menaechmus escapes their control only because his genuine anger and frustration terrify them. Yet the imminent assimilation of the two brothers is hinted at in the wild and extravagant language with which Epidamnian Menaechmus unwittingly repeats the style of his brother's more artistic representation of madness. Even more important for the swerve of the play as a whole towards the naturalistic perspective, the Epidamnian's rebellion here clearly fits the model of naturalistic rebellion, because his opponent, the doctor, who is convinced of his insanity, embodies the same kind of narrow-minded thinking that was represented by legal language in the earlier scenes. In those scenes, the Matrona and her father were labeled as illegitimate authority figures (thus ripe for overthrow in the mode of naturalistic comedy) be-

---

[46] Chiarini (1979: 40–41, 45, 69, 112–13, 119, 167) on acting ability as a mark of distinction in the comic morality. For *adsimulo* in role-playing deceptions, cf. *Bac* 962; *Truc* 390, 464, 472; *Am* 874, 999; *Capt* 224; *Mil* 1163. The use of literary models in this scene creates a complex joke by pitting Syracusan Menaechmus' and the audience's superior knowledge of the literary ancestry of madness against the blocking characters' ignorance of these models and insistence on the truth of their empirical perceptions. For his first outcry (835) Menaechmus makes use of the most horrific and antirational example of ritual ecstasy, that of the Bacchae. In the following lines this invocation gains additional humorous force from the implied inversion of gender roles; Menaechmus takes on the role not of Pentheus but of Agave, seeing his accuser as a rabid dog. But the religious and literary allusions of the rest of this scene fall into the realm of Apollo and Orestes (esp. 840). On the level of literary allusion, this farrago underlines both the ignorance of the blocking characters and the artificial nature of this madness, which is shown to be a patchwork of "Great Mad Scenes in Greek Tragedy." Leach (1969a: 39–40) argues that the madness of Hercules provides yet another model (she does not acknowledge the Orestes references) and emphasizes that for both Hercules and Pentheus "a fearful loss of identity places the hero in conflict with his closest kin."

[47] Segal (1987: 132–35) on the use of imagery of divinity to exalt the cleverness of slaves (see, e.g., *Bac* 640, *Asin* 712–13, *Ps* 109–110). Here we have a less extreme expression of the alignment between the divine order and the comic order.

cause they clung to a legalistic way of thinking and talking that prevented them from assessing the situation accurately. Here, the doctor's professional gibberish even more obviously clouds his vision. From his very first lines, the doctor shows his grasp of the differentiations between kinds of insanity with his list of technical terms, while completely missing the point that the Senex is interested only in restraining his raving son-in-law and not in the niceties of psychiatric diagnosis (889–93).[48] Thus, even though the Epidamnian brother is no more wise or moral than he has been all along, the characterization of his opponent in this scene makes him seem more like a naturalistic hero than a farcical rebel.

The third movement, then, has taken us from a point where the two brothers, with their differing authoritative and literary styles, were merely contrasted to a point where it has become clear that the Syracusan brother will win the day. But this victory is not a victory over his brother but a victory in which his brother will share, as together the twins escape the illegitimate authority that the Epidamnians have tried to impose on them. This victory delivers on the promise of the brothers' physical resemblance, namely, that by emphasizing the brothers' natural kinship, it prefigured a reestablishment of familial bonds. But the most important effect of the third movement is that it has made us forget that when we first saw Epidamnian Menaechmus rebelling against his wife we took him for the kind of mischievous rebel who knows that he must in the end submit himself again to her power. By the end of the third movement, both brothers have become the kind of morally justified rebels whose trickery exposes those tyrants who operate on illegitimate authority.

Wishes Fulfilled

The fourth and final movement (= Act V.6–9) is one of resolution and redemption. It begins with a monologue in which Messenio describes the ideal of the good slave, just as the first movement opened with Peniculus' explication of the principles of parasitism.[49] This monologue points to the specific language and ideas associated with the Epidamnian style of mastery and rejects them in favor of a stable, unambiguous mastery that emphasizes the slave's desire to avoid punishment more than his ambition to reap rewards. Again, in contrast to Peniculus, who gave advice to masters con-

---

[48] In parallel to my interpretation of the doctor here, Scodel (1993) argues that cooks are the comic butts in Menander precisely because their competence, especially in the area of sacrifice, is threatening to New Comedy's choice to privilege superhuman, diffused power.

[49] Leach (1969a: 36) notes the thematic opposition of these monologues.

ceived for his own advantage, Messenio gives advice to his fellow slaves shaped by the interests of masters.[50]

Messenio, the loyal slave, who has been consistently presented as the thematic opposite of the other three dependent characters, saves Epidamnian Menaechmus from the slaves trying to tie him up and reunites the twins, explaining everything to the two brothers who are still mired in confusion. Because it is the naturalistic perspective that shapes the end of this play, we have a good, obedient slave who orchestrates the resolution. In most other Plautine comedies, we expect to see the clever slave trying to placate his master who has discovered the fraud that has been perpetrated; here, the good slave acts to open the eyes of his master(s). Further, the casting of this denouement as a scene of questioning aligns it with the legalistic wrangling that took up most of the third movement. This final scene, however, replaces the disagreements and misunderstandings of the previous scenes of questioning with a formalized process that reveals the identity of the two brothers. This process is predicated on their giving exactly the same answers to the questions posed by Messenio, resulting in harmony and assimilation rather than in strife and difference. Thus the questioning process becomes an instrument of reconciliation rather than of hostility, as it was for the blocking characters. Finally, Messenio's manumission and transformation into auctioneer completes the process of distancing him from the usual slave heroes of comedy and makes him the means by which the brothers are freed from the material encumbrances of life at Epidamnus.

This final scene expresses the reunion and reconciliation between the two brothers in ways that further emphasize the role that material goods have played in marking out the social tensions in this play. First of all, the moment of recognition is also the moment when the two brothers are able finally to understand all the inexplicable things that have happened to them on this day. Along with explaining to each other what confusions they have experienced, they also reassert the correct relations to their property. Syracusan Menaechmus explains that he has eaten the dinner his brother ordered for himself, visited Erotium, and stolen both the cloak and some jewelry. When he passes the cloak back to the Epidamnian brother, we are momentarily returned to the image of hopeful liberation with which the

---

[50] Two details support my contention that the play is oriented towards the naturalistic mode here at its close. First, the Senex puts into practice the type of mastery Messenio has been advocating, by addressing his slaves unhesitatingly in authoritative language (990–91, 993). Second, Menaechmus calls for the aid of his fellow citizens (1000), and Messenio blames the Epidamnians for this act (1004): both uses of *cives* reinforce the idea that even this Menaechmus who has lived so long in Epidamnus cannot count on the help of its inhabitants and, in fact, is being victimized by them.

play began. The difference is that here the Epidamnian brother holds the cloak permanently: it will not be given to either of the greedy women. Nor does the cloak here "unman" him, because now he does not put it on, since he has no need to be sneaky about owning it. It is a symbol of his true liberation from the world-out-of-joint in which he had been living that he now can be both authoritative in claiming his goods and generous with his resources (1143). The Syracusan brother, whose authority never came into question, continues this connection between unapologetic ownership and generosity when he frees Messenio, having found out about the service he has done for his brother.

But perhaps the most telling detail of this final scene is that the resolution makes no attempt to rehabilitate the inhabitants of Epidamnus into the more perfect world that this reunion augurs. This play is not content merely to leave the blocking characters out of the final scene but goes further and enacts their removal from the new life of the two brothers.[51] The brothers will return to Syracuse and all the Epidamnian brother's household goods will be auctioned. The play ends with the newly freed Messenio announcing this auction and including Menaechmus' wife in the catalogue (1157–60). Thus ends the dilemma of how to integrate one's social ties with the economic relations such ties inevitably include: every relationship except for those defined through blood can be turned into cash. We are left with a vague sense that life back in Syracuse will be founded only on these "real" ties and will require no messy economic entanglements. In Syracuse, masters are masters and slaves are slaves, and everyone understands the value of money.

THE CAST OF CHARACTERS

Since each of the dependent characters has different attributes and a different relationship to the two brothers, it will be useful to clarify the characterization and dramatic function of each one before further pursuing the characterization of the two brothers. This discussion will include the three dependents of Epidamnian Menaechmus (Peniculus, Erotium, and the Matrona) and also Messenio, the slave of Syracusan Menaechmus. Each of the four is important in him- or herself, for what they do and say in this play, but each one is also an example of a well-developed type. An examination of these types (the parasite, the *meretrix*, the *uxor dotata*, and the good slave) will enrich the understanding of how these characters function here.

---

[51] Leach (1969a: 33) on this "satiric" ending, using Frye's definition of the satiric mode (1957: 180).

The primary characteristic of Peniculus is his self-conscious cynicism in manipulating the social forms with which he is familiar. The literary expression of this cynicism is his consciousness of the conventions of comedy. Although this play does not show the kind of explicit metatheatrical language and imagery as, for example, the *Pseudolus*, still it makes use of another kind of metatheater where the conventions of comedy operate as the fictional background experience of the characters.[52] Peniculus stands out as the most conscious of their joint comic past, as is particularly evident in his insistence on maintaining other characters' adherence to their comic stereotype. For example, in scene I.3, he and Erotium are openly hostile to each other, as rivals for Menaechmus' largesse. His hostility takes the form of undercutting Erotium's expressions of devoted submission by reminding the audience that she is, after all, a comic *meretrix*. Note, for example, their lines at 192–95, where Erotium extravagantly swears her loyalty and Menaechmus' power over her, and Peniculus comments by characterizing her as the typical flattering (*blanditur*) and greedy (*rapiat*) *meretrix*.[53] Similarly in scene IV.1, he supplies the Matrona with the habits from her comic past. At lines 569–70 when the Matrona plaintively asks for advice in accosting her husband, Peniculus reminds both her and the audience that this is one area in which she should need no help. These reminders are Peniculus' attempts to maintain his metatheatrical power in controlling the play, by refusing to admit the possibility of any deviation from the stereotype that might lead towards an unconventional characterization. But since here in the *Menaechmi* the naturalistic mode dominates the ending of the play, Peniculus' metatheatrical control will give him no stake in the final resolution.

In addition to this metatheatrical stance within the play, Peniculus and his parasite brethren have well-defined dramatic functions that shape the progress of the play as a whole. Peniculus' opening monologue in the *Menaechmi* should be compared to the monologues of parasites in the *Captivi*, *Persa*, and *Stichus*. All these speeches share certain features that differentiate them from most other monologues, even from most other opening monologues. The parasites' monologues are all direct addresses to the audience, with no semblance of a realistic dramatic motivation; the parasite is baldly introducing himself across the footlights. The artificiality of the

---

[52] Hunter (1985: 74): "The range of these activities in drama is so restricted that the total experience of comic characters may be limited to a group of commonly occurring dramatic situations. 'Everyday experience' for some comic characters is only that which is sanctioned by repeated appearance on the comic stage."

[53] Preston (1916: 23) notes that *blanda* is the stock epithet of comic *meretrices*. Again, at 204, Peniculus offers a cynical interpretation of Erotium's line at 203 by placing it in the context of comic stereotypes.

parasite's approach is heightened by the use of his own name and, in the *Captivi* and *Menaechmi*, an explanation of his nickname that obliquely hints to his contentious relations with the youth of the city, who are both his meal ticket and his tormentors.

But the most distinctive element of these speeches is the way they are so emphatically focused on the description of the "trade" of parasitism itself. There are parallels in the corpus,[54] but no other character type is so pervasively associated with such a distinctive subject matter and expression. These monologues serve to establish the unusually fixed (and unusually explicit) spectrum of characteristics of the parasite and to establish him in a close relation to the audience. His character, rigidly defined by comic convention, has so few traits that it is reducible to a single motivation, and therefore it is both more comic and more explicitly artificial than the other character types. Precisely because he is shown to be so completely a product of comic convention, no attempt is made to conceal his artificial nature, to claim any verisimilitude for him. Thus he is unified with the audience in their perception of the illusionistic world in which the rest of the characters act. Peniculus is in the strange position of maintaining this sort of distance while at the same time being an important catalyst in the plot (it is his betrayal of Menaechmus to the Matrona that adds the element of hostility to the confusion created by the twins).

Erotium's character bears many similarities to Peniculus', but the dramatic techniques through which it is presented and the social tensions it expresses are quite different. Like Peniculus, she too is defined by her ability to perceive and make use of what Menaechmus would like to hear. Erotium's manipulation of masterly expectations lies in her perfect impersonation of the devoted wife. Scene I.3 illustrates her deft use of the attitudes and language of marital propriety. She is submissive (186), flattering (192), and accommodating (207, 213, 215). But most important is the exchange at 202–3, where Menaechmus praises her for being accommodating (*morigera*), the ultimate wifely virtue, and she replies that she is only doing what decorum bids (*decet*).[55]

One difference between Erotium and Peniculus in dramatic terms is that, although both stereotypes emphasize rapacity and cynicism, hers is reinforced within the play by Peniculus' comments. Because he takes a metatheatrical stance and is able to interpret others' behavior for the audience, Peniculus comes off initially as a good-natured, if self-interested,

---

[54] Cf. the *lena*'s speech in *Cist* 22–41, the young man's at *Merc* 16–39.
[55] Segal (1969: 82).

rogue, while Erotium seems merely greedy. This difference can be explained by the differing levels of interiority each is granted (Peniculus' monologues give him a closer relationship to the audience, who feel that they see him from within)[56] and by the nature of the exchange in which each is involved. Unlike the parasite who exchanges deference for the sensual pleasure of eating, the *meretrix* preys on others' desire for sensual pleasure in order to pile up material wealth. Erotium's own calculating attitude towards Menaechmus is cleverly echoed by her maidservant (III.3).[57] Where Erotium is well practiced in the art of giving and getting exactly what she wants, this maid is rather more heavy-handed (*inauris da mihi . . . ut te lubenter videam, quom ad nos veneris*. "Give me some earrings . . . so that I'll be happy to see you when you visit here," 541–43). Her obviousness is both a foil for the careful and intelligent work of Erotium in the previous scenes and a preparation for the snappish Erotium of IV.3.

This aspect of the *meretrix* as somehow too controlled is illustrated in the *Menaechmi* in scene I.4. A very short and rather negligible scene in itself, it gives a pointed contrast between the spending patterns of Menaechmus and Erotium. In the previous scene we have witnessed Menaechmus' exuberant, unmeasured, and somewhat irrational spending (such as giving away cloak [see 205–6 on its value] and ordering an enormous feast).[58] Here Erotium carefully counts out for the cook the money to be spent on shopping and specifically tells him to buy just enough, neither too little nor too much (*neque defiat neque supersit*, 221). This scene also complicates the pattern of spending that we have charted. Usually in comedy it is the lover who does the shopping, as an expression of his submission to the desires of the *meretrix* and, on a practical level, as part of his outlay to recompense her.[59] Here Erotium is shown carefully counting out her own money and sending her own slave to the market.

In conjunction with the fact that we never see money changing hands between either brother and Erotium, we must acknowledge that her willing assumption of the characteristics of a wife to promote her business as a *meretrix* has been extended so far that she becomes inseparable from the Matrona in fundamental ways. First, she provides the food for the banquet and gets paid in return not with money but with clothes and jewelry (precisely the items Menaechmus claims should "buy" his wife's obedience):

---

[56] For the power of a monologue to put a character in a privileged relation to audience, see Slater (1985: 100, 155–58) and Averna (1983).

[57] Wilner (1931: 270).

[58] Ketterer (1986b: 52).

[59] Menaechmus' instructions here and Erotium's response to them are much closer to the passage at *Cas* 419–22, where a husband asks a wife to prepare a ritual feast than to, e.g., *Bac* 93–100, where the *meretrix* puts up a half-hearted fight to prevent her lover paying for the shopping (the lover wins, naturally).

later, like the Matrona, she has these luxury goods stolen from her. The irony of Erotium's mimicry of the forms of devoted wifehood is that her actions, fueled by a powerful self-interest, not only superficially imitate but in fact replicate in substance the pattern to which Menaechmus wishes his wife would subscribe. Erotium so clearly understands that her material comfort depends on adapting herself to suit Menaechmus (being *morigera*) that she has completely internalized the exchange of obedience for goods against which the Matrona rebels.[60] The wife and the prostitute, whom we would ordinarily assume to be polar opposites, are so fully assimilated that the ending of the play reverses both the normal outcomes of comedy: instead of a marriage we get a divorce and instead of looking forward to a night of pleasure with a *meretrix*, Menaechmus jettisons her along with everything else.[61]

A comparison across the corpus reveals that *meretrices* must be seductive and yet somehow withhold their favors for the machinery of the plot to run. In cases where there is a *leno* or *lena*, the *meretrix* can be all tenderness and her owner all withholding.[62] Independent *meretrices*, like Erotium, must combine these aspects within themselves; this is most characteristically accomplished by a metatheatrical recognition that the *meretrix* is merely acting the part of devoted lover.[63] The *Truculentus* provides the most extensive treatment of this theme. The specific paradox of meretricious greed producing wifely attitudes in Erotium is paralleled by a more developed version of the same pattern in that play. There, Phronesium's imitation of a wife is made even more extreme in her fictive maternity, and her greed is correspondingly inflated to an almost inhuman degree. Konstan's analysis of this play focuses on defining the process through which the usual bond between the *adulescens* and the *meretrix* is transformed into a satirical rejection of romantic values latent in such a plot.[64] He points to the fact that the warmth that Phronesium displays towards Diniarchus is consistently undercut by the revelation of greed as the engine of her emotions. As I have argued for the *Menaechmi*, this materialism, according to Konstan, is what produces the satirical ending of the *Truculentus*: "Whatever the resolution, it will not involve a festive union of hero and heroine" (1983: 150).

---

[60] Note that even at line 677, just before she will finally dismiss him, Erotium repeats her affability in almost the same language as at line 207: she is still willing to play the game.

[61] Ketterer (1986b: 58–59) emphasizes the similarity between the two women by arguing for the "mercenary" marital arrangements of the *uxor* rather than for the submissiveness of the *meretrix*.

[62] See *Asinaria, Cistellaria, Curculio, Persa, Pseudolus, Rudens*.

[63] See *Bacchides, Miles Gloriosus, Truculentus*.

[64] Konstan (1983: 142–64); see also Dessen (1977).

When we compare the two women in the *Menaechmi*, we can see that, although the contrasts between Erotium's erotic *voluptas* and the Matrona's domestic *industria* are well defined,[65] still there is a set of language that the Matrona and Erotium share, each using it strategically to defend her own realm of power. The clearest example of this shared language is the opposition between inside and outside. It is Menaechmus himself who introduces this theme in his first speech, the tirade against his wife (110–124). At line 113, he threatens to put her out of the house (*foris*), which would mean the end of her status and power. The negative meaning of *foris* for the wife is contrasted with the positive meaning of *foras* for the husband (114): the public world where he should be able to go without his wife's restraint (repeated at 116). At line 124, the general meaning of *foras* as "away from home" takes on the specific meaning of "at Erotium's house," thus both undermining Menaechmus' argument that a man should be able to conduct his business (which turns out to be monkey business) without his wife's nagging and also setting up the terms of tension between the Matrona's house and that of Erotium.[66] The opposition between the wife and *meretrix* along the axis of inside/outside is linked with the movement of material goods (130), which are central to the power of both women.

In scene II.3, however, we see a reversal. Rather than Erotium's house being part of the general "outside," she explicitly creates it as a rival inside to that of the Matrona's. In her preparations (351–55), she specifically gives directions for everything to be prepared inside, and she lists the components of this sensuous interior. But most explicitly at lines 361–63 she describes the meaning of an interior space not as domestic orderliness and restraint but as voluptuous pleasure (*magi' quam domu' tua domu' quam haec tua sit*, "since this house is more of a home to you than your own house"). The repetition of *intus* at 366 emphasizes that, like the Matrona, her strategy can work only by containing Menaechmus within the *domus*, though within a radically different *domus*.

In the two paired scenes of confrontation that make up most of Act IV (IV.2 between Menaechmus and his wife and IV.3 between Menaechmus and Erotium), this contest for the appropriation of the meanings of inside and outside is played out. First, it seems that Menaechmus has accepted Erotium's definitions rather than the Matrona's; at lines 603 and 630 he uses *intro* to symbolize the adultery that takes place at Erotium's house. Parallel to Menaechmus' redefining *intro*, the Matrona sums up her argument about the proper spheres of power for husband and wife by em-

---

[65] The contrast between Erotium and the Matrona, between *voluptas* and *industria*, is fundamental to Segal's interpretation. See esp. (1969: 79–80), (1987: 43–44, 46–47).

[66] See references in previous note.

phasizing the proper transference of material wealth from inside to outside the *domus*:

> equidem ecastor tuam nec chlamydem do foras nec pallium
> quoiquam utendum. mulierem aequom est vestimentum muliebre
> dare foras, virum virile.
>
> (658–60)

You don't see me giving away (outside the house) your cloak or mantle for anyone to use. Women should give away women's clothes, and men should give away men's.

The centrality of this debate to the themes of the play is demonstrated by the way that Menaechmus uses precisely this language of inside and outside to express his defeat at the hands of his dependents. At lines 668–71 he contrasts his ill treatment by his wife (*exclusit foras*, "she's shut me out") with the devoted welcome he expects to find at Erotium's house (669), and he neatly pairs them off in parallel clauses using *displiceo* and *placuero* (to displease and to please).[67] The play on *-cludo* compounds in this line is picked up again at lines 698–99 in his final disillusion. There the repetition of *-cludo* compounds and especially *exclusissimus* ("the most shut-out man in the world") reveals his own frustrated desires by mocking his expectations of line 671.[68] Furthermore, this echoing of what he said when locked out of his own house and the following line (699) reinforce the similarity and parallelism between the two houses and the two women. Their assimilation to each other supports the satirical conclusion in which neither of them is allowed to join the new society.

To understand the role of the *uxor dotata* in this and other Plautine plays, this character must be considered in the context of the two characters in juxtaposition with whom she is defined, that is, the *senex amator* and the *meretrix*. The preceding comments on the dramatic functions of Erotium have clarified the complementary ways that *meretrices* and *matronae* are defined against each other. Of the comedies in which the *senex amator* theme is prominent, the *uxor dotata* is the necessary balance to this displaced love interest. The *senex amator* himself usually is seen unsympathetically, as an indecorous older man trying to usurp the pleasures of youth. It should be noted, however, that he is disapproved of not because he is committing adultery but because his age itself prevents him from having any justified erotic interests. The "legislative proposal" that Charinus gives at the end of the *Mercator* (1015–26) makes this explicit:

---

[67] Cf. a similar rhetorical balancing at 189; see Segal (1969: 83).
[68] Fantham (1968: 176).

annos gnatus sexaginta qui erit, si quem scibimus
si maritum sive hercle adeo caelibem scortarier,
cum eo nos hic lege agemus. . . .

(1017–19)[69]

If we find out that any man sixty years old is consorting with prostitutes, whether he's married or even single, we will deal with him according to this law. . . .

Thus the insults aimed at the *senex amator* are consistent with comedy's privileging of youth over age, where sons get to cheat fathers of money and even reserve for themselves exclusive rights to the propriety of erotic escapades. The psychoanalyst Ludwig Jekels has succinctly suggested that where tragedy is an expression of "oedipal" guilt on the part of the son, comedy derives its manic pleasures from the release engendered when this guilt is transferred to the father.[70] Nowhere is this generalization better illustrated than in the father-son rivalries of Plautine comedy.

If we accept this structural explanation of the function of the *senex amator* (that he is the necessary counterpart to the reign of youth), how do we explain the role of the *uxor dotata*? Of the four comedies where the hostility between a *senex amator* and an *uxor dotata* is most important, the *Casina* presents a special case and will be dealt with in detail in the next chapter, but an examination of the *Asinaria* and *Mercator* will help to place the *Menaechmi* in context. First, it should be noted that while the *uxor dotata* is notionally the blocking character in each of these plays, in the *Asinaria* and *Mercator* this function is performed by a proxy for most of the play (by the *lena* in the *Asinaria*, and in the *Mercator*, Dorippa, the neighbor's wife, completely stands in for Demipho's wife, the real object of the deception scheme). Only in the *Menaechmi* does the *uxor dotata* actively obstruct and harass her husband throughout the play. Second, in the other two plays,

---

[69] The point of this "law" aimed at age-decorum rather than marital fidelity is even clearer when Charinus' proposal is compared to that of Syra in the same play (817–29), which focuses on the double standard for women and men in marital infidelity.

[70] Jekels (1952: 103): "In the last resort, this infantile phantasy of the father as the disturber of love is nothing but a projection of the son's own guilty wish to disturb the love of the parents." (104): "In each case [comedy and mania] we find the ego, which has liberated itself from the tyrant, uninhibitedly venting its humour, wit, and every sort of comic manifestation in a very ecstasy of freedom." Note how close Jekel's description of this phenomenon is to Frye's contention that the triumph of youth is fundamental to the comic spirit and results in "paradigmatic freedom" (1957: 169). Both of these should also be compared to Konstan's more anthropological statement of the same theme: "The competition between father and son is always the result of paternal encroachment, never of incestuous desires in the youth. By violating the connubial code himself, the father implicitly gives sanction to the son's impulse, and thereby weakens the status boundaries that are his obligation to uphold" (1983: 20).

the *uxor dotata* appears only at the end and is then successful in calling her husband's amours to a halt, thus incidentally helping the cause of her son in the rivalry. (Again in the *Mercator* the real struggle between Demipho, Charinus, and their wife/mother is displaced onto the family next door.) Even where she does not actively help the cause of her son, she does act in his favor by punishing the old man. In the *Menaechmi*, on the other hand, the *uxor* is unsuccessful in stopping her husband and, further, she herself becomes the object of punishment at the end of the play.

The key to the specific erotic pattern in the *Menaechmi* is that the doubling of the two brothers—as if they were two people with the "same" body—allows the central male character to be both a *senex amator* (Epidamnian Menaechmus) and a young man in love (Syracusan Menaechmus).[71] As in other comedies based on the *senex amator* theme, it is the son who finally wins the sexual favors and the father who ends up paying the price, both literally and in bearing the painful criticism from his wife. Epidamnian Menaechmus is thwarted and demoralized, as a *senex amator* must be, but his final integration with Syracusan Menaechmus allows him to escape the normal outcome of his wife's threats. Thus, where in other *senex amator* comedies the wife is unlikable but the bulk of the punishment falls on the old reprobate, here the wife is both unlikable and the recipient of the punishment displaced from her husband. As a result, she is more explicitly constructed as a blocking character than the wives in other plays, who share their function with other characters.

Yet the *uxor dotata*'s role as punisher of the *senex amator* and ally of her son does not in itself explain the specific necessity of her being richly dowered. Just as the *senex amator* is defined as usurping the role of the *adulescens*, the *uxor dotata*'s wealth usurps the proper role of the *senex*. The wife's undue power is an explanation for the husband's abdication of the decorum appropriate for his own age and the mechanism through which he is punished. In the *Menaechmi*, again because of the necessity of saving Epidamnian Menaechmus at the end, the wife's wealth is given even greater and more explicit prominence in explaining her husband's philandering. Unlike Peniculus and Erotium, whose relationships with Menaechmus consist of a simple exchange of wealth for deference, the Matrona is both a giver and receiver of household wealth. Thus her reliance on her dowry as a source of power echoes her husband's style of mastery, which is rejected at the conclusion of the play.

Furthermore, the primary axis of the complementarity between Erotium and the Matrona consists in their opposing relations to financial and erotic power; each is strong in one and lacking in the other. Menaechmus runs

[71] Contra Webster (1953: 68).

from his rich and sexually unattractive wife to the seductive *meretrix* whom he must pay. This situation reinforces Erotium's assimilation to what a wife should be (not rich) as it preserves the opposition between wealth and sexuality, which is implicit in the contrast between an *uxor dotata* and a *senex amator*. Both are transgressors against decorum, but the *uxor's* preference for wealth doubly alienates her from the sensual pleasures ratified by the comic worldview.[72]

The final dependent character who must be considered is Messenio, the one who stands in absolute contrast to the others and in whom is embodied the resolution of the tensions of the play. From his first introduction in II.1, his relationship to his master is diametrically opposed to those of the three characters already discussed. He manages to express both loyalty and absolute obedience, and yet he is not abjectly flattering or grovelling. In this he represents a humane ideal of slavery—an ideal in which the slave's devotion to his master is coupled with an acknowledgment of his own dignity, what Leach has called "freedom in slavery" (1969a: 36).[73] In II.1 he openly challenges the value of continuing to search for the lost brother, but he never comes close to questioning his master's authority. He also sees it as within the power of the loyal slave to advise his master about their financial troubles and about the dangers of Epidamnus (his tact is heightened by his deliberation before he speaks, 252–53). Even though he is outspoken about his opinions, it is clear that his master's welfare is his only goal. Where Peniculus is cynical in his own interest, Messenio is cynical (about the Epidamnians) in the interest of his master. Peniculus' cynicism, furthermore, is based on a knowledge of the characters' theatrically conventional attributes, while that of Messenio is represented as the attitude one might expect from a weary and wary traveler. His subordination of his own self-interest to that of his master is carried even further in his encounters with Cylindrus and Erotium. In contrast to Peniculus' undercutting Erotium (by pointing out the stereotype she is pretending to depart from), Messenio performs the same service by reminding Syracusan Menaechmus of the "reality" behind her appearance of hospitality, but he does it in his master's interest rather than in his own, and he remains within the fictional world, within the dramatic illusion.

[72] Schuhmann (1977: esp. 53, 64) emphasizes the aspect of money providing improper power to women as an explanation for the characterization of *uxores dotatae*; she links this to the historical circumstance of increasing numbers of women controlling large amounts of money. See now also Rei (1998).

[73] (1969a: 36); see also (1969a: 37–38) on Messenio as an agent of liberation countering the social "bondage" of the other characters. The chapter on the *Captivi* below will offer a much fuller discussion of this "humane ideal of slavery," esp. the importance of slave loyalty in masterly ideology.

After this strongly painted introduction, Messenio disappears for most of the action of the play, during the confusion and recriminations resulting from the deceptive appearances of the two brothers. His reappearance co-incides with the crisis of the plot, when Epidamnian Menaechmus is threat-ened with being tied up and completely losing his identity and his authority, but his presence is also key to the reestablishment of the proper relations of authority and dependence. His monologue of V.6 is the perfect foil for the biting cynicism of Peniculus' earlier monologue. It also functions dra-matically by closing off the section of the play dominated by the badgering dependents of Epidamnian Menaechmus (none of the Epidamnian's de-pendents appears on stage after the Matrona's fearful exit at 853) and pre-pares us for his own manumission, the reward for the slave who thinks about obedience rather than food and wealth.

He announces his comic function in the first line (966), by declaring that his advice is for the *bonus servus* (the good slave), that is, the comic type opposed to the *servus callidus* (the clever slave). He goes on to subvert all the assumptions of Peniculus' opening monologue, by focusing on his master's interest rather than on his own:

> Spectamen bono servo id est, qui rem erilem
> procurat, videt, conlocat cogitatque,
> ut apsente ero rem eri diligenter
> tutetur quam si ipse adsit aut rectius.
>
> (966–69)

It is the mark of the good slave, one who gives his master's interest care and foresight and energy and thought, that he protects the interest of an absent master as carefully or even more carefully than when the master's present.

At line 968 he makes explicit his contrast with the clever slave and, more broadly, with the whole world of slaves tricking their masters. The notion of a slave being as good or better *apsente ero* ("when the master's away") as he is when the master is present subverts a concept that is fundamental to slave scheming and the prodigality of youth, the central plot elements of the farcical outlook. In this play, loyalty to an absent master takes on even greater thematic importance since it directly opposes the kind of authority advocated by Peniculus and Erotium, in which the master must constantly exert himself, must expend money and energy in order to maintain his mastery. Lines 970–76 are the heart of the contrast with Peniculus. Both speeches foreground the subordinate's body, but where Peniculus empha-sized the body as the locus of pleasure, Messenio specifically rejects that image of the body in favor of the body as work engine and locus of punishment.

> tergum quam gulam, crura quam ventrem oportet
> potiora esse quoi cor modeste situmst.
>
> (970–71)

His back ought to count for more than his gullet, his legs than his belly, if the slave's got his priorities straight.

Next, the prevailing image that separates good from bad slaves is one of price and value (972–75), pointing to the role of material goods in maintaining mastery that is at issue in the play. The punishment for bad slaves includes both shackles (*compedes*) and hunger (*fames*), a direct rejection of the idea in Peniculus' monologue that a feast can be put before an unchained slave.

A new note is introduced with *malum metuo* ("I fear punishment," 977), the themes of physical punishment and of fear that will shape the rest of this monologue. Messenio continues to emphasize the contrast between his behavior and that of the rebellious dependents by setting up a series of opposites, phrased in punning language (977–79). The good slave gets *verba* (words) instead of *verbera* (beatings) and eats flour (*mōlĭtum*, i.e., bread) rather than provides labor (*mōlĭtum*). Again, what a dependent eats is central both to his character and to his dramatic function in the play. The contrast with Peniculus lies first in the food—bread rather than succulent pork chops (*sincipitamenta porcina* in Menaechmus' list at 210–12). Second, a comparison of this line with the end of Peniculus' monologue (104–6) will show that for Peniculus, the opposition is not between eating and punishment but between eating at another's expense and eating at his own expense. It is significant that the good slave keeps punishment in the forefront (see esp. 983–85) not in the exuberantly fatalistic manner of the clever slave (who takes delight in reciting knows the ghastly punishments in store for him and misbehaves anyway) but with genuine fear and humility.[74] This aspect of being a good slave is summed up in line 983a, that good slaves fear their masters even when they have not done anything wrong, that is, good slaves have internalized the master's ethos and carry it with them wherever they go. This imaginative union with the interests of the master is perhaps the most characteristic feature of the good slave and is the one noted in Messenio's first appearance, where his empathy with his master shaped his words and deeds. Line 985 repeats the sense of line 970 and the contrast with Peniculus: that they both conceive of their interests in terms of their bodies, but Peniculus confidently fixates on filling his belly, while Messenio humbly concentrates on protecting his back.

---

[74] Segal (1987: esp. chap. 5, "From Freedom to Slavery") gives a very good analysis of the elaborate descriptions of punishment that are central to the worldview of the clever slave; see also Chiarini (1979: 68–69). See now also Fitzgerald (2000: chap. 2).

A brief comparison of this monologue with those of the good slave Phaniscus and the clever slave Tranio in the *Mostellaria* (scenes IV.1 and V.1) will underscore this interpretation. Just as Messenio's speech is a reaction to the challenge presented by Peniculus, in the *Mostellaria* Phaniscus' monologue carries out an ongoing contrast between good slaves and clever slaves, a contrast that was introduced in the first scene of that play, where Grumio and Tranio engage in a verbal wrestling match over just this topic. The *Mostellaria*, however, preserves the farcical hierarchy in which the clever slave triumphs. There, the positions are switched, and Phaniscus plays the part of revealing the scheme to the blocking character (as Peniculus does here), while Tranio takes the stage near the end to introduce the final movement of resolution (as Messenio does here). As Messenio's monologue asserts the values of the good slave by subverting the language of Peniculus' first monologue, Tranio picks up the claims made by Phaniscus only to dismiss this ideal as unworthy of the high standards of comic slavishness. In particular he declares that slaves who fear punishment are no-accounts (1041) and disproves Phaniscus' prediction that the clever slave takes to his heels when he is found out by asserting that when he gets in trouble, he reacts by causing more trouble (1051–53; cf. 862). As clearly as Messenio sums up, codifies, and ennobles the manifesto of the good slave in the *Menaechmi*, Tranio does the same for the manifesto of the clever slave in the *Mostellaria*. The closeness of the parallels between the two plays, allowing only for an inversion between the values given to the good slave and the clever slave, shows how the *Menaechmi* turns the usual pattern of farcical trickery to the service of the naturalistic mode.

In this play of doubling, it is striking how the doubling of the brothers is echoed by opposed and complementary pairs of the supporting characters. Just as Erotium and the Matrona form a pair, so too do Messenio and Peniculus form a structurally and thematically complementary pair. Their structural complementarity is obvious in Peniculus' control and pervasive presence in the early part of the play, compared with Messenio's redemptive presence at the end. They form a contrast exactly at the thematic center of the play: the reliability of an exchange of food and material goods as the foundation of authority. Messenio represents a challenge to this notion of mastery, since he is an emblem of a slave-master relationship based on true personal authority rather than on the master's ability to provide material luxury. (Note his concern for his master, not for himself, at the sight of the empty purse.) Further, the contrast between Peniculus and Messenio also articulates the contest between the comic modes for control of the play, since Peniculus champions both rebellion and metatheater, while Messenio stands up for loyalty and naturalistic theater. This doubling of the supporting characters reinforces the themes of the play, buttresses the structural symmetry, and shows that these characters are as integral as the two brothers to the meaning of the play.

Since both the plot and the theme are based on the different personalities of the two brothers in the "same" body, much of the explication of the play has presupposed this opposition. The plot device of twinning, since it encourages us both to acknowledge and to suppress the fact that the Menaechmus brothers are two different people, creates a kind of compound personality,[75] a "person" who consists of two individuals and can thus contain within himself an enormous range of functions and values, even those that are mutually opposing. In this play the motif of twinning allows the brothers to combine (farcical) subversive energy with (naturalistic) authoritative confidence, forming a particularly flexible kind of hero. Other Plautine plays, those that lean towards the more farcical side of the spectrum, achieve this variegated heroism by jettisoning dramatic consistency and allowing characters' interests and motivations to shift from scene to scene. (The *Casina*, subject of the next chapter, provides an extreme example.) The *Menaechmi* conflates subversion and authority by exploiting two more naturalistic methods of introducing doubleness: the paradoxical difference/sameness inherent in the concept of twins and the moral ambivalence of the character type of the *adulescens*.

I argued above, in explaining the unique prominence of the Matrona among dowered wives, that the two brothers take on the structural functions of a son and father in the more usual comic pattern. Thus the contrast between the two brothers comprises three different levels of authority, each one of which must be understood in its relation to the others. The realistic authority of the *paterfamilias*, the farcical authority of the clever slave, and the "romantic" authority of the son are all contested throughout the course of the *Menaechmi*, and all end up located in the nexus of personality represented by the two brothers at the end. But it is the Syracusan brother who performs the function of the son for most of the play, and it is only by the final assimilation that the Epidamnian gets to share in the romantic authority.

Romantic authority, the authority of the son to defy his father in order to secure the girl he loves, is subordinated to the other two types of authority throughout most of the Plautine corpus. Since Plautus consistently prefers to focus on the contest between master and slave, the contest between father and son is proportionately diminished.[76] The importance of romantic authority for the *Menaechmi* is that it shares some attributes with each of the other types of authority, that of the fictive slave and that of the real

---

[75] Cf. Leach (1969a: 33), quoted above, note 21.
[76] Anderson (1993: 60–87).

master, and thus functions to support the balance achieved between them. Romantic authority is like farcical authority in that it creates an imaginative world in which the power belongs to those who are usually subordinated in real life. It is similar to naturalistic authority in that it upholds values coherent with those of everyday morality, that is, the lover triumphs because he is more open-minded, more tender, more altruistic than his narrow-minded elders.[77]

Although Syracusan Menaechmus is really motivated by his search for his brother rather than by a desire to marry an inappropriate girl (as is usually the case for *adulescentes*), still this goal partakes of the same moral values as the usual romantic goal: it puts human emotional relationships before the demands of propriety. His humane goal assimilates Syracusan Menaechmus to young men in love (and thus to the sympathy usually granted them), while it sidesteps the difficulties that the *senex amator* pattern itself presents. That plot type must structure the play around the opposed interests of the father and son, since their erotic rivalry is a zero-sum game in which one must lose for the other to win. And indeed, for most of the *Menaechmi*, all the Syracusan brother's successes come at the expense of his brother. But by maintaining the underlying motivation that he has come to Epidamnus to find his brother (cf. the *adulescentes* in *Miles Gloriosus, Rudens*, and other plays, who travel in search of girl unjustly enslaved), the play also keeps alive a more romantic plot type, where the Epidamnian brother fulfills the function of the *pseudo-meretrix*. In this latter plot type, the interests of the two brothers are far from opposed; on the contrary, everything the visiting brother does is done in the interest of the Epidamnian.

By framing the Syracusan as an *adulescens*, the *Menaechmi* uses the romantic authority of this character type to create a fusion between the fictive authority of the clever slave and the real authority of the *paterfamilias*. Further, the final union of the two brothers (a union that, like the marriage with which many comedies end, signals that things have now been put back into their proper places where they will stay forever) includes the Epidamnian brother within this compound heroism and thus also encompasses the farcical energy that he has brought to the play. Yet this fusion is a delicate structure, an optical illusion, in fact, created by the elision of certain circumstances. As long as no elaborate trickery is called for, nor any

---

[77] The contrast between the heavily romantic element in Shakespearean comedy and the heavily farcical element in Plautine comedy (emphasizing as it does the role of the clever slave over that of the son, and deception over emotion) shows how the same configuration of plot elements can take on radically different tone and meaning. The most concise illustration of this is in Shakespeare's treatment of the *Menaechmi*. *A Comedy of Errors*, despite its title, is a comedy of lost love and found trust, where melancholy Adriana replaces the screeching Matrona, and a faceless Courtesan replaces Erotium, that accomplished actress of domesticity.

harsh punishment meted out, the brothers can maintain the balance of these elements.

The ending of a comedy, however, often gives a clue to the stresses and strains that persist beneath the smooth surface. Most comedies manage to mediate between the world of the play and the moral constraints of the society in which the play is produced by having the clever slave and son triumph, but then gesture outside the world of the play to "tomorrow," the day when the master/father resumes his rightful place.[78] The satirical ending of the *Menaechmi*, which emphasizes getting rid of the old society more than building a new one, is a product of the peculiar conflict of values that has shaped this play. We cannot look forward either to the continuing triumph of the slave/son (as in, e.g., Shakespearean romantic comedy, and in Plautine comedy where a pimp is the primary blocking character, e.g., *Poenulus* and *Persa*) or to the renewed authority of the master/father (as in the usual deception comedies) without sacrificing one or the other side of the powerful containment of opposites that distinguishes the character of the Menaechmus brothers. Thus the hazy dream of a perfect life back in Syracuse allows the brothers and the audience to continue to enjoy this double life, to fortify themselves with the backing of both comedy and real life.

---

[78] Segal (1987: 159–60) on the ending of the *Mostellaria*; see also (1987: 161).

Chapter III

LOVE'S LABOUR'S LOST: *CASINA*

THE PROLOGUE of the *Casina* tells us that we are watching a typical story of a boy in love with an apparently inappropriate girl, a foundling raised in his parents' house; the epilogue tells us that she has been recognized as the daughter of the next-door neighbors, the story culminating in a happy ending of marriage. But the flavor of this play is best described by noting that neither of the two young lovers appears onstage; the entire play is taken up with the young man's father's attempt to get the girl for himself, an attempt that comes alarmingly close to being successful. The trickery that turns the tide is performed not by a clever slave but by a wily matron. Even more disconcerting is the play's apparent inability to follow any given course for long: it weaves and bobbles (albeit engagingly) through various plot types, making several false starts before entering what seems to be the "real" plot, a plot that itself is reversed in the final scene.

In all these ways and more the *Casina* seems engineered to unbalance the familiar structures and rhythms of romantic comedy.[1] This kind of entropy, a drive towards chaos and disruption, is most obviously associated with what I have labeled the "farcical aesthetic." Since the most characteristic elements of romantic/naturalistic comedy—marriage and the recognition of citizen status—are exactly the ones that are kept off stage, we can see the *Casina* as an attempt to represent romance through the distorting lens of farce.[2] In the Plautine play the essential story remains a story of

---

[1] It would be possible to argue, as Forehand has (1973), that the pointed undermining of romantic norms was Plautus' way of using the stock forms of New Comedy to express a more serious social comment than "all's well that ends well." However, I find this "bricolage" approach to meaning, while not impossible, unconvincing for reasons elaborated in chap. 1, note 14. Even what seem to be the comments of an individual author on a stale genre are, I would argue, the product of the self-conscious genre itself.

[2] Much of the earlier scholarship on the *Casina* focused on the questions of *contaminatio* and Plautine originality (e.g., Fraenkel [1922: 292–313 = 1960: 281–300], Jachmann [1931: 105–27], Cody [1976], Lefèvre [1979], O'Bryhim [1989]; see Cody's overview [1976: 461–72]). My interpretation of the play as it stands would vary only slightly if it turned out that Plautus had translated it word-for-word from a Greek play. However, it seems probable to me that the references to the characters who will not appear in this version (the slave who brings about the recognition [36–38] and the son [64–66]) offered in the prologue and the epilogue's brief resolution of the romantic story (1013–14) represent differences between Diphilus' play and Plautus' (cf. Abel 1955: 59); i.e., it seems probable to me that the plotting of Diphilus' play cohered more closely with the romantic story (on these terms, see next

young love, but the choices of plotting and staging have radically altered the romantic focus of the original.[3]

My treatment of the *Casina* will be organized around the idea that this play's blatantly inappropriate use of a farcical plot to tell a romantic story can help us to understand better the interaction of the two comic modes and the values and social forces that drive each mode. This violent restructuring requires three important changes from the romantic paradigm: first, the *Casina* substitutes the nonteleological structure of farce for the directed progress of romantic comedy; second, the functions and attributes of the character types become ambiguous; and last, metatheater takes over as the dominant organizing motif of the play.

The *Casina* flaunts its ability to hold the audience with its virtuoso comic bits, seeming to promise that the plot is making headway, but in the end, the only real development (the recognition of the foundling Casina and her marriage to Euthynicus, the son of her foster parents) is relegated to the epilogue, while the characters who have held center stage all along merely revert to the unsatisfying situations with which they began. Certainly the removal of the young lovers from the stage and the reduction of the theme of marriage to a single line in the epilogue expresses the play's nonteleological aesthetic. Just as important as these negative characteristics, however, are the positive characteristics of the *Casina*: the prominence of the *paterfamilias'* lust, which cannot lead to marriage and is in fact defined by contrast with marriage; the multiplicity of tricks, most of which end up having no effect on the situation; and the ending that makes much of the fact that it only returns the play back to where it started, the clearest opposition to a resolution of marriage, which looks toward the future.[4]

---

note). For a version of this play that shows how different it would look when given a naturalistic rather than farcical coloring, see Machiavelli's *Clizia*: he restored the plot line of young love and gave it great prominence, he tied up the logical loose ends by making cause and effect connect systematically throughout the play, and he clarified and sharpened the dramatic and moral opposition between the major characters by making the old man and his slave impious and dastardly, while showing the wife and her slave as god-fearing, hard-working, and truly interested in protecting Clizia as much as in thwarting the old man (she explicitly rejects the idea of helping her son's erotic goals).

[3] I will rely in this chapter on the Formalist distinction between "story" and "plot": the story consists of the events that happened; the plot is the shaping of those events into a narrative. In this case, we can say that the story of the *Casina* is a romantic one about young love triumphing over senile lust, but the plot is farcical since it emphasizes the lust of the father.

[4] The argument has been made by Slater (1985: 88–91) that a fundamental change does take place in the end, a change in Lysidamus' attitude. It will be argued below that far from being demoralized at the end of the play, Lysidamus in fact regains control. But even if we accept the possibility of his change of heart, it still would be unparalleled for such a change of heart to have no outcome in bringing young lovers together as does the miser's in the *Aulularia* and Menander's *Dyskolos*.

The *Casina*'s combination of a romantic story and a farcical plot reveals the differing temporal structures of these two modes of comedy: any linear development towards resolution to which the *Casina* can lay claim is the result of the romantic story, while the seemingly endless fooling that falls without effect all results from the farcical plotting. This difference in the temporal structures of the two modes is conditioned by the social difference between the relationship that drives romantic comedy, that of parent to child, and the relationship that drives farce, that of master to slave. The son's rebellion against the father expresses the necessary succession of generations, which is externalized on stage in the forward-looking marriage and the (sometimes imminent) birth of a child. The slave's rebellion against the master is limited by convention and by logic to the dramatic time of the play. It cannot look beyond the world of the play in any way except to envision repeated incidences of this limited action.[5] A son can replace a father and become a father himself without calling into question the fundamental relation between father and son. On the other hand, the relation between master and slave is necessarily conceived as atemporal: slavery as an institution would be meaningless if time could alter or reverse the positions of master and slave. This timelessness is at the heart of the style of comedy organized around the scheming slave. The persuasiveness of Segal's saturnalian vision of Roman comedy lies in his observation that the reversals of power are temporary; the slave's one day of freedom is both conditioned by and in turn supports a lifetime of servitude.[6] For this form of comedy to be successful, it must not create any lasting change in the situation and must thereby be endlessly repeatable.[7]

This pattern of endless rebellion that never changes the essential relation is easy to understand in the context of slave and master. We are, however, less inured to seeing such rebellion perpetrated by a wife against a husband. One of the most disorienting aspects of the *Casina* is its substitution of marriage for slavery as the relation governing deceiver and deceived. This startling shift reveals an important analogy between the two household

---

[5] See *Ps* 1333: *verum sei voltis adplaudere atque adprobare hunc gregem et fabulam in crastinum vos vocabo*, "If you are willing to applaud and express your approval of this company and this play, I'll invite you back for tomorrow" (spoken by the clever slave himself).

[6] Cf. MacCary (1974: 888): "At the end of it all they return to those normal relations and there is no expectation that male aggression or the authority of the *paterfamilias* will be any less obnoxious. Permanent change, however, is not the point; rather it is that purely momentary overthrow of taboos and reversal of roles which mark the Saturnalia of Republican Rome and the similar holidays of other people in other times. The *Casina* as comic drama fulfills this function of ritual."

[7] The comparison with TV sitcoms is helpful. Grote (1983) argues that at the heart of the conservatism of sitcoms is the requirement that each half-hour episode has to return the characters back to where they started, so any events that take place during an individual episode must be without long-term effect.

institutions. The farcical temporal structure makes us realize that, like slavery and unlike parenthood, marriage is an ongoing relationship that has no natural time limit and does not change in necessary or essential ways with the passage of time. This is the primary reason why an *uxor dotata* can hold the place of trickster-rebel in this play: because the farcical plot not only rejects the romantic view of marriage (by not allowing it to have its place as the marker of an optimistic resolution, a symbol of the new life that will begin) but also forces marriage into the farcical mold, which emphasizes its similarity to slavery. This refiguring of marriage has the effect of revealing something that Plautine comedy more typically conceals: wives, not husbands, are subordinated in marriage and so, according to the logic of farce, should have access to the imaginative liberation of being a rebel in comedy.[8] But the manner in which this reversal occurs and, especially, the failure of the final scene to follow through on the implications of the *uxor*'s rebellion make it doubtful that Plautus intended to express any social critique; rather, the critique of her husband's behavior appears, willy nilly, as a result of the social meanings embedded in the comic forms themselves, which Plautus manipulates in ever-new combinations.

As this play shows us how marriage is like slavery, it also shows us how slavery is like marriage. Although sex between masters and slaves is never very far from the Plautine stage, usually in the form of slave concubines or *pueri delicati*, it nowhere else has as central and pervasive an importance as it does in the *Casina*, where it supplies both the central plot line and many important details. The many ambiguities surrounding sex between master and slave in this play, especially the question of who is in control in each instance, reveal slavery to be not just a legal or economic relationship but also an emotional, social, and sexual relationship.[9] In fact, what some scholars have seen as an emphasis in this play on gender inversion[10] I would describe as an inversion of the properties usually attached to slavery and marriage. Because the relation between slave and master in comedy is almost always envisioned as a male-male relationship, the assimilation of this relationship to marriage also produces an assimilation of men to women;

[8] See comments on the husband as rebel in the previous chapter, pp. 39–40.

[9] See now Fitzgerald (2000) on the ways that the ambiguities surrounding master-slave sex get expressed in literary forms. See also his reading of the *Casina* (2000: chap. 4), which, while generally consonant with that I offer here, emphasizes the ways that slavery helps to articulate a continuum of relationships in the household. I am grateful to him for showing me this work in manuscript form and regret that, because I saw it only late in the development of this book, I have not been able to engage here fully with the rich conception of slavery in literature he presents.

[10] Slater (1985: 92–93), MacCary (1974: 888).

likewise, when the wife plays the part of the always male clever slave, she takes on qualities that could be described as masculine.[11]

Since the *Casina* applies to marriage a dramatic structure usually associated with slavery, it also forces the character types with which we are so familiar into strange new patterns. One of the primary places we should look for the influence of farce is in the identity and qualities of the comic hero or, in farcical terms, the rebel. My analysis of the *Menaechmi* demonstrated that Plautine comedy need not associate the role of rebel with the slave; this role can be appropriated by others, including the master. The analysis of the *Casina* offered here takes that argument further. This play shows that, not only is it possible for the comic hero to be someone other than a slave, but it is possible for the play to have no stable comic hero and no stable orientation towards maintenance or subversion of real morality. In the *Casina*, the function of rebel shifts from a married old man in lust with his slave girl to a wealthy and clever matron and back again. In an even more remarkable change from the usual pattern, each of these heroes uses his or her authoritative control of a slave to further the rebellion: in other words, in a stark reversal from what we are used to thinking of as comic norms, masters use slaves for their own rebellion.

As strange as this divided heroism may seem, shared as it is between characters whose interests are opposed, it is part of a broader phenomenon fundamental to the *Casina*'s distinctive oddness: almost all the characters who appear on stage are, to a greater or lesser degree, displaced from the function that they would normally (by the rules of comic convention) fulfill. This ambiguity of the characters' functions can be directly traced to the *Casina*'s rejection of the plot elements that its romantic story would seem to require. Since the goal of romantic comedy is to unite the young lovers, the usual attributes of the characters, their functions, and their claims to sympathy from the audience are determined by whether they support or oppose the lovers. Fathers, mothers, slaves, pimps are all labeled as good or bad solely by their relation to the love story. For example, in the *Asinaria*, the father is sympathetic in the beginning as he tries to help his son get the money for his girlfriend, but he becomes unsympathetic when he turns into a rival.

The removal of the son from the plot of the *Casina* throws into confusion this usual organization. Our first glimpse of the *paterfamilias* Lysidamus is as a light-hearted lover and schemer. Only after he is overheard making plans to gain access to Casina by placing her in a sham marriage with his slave Olympio does his sympathetic role as rebel against an overbearing wife deteriorate. Then his wife Cleustrata comes to the fore as an astute

---

[11] Cf. Slater (1985).

manipulator of appearances, with a series of elaborate deceptions designed
to thwart her husband's plans. In parallel with Lysidamus' metamorphosis,
Cleustrata is initially marked as an *uxor dotata* by her friend Myrrhina, who
delivers a sermon on the value of indulging a husband; this identification
is contradicted openly later when the same friend praises her as a consum-
mate *poeta* (860–61) since her schemes against Lysidamus and Olympio
have produced such excellent theater.

Adding to the ambiguity of the characterizations here is that the figures
of the *senex amator* and *uxor dotata* always contain a certain doubleness in
their relation to the rebellious impulses of comedy. The old man's rivalry
to his son makes him an enemy of youth, but his championing of sensuality
over responsibility and his rebellion against his rich wife hint at a more
sympathetic side. Likewise, the *uxor dotata* stands for greed, rigidity, hu-
morlessness—everything comedy is out to punish—yet it is through her
restraint of her husband that youth and romance triumph. The doubleness
of these character types is usually kept strictly in bounds by the focus provided by the romantic plot line. In the *Casina*, these ambiguities are exploited, and they further influence the presentation of the other characters,
for example, by blurring the distinction between the clever slave who aids
romance and the good slave who protects his master's interests. The ambivalence surrounding the two central characters, Lysidamus and Cleustrata, the lack of a clear and stable portrayal of one as the hero and the
other as the blocking character, is conditioned by the absence of a romantic
interest around which to organize the characters and is fundamental in
producing a play that scorns logic, clarity, and resolution.

In its preference for the inconsistent and the temporary and in many
other ways, the *Casina* embodies the aesthetic of the clever slave: spinning
out the pleasures of disguise, storytelling, tricking one's enemies, not for
any material or social gain but for the pleasure of the trick itself.[12] Since
the play as a whole echoes the playfulness of the canonical comic hero
himself, it is not surprising that metatheater takes over as a central thematic
concern in the *Casina*. When the markers of comic heroism shift from
Lysidamus to Cleustrata and back again, the function of the internal playwright, almost always the territory of the clever slave, shifts as well. But
Lysidamus' original scheme, to disguise his affair with Casina as her marriage to Olympio, pales in comparison to the elaborate and theatrical tricks
of Cleustrata. His failure to gain the high ground in this competition parallels his frustrated attempts to get Casina and can also explain some of his
most peculiar qualities.

[12] See Segal (1987: 61–63) on the clever slave's lack of interest in money and freedom; see
also Petrone (1983: 178).

The differing styles of trickery that Lysidamus and Cleustrata use are consistent with the position each holds in the household hierarchy. Lysidamus' attempts at constructing a false front behind which to hide his lust for Casina underestimate the difference between disguise and reality. Lysidamus' extreme confidence in his powers of transformation, expressed in his nearly pathological belief in himself as Jupiter, is integrally related to his style of theater. His tricks depend on being able to create a new reality (that he will be a young lover, that he will be immortal), though he seeks to disguise the content of that reality through the manipulation of appearances (pretending that he is upholding the office of *paterfamilias* by marrying off the slaves, when really he intends that Olympio's marriage somehow become his own).

Cleustrata's masterpiece of deceit, on the other hand, gathers its power precisely by playing on the gap between appearance and reality. In the climactic scene where she tries to disrupt the wedding ceremony by substituting for Casina the male slave Chalinus, the humor and subversive power of the joke come from the fact that Chalinus does not become a bride just because he is dressed as one. Cleustrata's theater emphasizes the pleasures of pretense itself and its temporary nature. Her three tricks all take their starting point from her outward obedience to her husband's wishes: she plays on the appearance of being a hard-working hausfrau or on the pretense of safeguarding Olympio from a dangerous bride, or on her apparent agreement to go along with the wedding ceremony. They do not attempt to create a new reality but to forestall Lysidamus' plans. To sum up, Lysidamus' style of trickery is the trickery of someone who is backed up by real authority: he believes he can create new realities that have real and lasting effect, though he acknowledges that he must also keep up appearances. Cleustrata's style of trickery is the trickery of those who are subordinated in real life: she knows that she cannot overturn the essential authority of her husband, but even by keeping within the bounds of apparent obedience she can make his authority impotent to bring about the results he wants, especially by checking his ability to act through his subordinates.

Comparisons of Cleustrata's style of theater and trickery to that of clever slaves reveals several parallels.[13] For these tricksters, the trick is a means to an end not, like Lysidamus' marriage by proxy, a construction that is intended to last beyond the end of the play. Their tricks are usually fictive situations designed to lure the blocking characters into betraying themselves through their own self-importance, greed, or desire to squelch a scandal. Equally distinctive is the role of stories in the tricks of clever slaves

---

[13] This comparison is in reference to such heroes as Chrysalus, Epidicus, Palaestrio, Tranio, Milphio, and Pseudolus, i.e., classic clever slaves without complications of character type (Curculio) or function (Toxilus).

and of Cleustrata. The nonpermanent nature of Cleustrata's tricks is emphasized by the fact that the first two are given prominence and then dropped, without really providing any necessary precedent for the final trick, the transvestite marriage. This nonpermanence is an expression of the nonteleological aesthetic of the clever slave and also accounts for the lack of relation of cause and effect in this plot and in others in which the clever slave is a prominent force.

Both at the level of the action of the play, where Lysidamus' desires are blocked without any fundamental change in the positions of power, and at the level of comic convention, where our expectations for how things work in comedy are thwarted and shifted, the *Casina*'s overriding property is that of reversal, negation, retarding. All the structural effects that have been discussed here—the assimilation of slavery and marriage, the ambiguity of characterizations, the prominence of metatheater—undermine the orderly progress of the play towards a meaningful resolution. In all comedies, the action is centered around reversing the hopes or perceptions of the blocking character; in the *Casina*, this reversal is not a plot device used to express a theme but has become the theme itself.[14]

A RAKE'S (LACK OF) PROGRESS

Through a linear overview of the play, we will see the concrete effects of the farcical aesthetic, especially the ways it distorts a romantic story of young love into a farcical plot of household warfare. I will divide the play into three movements, each of which has a particular dramatic function and is shaped by the prominence of a particular thematic element.

As the play opens, the rivalry between father and son is already established, and each has deputized a slave through whom he hopes to get access to Casina; Lysidamus' slave ally is Olympio, and Euthynicus' is Chalinus. But because the actual romance has been cropped out of this romantic comedy, the son never appears on stage; Chalinus and the *uxor* Cleustrata team up to promote Euthynicus' interests and to thwart those of his father. From this opening situation, the play follows Lysidamus' efforts to get Casina for himself, while pretending that her marriage to Olympio is his only goal. His scheme gives every appearance of imminent success, especially when he and Olympio win an apparently unrigged lottery intended to settle the question of which slave Casina will marry. But almost immedi-

[14] Fraenkel (1922: 303 = 1960: 291): "Die einzelnen Hindernisse, die sich dem Vorhaben des Lysidamus entgegenstellen, sind nicht so sehr Ausgangspunkte neuer Verwickelungen als um ihrer selbst willen da: ihre Bedeutung liegt gerade darin daß sie den Alten aufhalten und ihm sein Ziel, jedesmal wenn er ihm schon ganz nahe zu sein glaubt, wieder in die Ferne rücken."

ately after this lottery, Lysidamus' luck turns sour, and Cleustrata's clever schemes erect increasingly sturdy barriers between him and the hoped-for embraces of Casina. First, Cleustrata tries to upset Lysidamus' plans, which require the neighbors' house to be empty, by telling the neighbor Alcesimus that she has no need of his wife Myrrhina's help for the wedding preparations. Next, she tries to frighten off both Lysidamus and Olympio, by sending the slave girl Pardalisca to announce to them that Casina has gone mad and intends to run through with a sword any man who tries to marry her. Finally, when neither of these schemes has succeeded in derailing the wedding ceremony, Cleustrata sends in the cross-dressed Chalinus as bride in place of Casina. The final scenes have Olympio and Lysidamus coming back on stage from their honeymoon suite next door, humiliated and still somewhat puzzled over what has taken place there.

The relation between the first two movements is one of negation; they correspond to the reign and fall of Lysidamus. His power and his humiliation are expressed through the same images, including religion, food, and the metatheatrical control of events. In the first movement, these images are combined to show how his power is derived from and expressed through a godlike sense of subjectivity, a sense that there are no boundaries of experience through which he cannot pass, no transformations that cannot be accomplished. The most obvious instance of this all-encompassing subjectivity is his use of Olympio as a proxy, through whose marriage he will enjoy the sexual use of Casina. There is nothing delusional or mystical about this trick in itself, but the imagery of Lysidamus as Jupiter, of love as a spice, and of the *senex amator* as a justified romantic hero all contribute to extend the implications of the trick well beyond simple deception. Through these images, Lysidamus is endowed with almost mystical abilities of transformation; this kind of mystical or godlike control obscures how things get done, unlike the scheming of most clever tricksters, which, if anything, foregrounds the process over the product. This special kind of heroism is geared specifically to the *paterfamilias* as rebel, allowing him to take as far as possible his combination of real authority and fictive rebellion.

The second movement precisely reverses all the propositions on which the first movement was grounded and reveals a new set of meanings for the images of the first movement. The most powerful of these reversals shows that those in authority cannot effortlessly transcend the boundaries between subjects. Cleustrata's style of theatrical deception emphasizes the limits to the power of the dominant. She obeys her husband's wishes in setting up the wedding, but she sets it up in a way that reveals the many possible slips between the intentions of the dominant and the actions of the subordinates, thus undermining Lysidamus' mystical sense of control and ability to live through others. In a similar way, all the earlier evidence of Lysidamus' mystical transformations is inverted into proof of his naivete. For example, Cleustrata's plotting in the second movement reveals that food is more than a metaphor for the satisfactions of love; it is also a material commodity that can be given out or withheld to enforce control in the household.

The final movement embodies not resolution in the usual sense, since nothing brought up in the rest of the play is resolved but reversion to a new forced simplicity that merely ignores the issues raised in the central parts of the play.[15] We might expect, for instance, that the ending of the play would authorize either Lysidamus' viewpoint or Cleustrata's, would condemn either Lysidamus' lust or Cleustrata's sneakiness. But a final shift in the functions of characters brings the situation back to where it was at the beginning of the play. Lysidamus positions himself as a slave asking for the lenience of the deceived master, thus reclaiming his role as rebel and once again making Cleustrata act the part of the blocking character. This ending does not, however, justify his rebellion any more than it celebrates Cleustrata's cleverness; rather, it leaves Lysidamus' power and Cleustrata's opposition to it coexisting.

Lysidamus' Play

The most important function of the first movement of the play (89–228) is to introduce the characters in a context that shows Lysidamus' power over his household.[16] This section, culminating in the lot-drawing scene, reveals both Lysidamus' power and the threats to it. Since this first movement ends with the lottery scene, in which Lysidamus' erotic ambitions seem to receive divine sanction, it appears to place him on the brink of triumphant success, not abject humiliation. Of course, this imminent success could be perfectly consistent with Lysidamus' functioning as blocking character rather than hero: since the usual comic pattern consists in over-

---

[15] Forehand (1973: 251): "Without a change in the old man's character, which Plautus has no intention of providing, the only way to have a satisfactory comic conclusion is to end artificially, by admitting that we are dealing with a play which can be manipulated as the author chooses." My interpretation of the artificiality of this ending, however, differs substantially from Forehand's.

[16] O'Bryhim (1989: 96–97). Lysidamus' name appears nowhere in the extant text and is supplied from a scene heading in one manuscript. Duckworth (1938: 279–81), O'Bryhim (1989: 94–96), and Chiarini (1978: 119) have interpreted the *senex*'s possible namelessness in various ingenious ways (O'Bryhim argues that he is not nameless but is the mysterious Casinus of line 814); all three, however, see in it some kind of moralizing comment on his inappropriate sexual behavior. In keeping with my general argument about Plautus' lack of moral critique, I do not believe that we are justified in seeing any such subtle comment here. Consider the other examples in the corpus of relatively important characters being nameless, the best being the Matrona in the *Menaechmi* and the Virgo in the *Persa*.

coming the blocking character's control of events, this control must be established dramatically before it can be defeated. This movement of the play, then, can be seen as structurally consistent with a design in which Lysidamus is only a villain; but the structural requirement that the *senex amator* seem poised to win Casina has been met in a way that brings him close to being a hero rather than a blocking character.[17]

The play opens with hostile sparring between Olympio and Chalinus; it is not unusual to find this battling between two slaves of the same household in the early scenes of a Plautine comedy.[18] But there are several differences between this scene and others of its type, differences that alert us to the particular issues of the *Casina*. First of all, those other opening scenes pit a good slave, arguing for his master's interest, against a clever slave who seeks to deceive the master. With this background in mind, the spectator is stumped as to which slave is which in the *Casina*. The usual clues that separate good slaves from clever slaves are inconclusive here. At lines 95–96, Chalinus accuses Olympio of having tricks up his sleeve and declares that he has set himself up to prevent the enactment of those tricks, and so he seems to reveal himself as the enemy of deception. But at lines 106–8, Olympio asserts that Chalinus' watchfulness is not in his master's interest but in his own and also introduces the theme of erotic rivalry, aligning himself with the antiromantic forces that oppose young love, especially fathers and soldiers.[19]

This shifting of conventional functions is heightened by the use of two systems of imagery that have important meaning elsewhere in Plautine comedy: military language and the contrast between city and country. These two images are conflated in the slaves' agreement in using the military term *praefectura* to describe Olympio's duties as farm manager and his rural realm of power (99, 110; cf. *provincia*, 103). Yet the usual associations of these verbal patterns bring in conflicting nuances. Throughout the Plautine corpus, the city is consistently associated with license and deception. The country, on the other hand, is the locus of the ethical values of honesty,

---

[17] This contention finds corroboration in the observations of two translators who have produced versions of the *Casina* on stage. Both Tatum (1983: 88–89) and Beacham (1995: 254) note that *in performance* Lysidamus comes off surprisingly sympathetically.

[18] Esp. the *Mostellaria*, but also consider *Epidicus*, *Miles Gloriosus* (II.3), *Truculentus* (II.2, here of different households), and, what might be considered a variant on this type, the scene between Sosia and Mercury in the *Amphitruo* (I.1). Forehand (1973: 237–38) notes the parallels with *Mostellaria* and *Epidicus*.

[19] O'Bryhim (1989: 84) sees Chalinus as a *servus callidus*; MacCary and Willcock (1976: on 416) implicitly agree with this identification by declaring that he is the one "with whom the audience is expected to sympathize. . . ." Anderson (1983: 15) thinks that Chalinus has been lowered by his status of *armiger* and that Olympio's wit and aggressiveness give him the advantage in this scene.

obedience towards authority, and naivete.[20] Here, the unusual treatment of the spheres of city and country adds to the spectator's uncertainty as to whom to label as good slave and whom as clever slave: military language is used to describe rural duties (language usually reserved for comic slaves' urban escapades), and the country is identified as the realm of punishment for the rival (again, this kind of reveling in vengeance is usually reserved for the clever slave and takes place in urban environments such as before the praetor or the moneylender). The country is further citified here when Olympio envisions the sexual union that symbolizes comic resolution taking place there (109–10).

The country will be the site of Olympio's possession of Casina, and it will be the site of his punishment of Chalinus as well, the extravagant and sadistic details of which occupy the last twenty-five lines of this scene. This litany of punishments is closely related to the themes that will follow in the rest of the play, the denial of both food and sex. Note that the denial of food is phrased as a reduction to the level of animals (126–27), while the denial of sex is heightened by the torture of having to listen as Olympio enjoys Casina in his stead. This final image—Chalinus forced to eavesdrop on his rival's success while trapped in the wall like a mouse—powerful in itself, is emphasized by the extraordinary apostrophe in which Olympio anticipates Casina's beseeching plea to let her love him (134–38). The impact of this speech will reverberate throughout the play. It is an early and spectacular rendition of the themes that will guide this play: the use of sex as the instrument of vengeance, as the opportunity for impersonation, and as the object of a third person's gaze. This aggressively antiromantic view of sex, inverting as it does the romantic emphasis on the uniqueness of the beloved and the private world the lovers share, emblematizes the *Casina*'s twisted use of the elements of romance to the ends of farce.

It is not clear whether this extensive anticipation of Chalinus' punishment should be compared to the self-righteous speeches of good slaves gloating over the future punishment of clever slaves (never fulfilled within the bounds of the play) or to clever slaves' extravagant predictions of the successful outcomes of their schemes. The overall effect of this first scene is to establish the two slaves as equals, neither of them obviously having the upper hand. Nor is it clear by which scale of values, the farcical or the naturalistic, they should be judged. Although Olympio's long and rhetorically elaborate speech may seem to tip the balance in his favor, we must

[20] Cf. *Mos* I.1, esp. 15–24, 35–37; see also *Mer* 65–68. Again, the comparison with Machiavelli's *Clizia* (see above, note 2) is instructive: there the moral balance is realigned by having the propriety of country values embodied in the farm manager associated with the wife, who is waging a moral battle against her husband, not just trying to obstruct him for her own purposes and not trying to get the girl for her son.

also remember that the person in control and satisfied with the situation at the beginning of the play is often being prepared to be the butt of a joke.

This principle of balance between characters whom comic convention leads us to see as opposing one another is carried further in the next two scenes (II.1, 2). At the beginning of each of these scenes Cleustrata and her neighbor Myrrhina respectively are introduced in remarkably similar dramatic and verbal modes. Each turns back to address a slave and announces that she will be next door if her husband is looking for her (144–46, 165–67). The actions of each woman betoken her tacit assumption of household power, both in the authoritative voice with which they address their slaves[21] and in the emphasis for each on a traditional sphere of feminine domestic power—for Cleustrata the control over the household stores and for Myrrhina the responsibility to spin for the family's clothing.[22] But each scene develops the theme of women's domestic power in a different direction. Scene II.1 immediately shows that Cleustrata is using her power of saving and spending as a way of controlling her husband (see esp. 149–54). Her threatened punishment of her husband strangely echoes Olympio's sadistic fantasies: not only will she punish him by hunger and thirst (155; cf. 126–29) but she will also see to it that he leads the life he is worthy of (*faciam uti proinde ut est dignus vitam colat*,158; cf. 131: *noctu ut condigne te cubes curabitur*, "I'll see to it that at night you are bedded down in a way fitting for you"). As with Olympio, Cleustrata's vengeful language raises a question: is she to be compared to the clever slave plotting the overthrow of the master or to an irate *senex* swearing his revenge against his deceiver? In no other play does the blocking character realize that he or she is being tricked at the very beginning of the play.[23] The ambiguity of Cleustrata's position at this point is crucial to how we understand the action of the play as a whole: is it the justifiable rebellion of the downtrodden household members against a tyrannical *paterfamilias*, or is the ill-natured dowered wife exerting control over her fun-seeking husband? As with the earlier clash between Chalinus and Olympio, Cleustrata's and Lysidamus' positions in relation to farcical subversion are ambiguous; it is unclear whom we should see as rebel and whom as blocking character.

Scene II.2 makes everything much clearer, for the moment at least. Myrrhina's lecture on a wife's duty of submissiveness, especially in the area

---

[21] Tatum (1983: 88).

[22] Petrone (1988: 100).

[23] Fraenkel (1922: 294–99 = 1960: 282–87) and others have been greatly troubled by the fact that Cleustrata knows all about Lysidamus' lust here and yet seems surprised when she is informed of his plans by Chalinus in III.2. However, 531–33 clearly show that what Cleustrata has discovered there is not that her husband is in love with Casina but that the reason he asked her to invite Myrrhina over was to clear the coast for his tryst. There are several

of financial power, implicitly characterizes Cleustrata as a dowered wife who tries to control her husband through wealth. In particular, lines 203–12 bear strong resemblance to the argument between the Matrona and her father at *Menaechmi* 787–806 (scene V.2).[24] In both passages, the dowered wife's previous history of greed and desire to control is established not through her own actions but through the advice given her by a presumably well-intentioned advisor. This important scene is the first to give an unambiguous clue as to where the characters fit in the comic hierarchy, which should help the spectators label the characters as rebels or blocking characters. It should be noted, however, that this unambiguous definition of Cleustrata as *uxor dotata* and as blocking character, the only character function that has been clearly defined, will be the one most prominently reversed later in the play.[25]

The monody with which Lysidamus makes his entrance is important in establishing his character, his claim to the audience's sympathy, and the direction of the plot, for the rest of the first movement. In its structural features, this monody is similar to monodies in other plays (*Am* 633–53, *Cist* 203–28, *Mos* 84–156, *Poen* 210–32, *Truc* 448–64). These are all entrance monologues of important characters making their first appearance (except Phronesium in the *Truculentus*) after having been the topic of conversation of others; they all appear just after the first expository parts of the play; they all begin with either a generalization or a metaphor, then explicitly state how the character's own experience bears this out (in five of the six passages the transition between axiom and application is phrased in almost exactly the same language).[26]

Setting aside Lysidamus' monody in the *Casina* for a moment, we can characterize the dramatic and thematic content of the others. They are all rather philosophical reflections on the character's own temperament or state of mind, brought on by some strong emotional experience, most often love. The monodies present the character from within, sympathetically, and hint that the character is more complex, more honorable, and less silly

---

logical inconsistencies in this play, but this is not one of them. (Chalinus has less reason to be surprised in II.8.)

[24] Fraenkel (1922: 299–300 = 1960: 287–88).

[25] Petrone (1988: 101) sees the contradiction between Myrrhina's attitudes here and in the later scene as the author's attempts to guard Cleustrata from the charge of greed for power by establishing early on that both women recognize their proper sphere of power (the household), and it is only because of the enormity of Lysidamus' transgressions that they are justified in going beyond that sphere. On the contrary, as Petrone herself has ably argued elsewhere (1977: 19–20), the justification for trickery is never established in terms of naturalistic morality but in terms of *malitia*, which is the defining characteristic of all schemers.

[26] *Am* 637: *nam ego id nunc experior domo atque ipsa de me scio; Cist* 204: *hanc ego de me coniecturam domi facio; Poen* 216: *atque haec, ut loquor, nunc domo docta dico; Truc* 453: *ego prima de me, domo docta, dico.* Cf. *Cas* 224: *hanc ego de me coniecturam domi facio magi' quam ex auditis.*

than others of his or her type. Alcumena's almost theological reflection on the necessity of the link between pleasure and pain reveals her sincere love for her husband in a way that distances her both from unloving wives and from silly girls in love (*Am* 633–53). Alcesimarchus, like Charinus in the *Mercator*, may still act ridiculously but at least shows an objectivity, a recognition of his foolishness, lacking in most Plautine lovers (*Cist* 203–28). Adelphasium's witty critique of the extremes to which *meretrices* go to make themselves beautiful has more in common with the frequent masculine diatribes on women's extravagance than with the usual meretricious cynicism (*Poen* 210–32). Philolaches' description of his degradation through the metaphor of a falling house is moving in its clear-sightedness; like Alcesimarchus, Philolaches sees that love is ruining him, but he cannot resist (*Most* 89–156). Finally, Phronesium's monody in the *Truculentus* is the exception that proves the rule: the *meretrix* who cynically uses her fictive motherhood for all it is worth here uses the form proper to a mother reflecting on her fears for her child to express her fears that the trick might not go as planned (*Trac* 448–64). Although there are great differences in tone among these passages, with those in the *Amphitruo* and the *Mostellaria* being much more serious and emotional than the others, they share similar formal features and a similar dramatic function: to introduce a character and explain his or her motivation from within rather than by reference to the stereotypes of stock roles.

Whether we are sympathetic to Lysidamus' attempt to deceive his wife depends on his ability to walk a fine, even blurry, line: can he exhibit the appealingly naive qualities of *adulescentes* without abdicating his prerogatives as *paterfamilias*? conversely, can he exert his authoritative control without seeming like a blocking character? Although the balancing act he manages to pull off here will soon collapse as the play progresses, the entrance he is granted here achieves exactly this elusive fusion of opposing forces. Especially in the context of scene II.2 in which Myrrhina has just chided his wife for not allowing him sufficient freedom, this monody has the effect of proclaiming him the rebel in whom the values of farcical comedy are vested. The comparison with other monodies of its type only strengthens the impression that in this scene the conventions of the genre are being used to distance Lysidamus from the opprobrium that is always the response to old men in love. By contrast, in the *Mercator* and *Asinaria*, any positive qualities that we might attach to the old men's erotic declarations are precluded, because their sons have already taken the stage and declared themselves to be true lovers, worthy of our sympathy. Here in the *Casina*, Plautus' choice to remove the son from the stage puts Lysidamus' declaration in the forefront. This monody occurs at the point where in other plays we get the lovelorn speeches of young men.[27]

[27] Cf. *As* I.2, *Cist* II.1, *Epid* I.2, *Mos* I.2, *Trin* II.1.

The specific language and imagery of Lysidamus' monody are more elaborate, the metaphor here more extended than in any of the other examples except that of the *Mostellaria*. The controlling metaphor is that of love as a spice that has the power to transform the ordinary into the extraordinary. In many ways this extreme confidence in being able to change fundamentally the essence of things is central to Lysidamus' point of view.[28] Both the idea of turning gall into honey (223) and the idea of surpassing Charm itself with one's charms (225) make the recognizable attributes of things less reliable as markers of identity: gall becomes sweet, and Charm is no longer the most charming thing imaginable. His own vision of himself as transformed into a suave and charming lover by the addition of perfumes and unguents (226–27) is analogous to the belief that love can transform any food into a feast (221).[29] This monody gets at the heart of Lysidamus' point of view, in his self-image as well as in his approach to deception. Just as he believes he can transform himself with perfume, he believes that he can transform Olympio's marriage into his own.

Perhaps the most striking aspect of this presentation of Lysidamus is not the enormous inflation of his self-worth, nor the pathology of his notions of transformation, but the positive value given to these qualities here, the depiction of a *senex amator* in the language and form of a young lover. Whether or not Plautus found in his Greek model a speech by the old man in which he contemplated the changes wrought in him by falling in love with his son's beloved (a speech comparable to *Mercator* 262–67, perhaps), this speech as we have it can be seen as the result of grafting onto the typical kind of speech a *senex amator* might use to introduce himself elements from the speeches of young men, especially the extravagant praise of the powers of love and the confidence it gives them in their ability to do anything. While it is true that these young lovers are almost always depicted as impossibly naive, what matters here is that this depiction is unambiguously indulgent. In fact, its naivete is exactly what guarantees the merit of the young man's love.

This monody sets up the following scenes, which are the locus of Lysidamus' greatest power in the play. From the end of his monody through the

---

[28] Chiarini (1978: 115) notes that the metaphors introduced in this monody, especially those concerning smells and food, guide the development of the play, and, therefore, we could see Lysidamus as "il legislatore linguistico, e cioè in certo senso il 'poeta' della commedia." This observation coheres with the argument made here that initially Lysidamus does seem to be in a position to control the play through metatheater.

[29] Slater (1985: 76–77) makes a similar point: "Could [Lysidamus], like the young, live on love? No, love is not *food* to him, it is a spice. . . . Love is an additive, which can change how something registers on the senses (the bitter made sweet, 223) without changing the nature of the thing. Lysidamus' perfume works much the same way: the old goat thinks he can become a

end of the lottery scene (229–423), Lysidamus seems to be in control of all the forces of wit, authority, religion, and rebellion. But as these scenes progress, the increasing need to exert his authority threatens to undermine the delicate balance of opposites on which the figure of *paterfamilias*-as-rebel depends. The strategy of his entrance monody was to effect a conjoining between the *adulescens* figure and the *senex* figure by expressing his special, mystical kind of heroism in the dramatic forms usually used by love-struck young men. For the rest of the first movement, this strategy alternates with another strategy, superficially similar but with very different implications: using the image of himself as Jupiter again defines Lysidamus' heroism as mystical, but now in the unsentimental language of clever slaves.

In successive scenes (the end of II.3, II.4, 5) he displays his authority over his wife, Chalinus, and Olympio. None of these displays of power is without rankling from those who submit, but they do submit. Lysidamus' ascendancy in this part of the play is expressed by emphasizing his strangely unfettered view of his own subjectivity as evidenced in the imagery of divinity (Jupiter and Juno theme) and in the proxy relationship through which he hopes to gain access to Casina. The height of both these systems of imagery comes in the lottery scene (see esp. 404–8). This proxy relationship is brought into question elsewhere in the play, but here it has a logic of its own and seems perfectly plausible. Not only does it seem in this section that Lysidamus might succeed in his plans, but the more surprising trick (in light of the rest of the play) is that it seems as though he ought to succeed. He is given the language of military boldness with which to describe his plans and his commitment to seeing them carried out (see esp. 307–8, 344, 352), a use of language that associates him with clever slaves. Even the claim of his own divinity, which alienates us when we know what he will be in the rest of the play, in the beginning could be assimilated to the similarly expressed arrogance of clever slaves.[30] And, although his scheme is not particularly elaborate, we are inclined to view it as a clever deception, since it is the only scheme of deception presented so far.[31] The difference between Lysidamus' scheme and those of other comic tricksters is that it lacks exactly the kind of theatricality that subtends the performance-oriented aesthetic of clever slaves and, as we shall soon see, Cleustrata; instead of taking pleasure in managing the details of the disguise scheme, Lysidamus merely exudes a confidence that everything will turn out his way.

---

sweet young thing merely by perfuming himself . . ." (emphasis in the original). See also Chiarini (1978: 118).

[30] MacCary and Willcock (1976: 30–31).

[31] Slater (1985: 90): "He is thus in a small way, though nowhere explicitly, a *poeta*." Cf. Chiarini (1978: 115) quoted above in note 28.

(Moreover, up through the drawing of the lots, he is right.) But, by putting Lysidamus in a position of power over his household and using stylistic and dramatic clues to show this power as analogous to that of comic rebels, this movement of the play is very close to the effect of the *Menaechmi* as a whole; it creates a *paterfamilias* who embodies at the same time the official authority of the master and the subversive authority of the rebel.

The section following Lysidamus' monody (235–48) reverts to the most canonical forms of byplay between a dowered wife and an aged lover.[32] However, at lines 249–51 there is an abrupt shift, where Lysidamus remarks, in a metatheatrical way, that he has had enough of the conventional dowered-wife gags and seems to intend to stop the momentum of the play from going in its accustomed direction. Like the clever slave who assents to his master's beating him tomorrow, as long as he can get his way today, Lysidamus tries to sidetrack Cleustrata from her dowered-wife role (blocker of the *senex*'s amours) into the role of deceived master by asserting that tomorrow she can do all the haranguing she wants (*cras quod mecum litiges*).[33] Like his monody, this attempt to take over as playwright and, even more, his assuming the control of today while allowing Cleustrata to control tomorrow mark Lysidamus as the clever rebel.

Scenes II.4 and II.5 establish Lysidamus in relation to his two slaves, continuing the theme of the grudging acceptance of his authority. At the beginning of scene II.4, Lysidamus' form of mastery is articulated through emphasis on the extremes of masterly language. At lines 281–83 he first demands complete obedience and respect by reminding Chalinus of his power and forbidding any other facial expression but one of serene obedience, but then he immediately drops to the most humiliating forms of persuasion: flattery and lies.[34] The scene then continues to focus on mastery, presenting the complex problems of using manumission as a weapon in the master's arsenal. Similar to the questions that had much fuller expression in the *Menaechmi*, this scene raises the question of how the master can simultaneously convince the slave that slavery is not so bad and yet that manumission is worth working for and being obedient for. Chalinus makes this trick even more difficult for Lysidamus by playing both sides against the middle: at lines 284–5 he asks why Lysidamus has not already manumitted him if he thinks so highly of him, and at line 293 he declines

[32] Slater (1985: 77–78) notes the adherence to stereotypes in this part of the scene and Lysidamus' use of asides to "bid for the audience's favor."

[33] Note that legal language in general and especially *litigo* is a marker of *uxor dotata* discourse; see note 37 below. For the *hodie/cras* motif, cf. also Tranio's pardon at *Mos* 1178–79.

[34] The alliterative language of 282 and the *figura etymologica* on *potestas* may be intended to give this line a religious ring, in keeping with Lysidamus' open identification of himself as Jupiter in the next scene. Cf. the explicit divine imagery of his similar command to Cleustrata at 230, there too bolstered by *blanditia*.

to be manumitted (on the condition that he gives up Casina) by pointing out the advantages of being kept at his master's expense rather than his own.[35] Chalinus' rhetoric here is unsettling because it demonstrates how the slave can use the master's apparent show of generosity against him.

But unlike the *Menaechmi*, where this subversive point of view was opposed by Syracusan Menaechmus' convincing combination of mastery and comic heroism, in the *Casina*, significantly, Chalinus' point of view is allowed to stand unanswered but is also left unsupported. This scene is a good illustration of how this first movement reveals on stage both Lysidamus' implacable power and the opposition to it. Chalinus never backs down from his arrogance. His open acknowledgment that his very existence is a thorn in his master's side sums up the slave's powerful knowledge of how difficult mastery is. Yet at the end of the scene, he is obeying Lysidamus' orders to bring Cleustrata and the lots from inside, lots in which Lysidamus' hopes seem unjustifiably high.

Scene II.5 establishes Olympio as a fitting aide to Lysidamus, emphasizing his hot-blooded defiance of Cleustrata and his knowledge of the language appropriate to the comic stereotype of the *uxor dotata*.[36] In response to Lysidamus' question (317, phrased in the legal idiom, *litigas*, common to *uxores dotatae*; cf. 251),[37] he invokes comic stereotypes as past experience, showing himself to be an astute participant in comic life and reinforcing our impression that Cleustrata can be completely accounted for by our usual expectations for the rich wives of comedy.[38] It is important that he reinforce this stereotype at this crucial point, because Lysidamus' position as a sympathetic comic rebel has been eroding ever since its high point in his entrance monody. The reminder here that it is Cleustrata who is the blocking character serves to prop up Lysidamus at least a little longer.[39]

From line 321 to the end of the scene, the focus shifts to Lysidamus' strange self-concept and its influence on his mastery. The ambivalence in this scene with regard to Lysidamus' claims to divinity is integrally related to the ambivalence of the play as a whole. From a moral perspective and

[35] Note that at lines 504–6 Chalinus explicitly renounces any chance at freedom for the pleasure of seeing his master's plans exposed and foiled—very characteristic of a clever slave, as Slater notes (1985: 82–83).

[36] He loudly and scornfully rejects Cleustrata's arguments, in contrast to Chalinus' equally rebellious but calmer and more cynical refusal of Lysidamus' offer. This contrast builds on the difference between the two slaves established in the first scene, where Olympio's extravagant vindictiveness was set against Chalinus' more cagey spying.

[37] Cf. *Men* 765, 784; *As* 914.

[38] Cf. Peniculus' similar use of stereotypes at *Men* 569; the dog joke is also paralleled in the *Men* at 714–18.

[39] This technique is repeated in the jokes of 325–27; both the phrase *in fermento totast* and the word *turget* are used elsewhere of the anger of *uxores dotatae* (*Mer* 959 and *Mos* 699 respectively).

from the perspective we gain from knowing the outcome of the play, his declarations here seem to be hubristic and make his punishment inevitable. Yet from the point of view that has been developed in the play so far, although there is plenty of discontent and he has not been able to persuade either his wife or Chalinus to give in, the events bear out his contention that Olympio has more to worry about in displeasing him than in displeasing the "minor gods" (*minutos deos*, 332). In fact, his failure to persuade only heightens the effect of sheer authority and of the divine imprimatur he will receive in the next scene.[40]

Again, as with Lysidamus' entrance monody above, we can see the skeleton of a play in which the father was a tyrannical old lecher, and his triumph in the lottery scene would have functioned only to increase the danger of Casina being sacrificed in marriage to a slave, a danger that is necessary to set up her final salvation as the wife of a citizen man. But the way Plautus chose to flesh out this skeleton uses the *senex*'s delusions of grandeur not just negatively, to set up the dramatic context for recognition and romance, but positively, as if Lysidamus is himself the rebellious schemer. The difference between Lysidamus' ambitions and those of a clever slave lies in his ability to use his domestic authority in the service of his subversion, requiring others to abet his adultery, and in the sanctioning of his desires by other authorities (here, the gods). Furthermore, the substance of his subversion is completely different from that of slaves or sons; in fact, one can hardly call it subversion at all. But the depiction of Lysidamus as a schemer, and the initial portrayal of Cleustrata as an *uxor dotata*, seem to engage the challenge of how close a *senex amator* can get to being a sympathetic rebel.

The lottery scene parallels the wedding scene at the end as a schemer's triumphant use of ritual.[41] The great difference between them lies both in the contrast between Lysidamus' triumph here and that of Cleustrata in the later scene and in the contrast between the mystical nature of his control and the metatheatrical nature of hers. The latter scene fits with the norm of Plautine comedy by creating a fictive situation that uses the ap-

---

[40] Although Lysidamus' arrogance may seem to support his role as blocking character rather than his potential heroism, the ways he expresses his extreme self-confidence have important parallels to the language of young lovers and clever slaves. For young lovers declaring their own divinity, cf. *Cur* 167 and *Mer* 601–2 (in both cases the fool in love is contradicted by a more earthy companion, as Lysidamus is by Olympio here). Cf. also *Truc* 372, where Diniarchus in love declares that he is better off than Jupiter. Moreover, throughout this movement, Lysidamus' confidence is expressed in military vocabulary—a positive depiction since comic convention associates this vocabulary with the successful scheming of slaves; see esp. 297–98, 307–08, 344, 352, 357. See also Chiarini (1978: 108–10, *passim*).

[41] MacCary and Willcock (1976: 35–36, on II.6) name this as the first of the "three spectacular scenes" around which the play is structured (the others are III.5 and IV.4) and which they claim reveal the *Casina*'s affinities to the *Rudens*, also from a Diphilean original. See also MacCary (1973: 194–95).

pearance of ritual to ensure the effectiveness of the trick. The lottery scene, on the other hand, is a real ritual that is not manipulated by any of the characters and seems to express naturalistic authority (in the form of religious authority) rather than the farcical authority of a trickster.

In both scenes the married couple are less prominent in the wrangling than are their slaves. Here and in the wedding scene, Cleustrata and Lysidamus are trying to profit from seeming to be calm, dignified, and removed from the conflict. In the lottery scene, that attempt breaks down prominently in two places, at lines 365–70, in Lysidamus' "Freudian slip," and at lines 404–11, where the outbreak of violence and carping serves only as an index to the strategy of the rest of the scene. In the first instance when Lysidamus almost gives himself away by referring to himself rather than Olympio as the bridegroom, we have one of the most obvious examples in the first movement of the weakness of Lysidamus' position, which will be fully revealed in the second movement. We can interpret this slip as generated either by his complete identification with Olympio in the pursuit of his erotic goal or by his lack of acting ability, which comes through as "breaking character."[42] His mistake is bound up with his unwillingness to recognize the boundaries that separate him from others. This error in turn gives rise to his sense of theater, which seeks to create new realities rather than merely mask or disguise realities.

In the second instance, the couple strike out at each other through their slaves, and this displacement is explicitly justified by comparing them to Jupiter and Juno.[43]

> CL: quid tibi istunc tactio est? OL: quia Iuppiter iussit meus.
> . . .
> LY: quid tibi tactio hunc fuit? CH: quia iussit haec Iuno mea.
>
> (406, 408)

CL: What business do you have hitting him? OL: Jupiter here ordered me to do it.
. . .
LY: What business do you have hitting him? CH: Juno here ordered me to do it.

This short exchange is a microcosm of how the couple uses their slaves to combat each other in the rest of the scene (and, in fact, in the whole play) while seeming to maintain a godlike distance from the conflict.[44] Outside these lines, Cleustrata, like a proper wife, speaks very little and confines herself to short, simple statements. Lysidamus acts the part of a *pater-*

---

[42] Petrone (1983: 91–92).
[43] Segal (1987: 25), Forehand (1973: 244).
[44] See Way (1998) on the dynamics of physical distance and social status in this scene.

familias in organizing the drawing of the lot and in restraining Olympio.[45] Thus this scene functions as the summation of the first movement in showing Lysidamus to be successful without the tricks that are usually necessary for success in comedy, as the mystical power of religion, the ultimate authority, justifies his seemingly outrageous confidence.[46]

The premature sense of closure imparted by Lysidamus' seemingly imminent triumph will be revealed as incomplete and wrong by the following movement, which reverses almost every aspect of the progress of this movement. This reversal brings the *Casina* into line with our expectations for Plautine comedy, that is, the overthrow of authority by theatrical trickery. However this eventual alignment of the plot with the expected comic goals has been deferred throughout the first movement by characterization that leaves us in doubt as to the comic functions of the characters and by the identification of the *senex* as hero. This identification allows Lysidamus to partake of both the farcical authority of being a rebel against his wife and the naturalistic authority that grants him power of his household and the blessings of the gods. This is not to claim that Lysidamus' rebellion is presented as unambiguously justified (the loopholes in his self-presentation will be exploited in the coming scenes). But, during the first movement, the entire play is structured around the possibility that Lysidamus might get what he desires. He may not be a complete comic hero in this part, but no

---

[45] The interpretation of this scene is muddled by the manuscript problem of the attribution of lines. Unfortunately, any decision about the attribution of lines must be guided by an understanding of the characters and plot, an understanding that is in turn frustrated by the *Casina*'s extreme lack of coherence. I have argued above that the functions of Chalinus and Olympio are ambiguous, that we cannot tell who is meant to be the clever slave and who is meant to be the good slave. But from my remarks on the previous two scenes (II.4, 5) it will also be clear that they do have distinctive characteristics and styles of speaking, which can help in sorting out the lines here. With that in mind, I agree with the attributions printed by MacCary and Willcock in their 1976 edition (derived from Groh at 379–81), which continue the characterization of Olympio as "surly and suspicious," in keeping with his more violent defiance as outlined above. Chalinus in this scheme gets more of the lines that reverse blessings to curses (e.g., 382–83) in keeping with my contention that he operates by more indirect methods. The problems of attribution are less difficult in the lines of Cleustrata and Lysidamus, since enough remain undisturbed to show that (except for the passages cited) they act with a modicum of restraint in this scene (see MacCary and Willcock on 381).

[46] Olympio's emphasis on piety as the assurer of their victory (383) is set off against Chalinus' repeated strategy of turning his prayers into curses (382, 389, 390; at 396 the joke is that he turns his own prayer into a curse) as well as against his own paranoid attempts to forestall any tricks from the other side (380, 384). The surprise here for anyone schooled in Plautine comedy is that the piety turns out to be effective and the tricks nonexistent. L. R. Taylor (1966: 72–73, 112–23) makes two observations relevant to the current argument. First, that lot drawing with the particular apparatus described in the *Casina* is specifically Roman, not Greek. Second, and more important, she notes the role of religion in the lot drawing process, in particular the authority of augurs as the guarantors of the sanctity of the lot and the identity of Jupiter as the god presiding over the *comitia*.

one else is allowed to develop into one either.[47] The play so far has teetered on the brink between affirming Lysidamus' ambitions (by taking seriously his claims to mystical control) and utterly destroying his plans (by exposing him as hubristic).

The first movement is an attempt to create a successful *senex amator*, an attempt that is itself produced by the rejection of the romantic plot line and entails further dramatic consequences. But although the *Casina* comes as close as possible to bringing off such an unlikely heroism, even this ebullient farce cannot meet this extreme challenge. The underlying concept of the *senex amator* is that this character type tweaks the usual structure of comedy by making someone who is usually in power in real life attempt to claim the place of the rebellious hero in the fantasy world of comedy. If this attempt were successful, it would radically change the structure of Plautine rebellion, since it would allow socially dominant members of the audience to experience liberatory release through a socially dominant figure on stage rather than having this release routed through the fictive characters of subordinates. Most *senex amator* comedies "punish" the *senex*'s attempted assault on comic heroism, thus preserving the illusion that comic rebellion is wholly in the service of those who are more obviously subordinated in real life.

The *Casina* pulls together all the elements that would be neccessary for such a coup: a clearly defined blocking character as wife, the removal of the son as sympathetic character, the introduction through an elaborate and imaginative monody, and the maintenance of household authority in addition to romantic authority. But even this supportive context is not enough to allow the *senex amator* to overcome the logic of farce, which requires that social subordinates take center stage and may even require some genuine subversion.[48] Contrary to what we might expect, what is needed to overcome this law of farce and create a successful *senex amator* is not a more easy-going characterization of the *paterfamilias* but one with even more absolute authority. The evidence for this lies in the only play that does manage to create a successful version of the *senex amator*: the *Amphitruo*. In a later section of this chapter I will discuss in more detail how Jupiter in that play can help us understand Lysidamus in the *Casina*,

---

[47] Slater (1985: 84) notes the play's failure to get in motion until after the lottery scene, thus equating the *Casina* with Cleustrata's metatheatrical play.

[48] It is useful to compare the situation here with that of the *Menaechmi*, where it was possible for a figure like a *senex amator* (Epidamnian Menaechmus) to be successful. Two important factors account for this different outcome. First, although that play makes great use of the elements of farce, naturalistic comedy maintains control of the plot. Second, Epidamnian Menaechmus' success was achieved both by abandoning his domestic authority (remember how impotent he was to control those who should have been obedient to him) and through an assimilation with the young lover (the Syracusan brother), not in opposition to him.

but for now, we should note that the greatest hope Lysidamus had of getting his way was not in persuading his household that he was a good guy who ought to be indulged but in relying on a godlike sense of his ability to act through others and in opposition to their wishes. The imagery of divinity, uniting the spheres of farcical and naturalistic power, is successful when taken literally as in the *Amphitruo*. Here, where it is only a metaphor, it merely delays Lysidamus' ultimate downfall.

Cleustrata's Play

It is characteristic of the farcical aesthetic that the first movement only negatively lays the groundwork for the second. It does not create a situation that will be elaborated and ultimately resolved but one that will be turned inside out. Throughout the first movement we have seen an ambiguity surrounding the characters' relation to the usual functions of the comic structure and an unusual portrayal of Lysidamus, which emphasized his assumption of a godlike power in dealing with his household. The reversal of Lysidamus' hopes and dreams creates the framework for the second movement. Within this framework, three important themes become activated. First, the similarities between slavery and marriage order this part of the play, because Cleustrata's role as trickster assimilates her to a comic slave and because the tricks all revolve around the force of sexuality in relations between masters and slaves. Second, Cleustrata's metatheatrical style points up the contrasting social meanings of comedy in Lysidamus' play and her own, namely, the contrast between a trickster who has some authority outside the play and one who has authority only within the fictive world of the play. Finally, the increasingly insistent theme of delay and lack of progress works in this movement within the play to forestall Lysidamus' plans. In the last movement of the play this theme will work metatheatrically to forestall the *Casina*'s own ambitions to be anything more than an afternoon's entertainment.

As surely as the first movement belongs to Lysidamus does the second movement (424–854, II.7 to IV.4) belong to Cleustrata.[49] In what seems like the blink of an eye, all the aspects of Lysidamus' power are turned into evidences of his weakness. Lysidamus' fanciful scheming in pursuit of an erotic goal (highly admirable in comic terms) is revealed to be merely the lustful delusion of an old man. The precision with which every expression of Lysidamus' and Olympio's imminent triumph is reversed into an instrument of their defeat is truly impressive. The transition between Lysidamus' triumph in the lottery scene and his discomfiture to follow is heralded by

[49] Lefèvre's (1979) main argument is that Cleustrata and her female allies take on the divine function played by Tyche in the Greek original (i.e., the undermining of Lysidamus' plans and the promotion of the son's).

several details of Chalinus' short monologue of II.7, almost giving it the status of an internal prologue. First, he asserts that it is not so much his loss that troubles him as the eagerness of the *senex* to have Olympio win (429–30), setting up his discovery of the proxy relationship between the two men. Next, he introduces the important motif of hurrying (*ut festinabat miser!*, "what a hurry the poor man was in!" 432), which foreshadows Lysidamus' future pointless expenditures of energy. Finally, this short speech also contains a hint of the theme of reversal that will be fully expanded in Chalinus' speech at the end of the next scene. Here, the line "out of this ambush, I'll ambush them" (*hinc ex insidiis hisce ego insidias dabo*, 436), prepares for the theme of turning Lysidamus' plans against him.

Scene II.8 proves to be almost exactly a reversal of the punishment Olympio promised to Chalinus in scene I.1. Chalinus, hidden between the walls, like a crab (*recessim dabo me ad parietem, imitabor nepam* "I will retreat backwards into the wall like a crab", 443: cf. 140: *quasi mus, in medio parieti vorsabere* "You'll squirm inside the wall, like a mouse"), overhears not Casina as promised but Lysidamus beg Olympio for the favor of a kiss (453; cf. 136).[50] Thus, near the beginning of Cleustrata's play we have a scene that exactly inverts the expectations set up by the opening scene in Lysidamus' play, since Chalinus achieves profit, not punishment, from being hidden in the walls and overhearing this attempted seduction. In the earlier scene, Olympio had represented his destined possession of Casina by ventriloquizing her desire for him, implying that the desiring subject can orchestrate everything on his own terms, including the behavior and identity of the desired object. This erotic control offers clear parallels to the kind of theatrical control that Olympio attributed to himself: like Casina, the perfectly malleable object who speaks the words supplied for her, the audience in Olympio's scheme is merely passive and has prescribed for it the emotions it must feel. Olympio's vision of sex as theater, then, coheres with Lysidamus' theatrical vision: it extends the logic of the master's authoritative control of his slaves to the relation between actor and audience. The vision of theater that will guide Cleustrata's play is one in which the passive participant (the audience) exerts some control. Cleustrata's theater does not seek to create new realities by fiat but rather emphasizes the irreducible necessity for negotiation, that is, that seemingly passive subordinates (wives, slaves, the audience) can block or twist the effect of the desires of the authoritative.

---

[50] The similarity of this situation to the one imagined by Olympio in I.1 is emphasized by the dialogue between Olympio and Lysidamus at the beginning of the scene. This dialogue recaps I.1 in its division between the city and the country (437–38), in the slave's promise to punish Chalinus by turning him into a *carbonarius* (cf. 124–25: *ita te aggerunda curvom aqua faciam probe / ut postilena possit ex te fieri*), and in Lysidamus' desire to add to Chalinus' woes by forcing him to help with the shopping for his rival's wedding (440–42).

This new emphasis on negotiation contrasts sharply with Lysidamus'
mystical control, which sought to obscure the processes of social life, and
it radically changes the terms on which slavery and marriage are associated.
In the first movement, slavery was associated with marriage in the context
of the master's control of both: Lysidamus was confident in his ability to
use a shadow marriage between two of his own slaves as a cover for his
sexual appropriation of Casina, and he was successful in controlling his
own wife. Here, in Lysidamus' attempted seduction of Olympio, surprisingly, this slave, uses about himself the language of a properly submissive
wife (see esp. *opsequens*, "obedient," 449; *morigerus*, "obliging" 463),[51] but
also, like Cleustrata in an earlier scene (cf. 229–35), resists Lysidamus'
erotic advances. In the earlier scene, Lysidamus made clear through asides
(227–28, 234) that he was sweet-talking his wife only to further his plan to
get Casina; in this scene, his motivations are left ambiguous: it is not clear
whether his desire for Olympio is genuine or merely strategic. But in either
case, master-slave sex in this scene carries a new charge of meaning: it is
not just an expression of the master's power but a point of delicate negotiations in which each party tries to get something from the other while lim-
iting his own exposure to the other's control.

Chalinus, watching from the sidelines, recalls a similar instance in his
own experience (460–62), when Lysidamus tried to extort sexual compliance from him. As a way of shifting the audience's interpretation of the
actions on stage, this information redefines the old man's erotic ambitions.
I have noted Plautus' general tendency to create from stereotypical comic
situations a history for each character that will give the audience the clues
it needs to situate that character in the system of comic conventions. For
example, in scene II.2, Myrrhina berated Cleustrata for her attempts to
control her husband through her dowry, telling the audience that Cleustrata has the habit of unreasonably reining in her husband's romantic pleasures, the trademark of the *uxor dotata*. Here we are given a distinctly differ-
erent view of this couple's past life; Lysidamus' longing for Casina can no
longer be seen in the rosy light of romantic love, as it was in his entrance
monody; it is immediately transformed into the act of a man who uses his
domestic authority to impose his erotic will on his slaves. Chiarini (1978:
113) has observed that this scene marks the height of Lysidamus' delusions,
as he calls adultery "marriage" (486) and his neighbors' house "the country" (485). It also contains a few more examples of his belief in his own
powers to transcend the boundaries between subjects, especially in his extravagant claims of identification with Olympio.[52] But because the frame

---

[51] O'Bryhim (1989: 98–99).

[52] See 456: OL. *ecquid amas nunc me?* LY. *immo edepol me quam te minus*, and 464: *ut tibi,
dum vivam, bene velim plus quam mihi.*

within which we view the actions has been subtly but definitively reoriented by Chalinus the eavesdropper (the resisting audience), his self-confidence comes across not as the charming arrogance of the trickster but as the despicable self-delusion of a dirty old man.

This important scene marks the transition between the play Lysidamus has been scripting, a play marked by the mystical lack of boundaries between subjects, and the very different play that Cleustrata will produce. It closes with Chalinus' explicit expression of the relation between these two plays:

> ibo intro, ut id quod alius condivit coquos,
> ego nunc vicissim ut alio pacto condiam,
> quo id quoi paratum est ut paratum ne siet
> sietque ei paratum quod paratum non erat.
>
> (511–14)

I'll go inside so that I can season to my taste what another chef has cooked up, and to unprepare what has been prepared, and prepare for him something quite different from what he prepared.

The cooking imagery in this statement of intent is yet another indication of the imminent reversal of Lysidamus' dreams, picking up as it does on the culinary language of his memorable monody.[53]

After this preparation for the shift from a play controlled by Lysidamus to one controlled by Cleustrata, scenes III.1 through III.4 present the first of three tricks when she tells her neighbor Alcesimus that she has no need of his wife's help in the wedding preparations, thereby foiling Lysidamus' attempt to use his neighbors' house as a trysting place. This first trick is an extreme statement of the style of theatricality of clever slaves because it involves much acting but produces no result, except to get the two male neighbors angry at each other. (This anger is itself without result, since Alcesimus quickly vanishes, never to be seen again, though the epilogue tells us that he is Casina's father.) Cleustrata has no interest in keeping Myrrhina from coming to help her, and in fact she is glad to have her join in the fun. Unlike Lysidamus' style of theater, which seeks a lasting situation, Cleustrata's is not even interested in the proximate result, only in the trick itself. Lysidamus' interchanges with Alcesimus in scenes III.1 and III.4 emphasize the change in plot line from the first part of the play by explicitly pointing to all the usual markers of *senex amator* comedy, emphasizing the inappropriateness of this infatuation at his age.[54] These markers label Lysi-

[53] This scene also extends and expands the theme of delay, by pointing to Lysidamus' impatience: see 472–74, 491.

[54] Cf. especially the neighbor's advice in *Mer* II.2, III.3.

damus as an old man who does not realize or admit that the pleasures of Eros belong to the young.

Cleustrata's scenes here (III.2, 3) reveal her transformation from complaining wife to accomplished actress. Her conversations with Alcesimus and with Lysidamus show her relying on their belief in the attributes of a good wife to trick them. To Alcesimus she plays the part of a calm, self-sufficient housewife who would rather do all her work herself than either call on the help of a friend or indulge in leisurely companionship. Her performance is so convincing precisely because she acts the part of the ideal wife; if she had allowed herself even a single complaint or question about her husband, Alcesimus would suspect the truth (554–56). Likewise with Lysidamus, her portrayal of a wife with an overactive sense of propriety (585–86) is precisely what turns his anger away from her and towards his neighbor.

Cleustrata's use of the stereotypes of her own role in order to trick the two men is the best illustration of how her sense of theatricality differs from that of Lysidamus. Where Lysidamus believed in the power of disguise to change the essential attributes of people and things, Cleustrata puts her faith in her own manipulation of the gap between appearances and identities. She realizes that her performance of the good housewife can be radically different in substance, depending on the meaning with which she invests it. Her sensitivity to this gap between appearances and reality will be the key to her theatricals in the rest of the play; it is shown here in her distancing herself from being a good wife by merely playing a good wife.

The second trick too, like the first one, seems to be invented only to fall into the void. Cleustrata sends the slave girl Pardalisca out to "warn" Lysidamus that Casina has turned into a raving madwoman, ready to kill in order to prevent this wedding. Pardalisca's messenger speech surely needs no other justification than the extravagant pleasures of parody, irony, and spectacle it provides. The fearful possibility that Casina is wielding swords with which to kill any man who tries to marry her surfaces again in a memorable joke in the final revelation, but, strictly speaking, it does not have any dramatic result in the situation.[55] This scene presents and comments on Cleustrata's vision of theatricality (as introduced in the previous four scenes) and emphasizes the difference of this vision from that of Lysidamus, which governed the earlier part of the play. It provides exactly the theatrical elements that Lysidamus' stage direction left us hungry for: nar-

---

[55] Lefèvre (1979: 317) adduces this lack of coherence between Casina-as-fury and the silent, passive bride who appears later as evidence of contamination, with the break between Act III and Act IV as the seam between two plays. Further (1979: 332), he singles out this scene as a good example of the replacement of the mystical agency of Tyche by the farcical action of the "Triummatronat": "Wurde bei Plautus der ganze Auftritt seiner tieferen Bedeutung entkleidet und auf die Ebene der reine Komik und des Klamauks transponiert. . . ."

rative and the parody of tragic language and themes.[56] Compare the stories about pirates, a haunted house, the plight of a war captive, and the pains of childbirth that animate the *Bacchides*, *Mostellaria*, *Persa*, and *Truculentus*. Paratragic language and themes are central to the theatrical worldview of clever slaves, because this kind of performance simultaneously foregrounds acting ability and a metatheatrical knowledge of the relation of this particular play to the dramatic tradition.[57] Pardalisca's star turn forcefully impresses upon us her acting ability, her knowledge of tragedy, and Lysidamus' corresponding ignorance.[58]

Further, corresponding to what Cleustrata did in her performances, Pardalisca uses the expected attributes of her role to achieve her goals. Her role as female house slave has two competing aspects, and she makes use of both of them. First, for the benefit of the audience, who might associate her type with the maids of *meretrices* in other plays (cf. *Menaechmi*, *Truculentus*), she tricks Lysidamus into a compromising position by pretending to be faint with fear (634–41).[59] Then, in her most emphatic performance, she turns to playing the part of a devoted and deferential slave.[60] Her deference is portrayed through little touches, like the frightened "oh master, you're too angry" (*ere mi . . . nimium saevis*, 646–47), the excuse "fear has tied my tongue" (*timor praepedit dicta linguae*, 653), and the perfect irony of the diminutive in "you make that mistake a tad often" (*saepicule peccas*, 703). Like Chalinus, she declares her allegiance to the party of theater over the party of wealth when she seemingly assents to Lysidamus' bribes, only to lure him further into the trap (708–17).

Scene III.6 degrades Lysidamus further, interestingly by using a strategy that is only a slight change from the strategy that supported his potential heroism in the early part of the play. I noted in the previous section that one possible escape for Lysidamus from the unsympathetic characterization of *senex amator* rested on his assimilation to an *adulescens*. But while his monody and other hints in the first movement associated him with the youthful optimism of these lovers, this scene removes any last shred of dignity he

---

[56] Fraenkel (1922: 342 = 1960: 326) on paratragedy here.

[57] MacCary and Willcock (1976: on 621–29). Another reference to dramatic traditions enlivens this scene: it is a female slave's rendition of the running-slave scene in which she uses fear, faintness, and melodrama to delay the delivery of the message, rather than the usual (male) running-slave's determination to get people out of the way.

[58] Cf. Syracusan Menaechmus' use of paratragedy in his mad scene at *Men* 835–71, as discussed in the previous chapter.

[59] MacCary and Willcock (1976: on 641) adduce *As* 668 as evidence that holding the ears is a synecdoche for kissing. This also raises the possibility that even passive sexuality (as the position Pardalisca puts herself in here) could be masking a manipulative power.

[60] Tobias (1979: 12) notes that Pardalisca's bacchiacs here (common in slave-master dialogue) "emphasize the seriousness of [her] warning and her pretended deference toward Lysidamus."

might have had by attributing to him the helplessness and cowardice that makes these young men completely dependent on their slaves. Like those hapless souls, who grovel at the feet of their slaves to secure help in obtaining the girl of their dreams, Lysidamus is willing to call himself Olympio's slave (738–41) in return for defense against Casina's swords.

In addition to giving Lysidamus the comical attributes of young lovers, rather than their romantic attributes, this scene further de-romanticizes him by repeating (from scene II.8) his unsuccessful attempt to seduce Olympio.[61] Like the earlier scene, this attempted seduction inverts the meaning that Lysidamus' play tried to attach to master-slave sex. Not just because it was heterosexual desire but also because it emphasized the mystical bond that unites the lovers and the transformative power of love (especially in his entrance monody), Lysidamus' desire for Casina in the first movement seemed like the kind of love we are used to seeing crowned by marriage in the final scene. But Cleustrata's play seeks wherever possible to invert slavery and marriage. Thus, in scene II.8 and again here in III.4, we see in Lysidamus a kind of desire (homosexual, shaped by master-slave dynamics, and—most importantly—resisted) that is the exact opposite of the desire that forms the pivot of romantic comedy. In place of the mutual, mystical, unique longing of two young lovers, Cleustrata's play offers rather sordid negotiations, which make obvious the extent to which sex (especially master-slave sex) is implicated in everyday hierarchies. Although his choice of objects in this second movement (the full-grown male slave Olympio; see 465–66) provides the mechanism through which his sexual desire is de-romanticized, it is not so much the homosexuality of his later attempts as the fact that they are embedded in complex domestic negotiations that effectively deprives Lysidamus of any sympathy he might have had as a lover. In addition to showing that he is acting as a master rather than a lover in his pursuit of Casina, Cleustrata's play adds insult to injury by showing that his mastery is not even a very reliable way to get what he wants. The final blow to the self-image Lysidamus had built up in the earlier part of the play is Olympio's chilling reply to the suggestion that he go in first to brave Casina's swords:

> OL: tam mihi mea vita
> tua quam tibi carast.
>
> (757–57a)

OL: My life is as dear to me as yours is to you.

---

[61] Cody (1976: 456–57) notes both the master/slave role-reversal in this scene and the culinary language in which the sexual offer is phrased (see 726, 727, 730–32a, 742–43 [where she posits a sexual meaning of *recreas me*]). See also Lefèvre (1979: 333), Slater (1985: 86–87).

This reply, even more than his earlier reminder of his master's mortality, undermines the belief in a godlike sense of self, which is the cornerstone of Lysidamus' image of his own power. The assertion that other people are subjects in their own right and not channels through which divine or masterly will can be exerted is the exact reversal of the pattern on which Lysidamus has constructed his authority.[62]

The next two scenes (IV.1, 2) begin to solidify the connection between the vision of theatricality that has been demonstrated in the third act and the increasingly important theme of delay and frustration. Although the use of the words *propero* and *festino* and the corresponding use of *moror* have been frequent in the third act,[63] this theme of obstructing the ever-more-fervid desires of Lysidamus is now made concrete when Pardalisca reveals that the lengthy preparations within will not only stall Lysidamus' satisfaction but the third trick, the substitution of Chalinus for Casina as bride, will prevent his satisfaction completely. Her speech brings to fruition the hint that Chalinus gave, that the "feast" of which Lysidamus had dreamed will be replaced with the meal of his nightmares. While Lysidamus' sexual frustration is foreshadowed in his hunger,[64] the success of the plan of Cleustrata and her allies is envisioned in the promise of their satiety. I will discuss more fully in the final section of this chapter the peculiar economy of food and sexuality in this play, in which the scheming women, rather than using sexual wiles as scheming women do wherever else they appear (e.g., *Miles Gloriosus, Truculentus, Bacchides*), are specifically segregated from any sexual role and instead their cleverness and their satisfaction are represented in terms of food.

In scene IV.2 Lysidamus' repetition of his language about the country and his military vocabulary reminds us of his delusive state of mind and prepares us for a reversal,[65] as does his repeated assertion that he can live without food as long as he has love, an assertion that sounds more and more hollow. One element of his speech here looks forward to his future discomfiture rather than back to his own vision of power. Unlike scene II.3 where he waived his rights to tomorrow in exchange for his freedom today (251), he claims here that he will get his dinner tomorrow while his wife and her friends eat today. In the terms of the comic code, this constitutes an acknowledgment that he has become the blocking character. Since food in this play has represented control and the satisfaction of desires, conceding his dinner until tomorrow is tantamount to conceding his authority.[66]

[62] Again, note the insistence on delay in this scene (744–45, 749–50).
[63] See notes 53 and 62 above; see also lines 532, 588, 618.
[64] Lefèvre (1979: 319), Chiarini (1978: 115).
[65] Chiarini (1978: 110).
[66] Cf. *As* 935–36.

The preparation for the culminating scene expresses the major dramatic force of the play, delay, in the sexual idiom. Scene IV.3 depicts Lysidamus' lack of progress sexually, making it parallel to and differentiating it from Olympio's rumbling stomach (801–3).[67] The interminably deferred climax of the play is symbolized in Lysidamus' claim that he is about to burst with his own frustrations (809–10). Neither Lysidamus' sexual satisfaction nor any real dramatic resolution will be achieved, since this play frustrates his sexual desires by frustrating the forward movement of the dramatic situation.[68]

Although the wedding scene (IV.4) is a short scene, it is perhaps the funniest in the play and certainly one of the most powerful in summing up the themes that have been woven throughout. The parody of ritual is emphasized by Pardalisca's using ritual language[69] to express the manifesto of the clever slave instead of advice of submission to the bride.[70]

> Sensim super atolle limen pedes, nova nupta;
> sospes iter incipe hoc, uti viro tuo
>   semper sis superstes,
> tuaque ut potior pollentia sit vincasque virum victrixque sies,
> tua vox superet tuomque imperium: vir te vestiat, [tu] virum despolies.
>   noctuque et diu ut viro subdola sis,
>   opsecro, memento.
>
>   (815–24)

> Carefully lift your feet over the threshold, newlywed; begin this journey safely, that you may always outlast your husband, that your power may be more potent, and that you may conquer your husband and stand victorious, that your voice and your authority may emerge triumphant: let your husband clothe you while you despoil him. By night and day, remember to deceive your husband, I pray.

Just as Lysidamus' play ended with a spectacular ritual scene, which exemplified his theatrical style (relying as it did on mystical confidence and the sanction of authority), the wedding scene is a fitting climax to Cleustrata's extravagant show, expressing in the most entertaining possible way the substitution of a slave for a wife and a wife for a (clever) slave. Although Cleustrata is a slave only at the level of comic convention (where all tricksters are measured against the template of the clever slave), because these conventions are themselves shaped by the real social attributes of slaves, even

---

[67] Forehand (1973: 245).

[68] Note also the repetition of Olympio refusing Lysidamus' offer of sex (811–13).

[69] Fraenkel (1922: 362 = 1960: 343).

[70] O'Bryhim (1989: 90).

this kind of metatheatrical connection to slaves inverts the institutions of slavery and marriage. This inversion of slavery and marriage does more than merely flatten out the differences between the two institutions, it tantalizingly displays both the similarities and the differences of these two household hierarchies.

Plautus' Play

If the first movement is that of Lysidamus' triumph and the second is that of Cleustrata's, whom can we say the third and final movement (855–1018, Act V) exalts? It is indicative of the peculiar structure of this play that the final scenes, just where we would most expect resolution and definition, are even more uncertain than those that came before.[71] The theme of delay and lack of progress, which was previously aimed exclusively against Lysidamus' plans, in the end swallows up the entire play.

Cleustrata's trickery in the second movement fulfilled our expectations for imaginative Plautine deception. Although her trick was successful, in this final movement her characterization as trickster will falter. Like her clever counterparts in other plays, Cleustrata is not permitted to imagine that her power will last beyond the end of the play, since that would imply a fundamental and permanent change in the relation between (usually) master and slave or (here) husband and wife. But even beyond this check on Cleustrata's triumph, there is another that puts an end to her power within the play (clever slaves are usually permitted to reign at least until the very end of the play). That is the surprising conversion of Lysidamus himself into a slave on the metatheatrical plane, when he uses the final scenes to extort forgiveness from his "master." When he usurps the function of slave, he forces Cleustrata into the function of master, and comic convention decrees her pardon in this circumstance.[72] In the end, Lysidamus embraces farce by assimilating himself to a clever slave and abandons his attempt to win the indulgence granted to *adulescentes*; thus, he can end on a triumphant note, but only on farce's terms, in which the hero within the play must abdicate any authority outside the play.

One of the most reliable rules of Plautine comedy is that clever slaves get off scot-free. When their trickery comes to light at the end of the play, masters may rant and rave, but they never really punish the trickster slave, since clever slaves embody contradictory qualities for the master; their

[71] Part of this problem is due, of course, to the state of the text. The interpretations offered here will be an attempt to make sense of the portions of the manuscript that we have without resorting to reconstructing what was conveyed in the gaps in any particular way.

[72] O'Bryhim (1989: 101) does not see the reversal in terms of master and slave but argues that Cleustrata, by punishing her spouse for adultery, has become a "husband."

ebullient rebellion captures for the audience a sense of liberation while their childlike simplicity disarms the potential danger of slave rebellion. When the master forgives the slave's antics, these disparate functions are at their most extreme: the slave succeeds in escaping his due punishment but at the same time happily anticipates future repetitions of this insubstantial rebellion, giving up any attempt to end his servitude.

There is no easy way for the *Casina* to adhere to this pattern without introducing troubling consequences. To play out the normal scheme of having the rebel (Cleustrata) forgiven in this case would be to push even further her similarity to clever slaves, and this would make both too much and too little of Cleustrata's rebellion. It would make too much of it because it would imply that this is just one of an endless string of assaults against her husband. Although Plautine comedy is comfortable with assuming that marriage is a form of ongoing warfare between the spouses, to make a wife into the kind of permanent enemy within the household that the slave represents would understate the coincidence of social and economic interests between the husband and wife.[73] This may be evidence of Roman wives' more central role in the household (compared with Athenian wives, e.g.), but it almost certainly implies that slaves are not just less powerful members of the household (a possible paternalistic view of slavery) but of a fundamentally different order whose interests are by definition opposed to those of the *paterfamilias*. On the other hand, if Cleustrata were forgiven by Lysidamus in the way that clever slaves are forgiven by masters in other plays, it would make too little of her rebellion against Lysidamus' high-handed behavior. Although Cleustrata has been shown to be very different from the usual humorless *uxor dotata*, she still does have right on her side when she punishes her husband's selfish and indecorous behavior. This separates her from clever slaves whose rebellion is aimed at reveling in *malitia* (the desire to do what we know we should not), rather than at correcting the master's morals.

The play finally negotiates this thicket of conflicting energies by opting, once again, to abandon one line of dramatic development and pick up another. The final movement combines elements of the comedy of rebellion we have been witnessing all along with a related but distinct type, the comedy of humors. The comedy of humors, best exemplified in ancient drama by Menander's *Dyskolos* and Plautus' *Aulularia* and later brought to the height of its form by Jonson and Molière, may have a romantic story centered on two young lovers separated by the unreasonable strictures of their

---

[73] Rei (1998: 104) emphasizes the solidarity between husband and wife that the ending of this play expresses, and esp. the effect of this solidarity in clarifying the division between slave and free in the household.

elders, but instead of focusing on the love story, it focuses on correcting the *idée fixe* (the "humor") that caused the blocking character's antisocial behavior. When applied to the *Casina*, this comic paradigm produces a dénouement in which Lysidamus admits he was wrong and promises never to act that way again. But we must also acknowledge that along with this new paradigm the comedy of rebellion persists. Since the persona through which Lysidamus chooses to express his humiliation is that of the slave, he simultaneously reasserts his claim to the role of rebel, which he played in the first movement; thus, Cleustrata ends up supporting moral values, Lysidamus ends up as champion of *malitia*. Although this type of ending gives credit to Cleustrata, the person who has cleverly contrived to show the humorist the error of his ways, in doing so it changes the basis of her rebellion from *malitia* to social justice: this ending backs away from the possibility that a *matrona* could be a farcical trickster and, as a result, backs away from the strongest statement of the analogy between slavery and marriage. The final movement, then, is fundamentally conservative: it denies any real social change, and it returns to comedy's "official version" of marriage, in which it is the husband who has a right to rebel against his dour, rich, and unattractive wife.

Trickery as clever as Cleustrata's has been deserves recognition, even if that recognition comes as a swan song just before she must revert to being a *matrona*, enforcer of decorum. Scene V.1 is the most explicit statement in the play of Cleustrata's identity as the clever slave and playwright of this farce. Myrrhina describes her with words that clearly fit the vocabulary of metatheatrical control (*ludi*, *fallacia astutior*, *poeta*, and *fabre*). Further, that Cleustrata expresses the desire to humiliate Lysidamus and make him a laughingstock (*ludibrium*) is in keeping with the common goal of all clever slaves (862–63, 868). Thus, just before the final swerve that will reinstate Lysidamus, this scene establishes Cleustrata's function as comic hero and grants her the praise she deserves for a well-constructed farce.

Food is especially important in defining the heroism of Cleustrata and her female allies. This scene shows Cleustrata, Myrrhina, and Pardalisca emerging from the house after having dined sumptuously (855; cf. 775–79). This comic banquet is different from those we see in other plays (e.g., *Stichus*, *Rudens*, *Persa*) in that it takes place before the final scene of the play. Because the festive banquet is always a marker of resolution, and because in this play the ability to satisfy one's appetite has been equated with the ability to exercise control over events, this strange banquet offers more evidence that Cleustrata's role as hero is coming to an end. Although her script has given us the most memorable scenes, this premature festivity makes clear that Cleustrata's play is not coextensive with the *Casina* and must yield the stage for the final scenes.

Scene V.2 begins the transition by which Lysidamus will be transformed into a clever slave worthy of forgiveness. The most obvious theme in this section is the repeated expressions of shame on the part of Olympio (876, 878, 879 bis, 897–98, 899, 902, 911).[74] Comparison of this scene to scenes of humiliation for old men in love will show that Olympio's is the language usually reserved for these repentant husbands when faced with their angry wives.[75] Olympio's assumption of this language, and the consequent displacement of this part of the *senex amator* paradigm onto him, helps to preserve the structure of a *senex amator* ending, while leaving Lysidamus free to enact the part not of an old lover but of a clever slave who has been caught in his wiles.

Furthermore, this scene once again makes reference to the striking speech of the first scene in which Olympio plans his revenge. Here, as in II.8, the situation is reversed so that instead of seeing Chalinus tortured with the sounds of Casina begging to make love to Olympio, we see Olympio recounting his own humiliating experience of begging for a kiss from "Casina" and being physically abused in return. Particularly affecting is Olympio's echoing of his own voice (882), similar to the way he ventriloquized the voice of Casina in the opening scene. There he assumed her voice in an imagined moment of submission; here he mimics his own voice, both representing and repeating his own humiliation. This final reworking of the opening scene also shows again how far Lysidamus and Olympio are from understanding how to control the presentation of drama before an audience. Far from being able to control what the spectators see, they are put in the position of dupes in Cleustrata's masterfully planned show.

The final two scenes of the play radically depart from the moral and dramatic structure of Cleustrata's play, which has dominated the stage since Chalinus' eavesdropping in scene II.8. The course of the play since then has consistently asserted Cleustrata's cleverness, heroism, and farcical authority. These last two scenes unexpectedly reverse this course to make Lysidamus the clever slave who knows that he must be forgiven at the end of the play for any wrongs he has committed. By becoming slavelike, he implicitly claims that his actions were in the interests of sensuality, rebellion, and upheaval, like the extravagant acts of comic heroes, and he denies that they were acts of erotic trespassing and failure to understand the nature of theater, the crimes committed by blocking characters. His usurpation of the role of clever slave forces Cleustrata, his opponent, into the function of blocking character as she was at the beginning of the play.

---

[74] Cody (1976: 458–59); Forehand (1973: 247, 249) notes the contrast between the slave's contrition and Lysidamus' attempt to escape punishment.

[75] E.g., *As* 933, *Mer* 983, and the Matrona's attempt to apply this paradigm at *Men* 708, 713.

Lysidamus takes on the persona not just of any slave but specifically of the clever slave.[76] This specific persona is established both through the situation (his attempt at deception has failed, and he faces punishment) and through language that he shares with clever slaves in other plays. In particular, the language that he uses to imagine his punishment is familiar from the lexicon of clever slaves. For example, he declares that his shoulders are in danger if he returns home (955–56) and that he does not want to be beaten, even though he knows he deserves it (957–58). Beginning at lines 967–68, he begins to use the colorful and inventive language in which clever slaves describe their future punishments (*defloccabit* and *lumbifragium*) and witty manipulations of proverbs (970–73). Finally, perhaps the most telling evidence that he is modeling himself on a slave like Pseudolus is his extragavant promise that if he ever misbehaves in the future, he will offer himself to be beaten while hanging (1001–3), and willingly undergo the punishment he is now so strenuously avoiding. This offer is received by Cleustrata and by the audience with the appropriate degree of amused scepticism: no one could believe that he will live up to his promise of good behavior, and yet he has skillfully maneuvered to claim for himself the farcical high ground, and thus he cannot be denied amnesty.

And where does Lysidamus' conversion leave Cleustrata? Not as badly off as one might expect. Although Lysidamus has usurped the role of farcical hero by assimilating himself to a clever slave and by extorting forgiveness from her, Cleustrata's characterization at the end of the play is the softest possible version of a blocking character. She fulfills the function of a blocking character in agreeing to pardon her wayward husband, but the way that she does this takes her as close to being a hero as a blocking character can be.

> propter eam rem hanc tibi nunc veniam minu' gravate prospero,
> hanc ex longa longiorem ne faciamus fabulam.

(1005–6)

The only reason I'm now advancing your pardon less grudgingly is to avoid making a long play even longer.

In granting her pardon "less grudgingly," she is distancing herself from other blocking characters, whose forgiveness is grudging in the extreme.[77] But even more importantly, the reason she gives for her leniency is a meta-

---

[76] Scholars have been quick to see the slavelike attributes of Lysidamus here but have explained them in the context of humiliation rather than aggrandizement (Lefèvre [1979: 337], Cody [1976: 461], Slater [1985: 89–90], Forehand [1973: 249], Rei [1998: 101]). This interpretation, however, ignores the role of the slave in comic convention and the prevailing structure of final scenes, which always pardon the trickster slave but never pardon *senes amatores*.

[77] Cf. particularly *Bac* 532.

theatrical reason—the strongest way of showing that Cleustrata here is more than your usual humorless matron; she is also a perceptive student of theatrical life, who realizes that this time she must relinquish center stage and play a supporting role.

Chalinus' final speech deserves close attention. In lines 1010–11 we find out that, despite the wild frenzy we have observed throughout the latter part of the play, "nothing happened." This negation applies equally to Cleustrata's trick and to Chalinus' "marriage." In the end, this play backs away from the transformations of a wife into a clever slave and a slave into a wife that we thought we were witnessing. The denial of these transformations further implies that the statement "nothing happened" could be applied to the play as a whole. Thus, like Cleustrata's play, which gloried in multiple tricks without following out the consequences, Plautus' play has been an elaborate arrangement that forcefully presented the possibility for all kinds of strange permutations of the comic code (that old men could be lovers, that rich wives could be tricky), only to retract that possibility at the final curtain.

The epilogue repeats in miniature the effect of the play as a whole. It grants but two lines to the romantic tradition: one line to the recognition of citizen status (1013) and one line to the ensuing marriage (1014). The final four lines of the play, in contrast, focus on the *senex amator* and, surprisingly, hold out the possibility of his success.

> nunc vos aequomst manibus meritis meritam mercedem dare:
> qui faxit, clam uxorem ducet semper scortum quod volet;
> verum qui non manibus clare quantum poterit plauserit,
> ei pro scorto supponetur hircus unctus nautea.

$$(1015–18)$$

Now it's only fair that you give us our hard-earned pay with your applause: whoever does so will always enjoy the tart whom he desires without his wife finding out; but anyone who does not applaud as loudly as he's able, will find his tart supplanted by a goat perfumed with bilge-water.

If only a *senex amator* will agree to go along with the spirit of comedy and applaud this vaudeville farce, he will be granted his desires not just once but whenever he wants.[78] The *paterfamilias* who fails to understand that

---

[78] Forehand (1973: 252–53) compares the epilogue to that of the *Mercator*: "In the *Mercator* there is a call for general license to youth and denial to old age. . . . In the *Casina* the final comment forfeits any claim to decency or propriety. In fact, Lysidamus' fondest wish will be granted to the audience: to philander at will and have no fear of their wives." In keeping with my argument about comedy's "official version" of marriage, I would observe that the epilogue pretends that the audience is made up exclusively of men who want to escape restrictive marriages.

farce is the source of his salvation will be punished as Lysidamus was, by the substitution of his love object.

COMIC HUSBANDS AND WIVES

Much of this analysis of the *Casina* has depended on the conventions governing how marriage is represented in comedy and the ways that this play brings into focus similarities between marriage and slavery in the comic world. I would like to close this chapter by situating against the background of other plays in the Plautine corpus the husband and wife we have seen here; even though Lysidamus and Cleustrata are unusual instantiations of their character types, the premutations of the *senex amator* and *uxor dotata* in the *Casina* are essentially related to the structural and thematic functions of these characters elsewhere in Plautus. Finally, a brief look back at the *Menaechmi* will clarify the similarities and differences between these two comic households.

The first part of the *Casina*, Lysidamus' *aristeia*, is surprisingly parallel to the career of the only successful *senex amator* in the corpus: Jupiter, in the *Amphitruo*. That Jupiter fulfills this comic function is obvious not just from his status as the father of gods and mortals but from the corresponding filial positions of both Mercury and Amphitruo. Jupiter's appropriation of Alcumena from his "son" corresponds to the unfulfilled desires of the fathers in the *Mercator, Asinaria*, and *Casina*. The ability to take on the identity of another is literal in the case of Jupiter and therefore successful.[79] Lysidamus' attempt to "marry" Casina through the agency of her true husband Olympio is less promising. The *Casina* cannot entertain this possibility beyond the first part of the play, since the kind of mystical control on which it rests can be motivated dramatically only in the case of a god. Instead, this play partway through renounces its own attempt to give a mortal *senex* the powers of Jupiter by reconfiguring Lysidamus' nearly divine powers as hubris and finally can only make him a hero by making him a clever slave, with all the ambiguities entailed by that kind of heroism.

Lysidamus' inevitable failure to obtain the object of his desires is not the only difference between the *Casina* and the *Amphitruo*. Another important difference is the removal of the girl Casina from the stage, with the result that her claim to sympathy is purely structural, not—as for Alcumena— also derived from her personal qualities. Jupiter's greater power makes it possible to strengthen the position of those who are opposed to him without risking his complete loss of authority (though many modern readers feel that this danger is not completely avoided). For Lysidamus, on the

---

[79] Bettini (1982: 70–71) shows that Jupiter's divinity is what makes the adultery conceivable.

other hand, although his position as *paterfamilias* and light-hearted lover allows him a certain amount of power in both the farcical and naturalistic realms, the sympathy he attracts in the first movement is extremely fragile and would be completely undermined if Casina herself were to appear on stage as an appealing and helpless young girl.

A further difference between the two plays is that the *Casina* reduces the importance of the marriage that is being violated by female adultery by making it a slave marriage. The prologue (67–74) calls our attention to the dubious nature of such a marriage and so weakens the charge of adultery while still implicitly advertising the transgression involved in such an affair. Furthermore, the uncertainty of the character functions and attributes in this early part of the play are the direct result of avoiding any stark alignments of sympathy that would threaten Lysidamus' tentative escape from the strictures on mortals and on comic old men. The only unambiguous identification of character function in these early scenes is that of Cleustrata as *uxor dotata* and, therefore, as blocking character, precisely the one identification necessary to depict Lysidamus as a rebel and safeguard him from the normal opprobrium of the situation.

In this context, we must consider the surprising absence of Juno in the *Amphitruo*. Because the mythological tradition of Hercules' (=Hera*cles*) birth emphasizes Juno's/Hera's role as antagonist and because in Plautine comedy bickering mortal couples are sometimes compared to Jupiter and Juno,[80] we might reasonably expect Juno to play an important role. In fact, as I argued for the first movement of the *Casina*, the *uxor dotata* is a necessary component of the *senex amator*'s potential heroism, because it is only in contrast to his wife (rather than his son) that the older man can seem like a morally justified rebel, not just a rebel fueled by *malitia*. But in the event, Jupiter's ability to play the role of the rebel and, thus, his success as *senex amator* comes from his truly divine power to take on any appearance or personality he likes rather than from his (explicit or implicit) subordination to his wife; in the *Amphitruo*, this ability is assimilated to the comic trickster's talent for disguise. Conversely, we can say that Lysidamus fails (and thus opens the way for the very different logic of Cleustrata's play) not because he is too much the domestic tyrant but because his tyranny cannot go the final distance to make him completely impervious. The tantalizing possibility glimpsed in the *Casina*, but realized only in the *Amphitruo*, is the possibility of bringing on stage a literal instantiation of the rebel who is also an authority figure, an ideal that elsewhere in comedy must always operate through metaphor, that is, through the audience's cross-identification with the low-status hero.[81]

---

[80] Besides the examples discussed in the *Casina*, see *Mer* 690, 956.

[81] I am grateful to Matt Pincus for conversation that helped me to clarify the argument of this paragraph.

Finally, the difference between the two endings is the most forceful demonstration of the insuperable differences between gods and mortals. A god can be a successful *senex amator* and can even turn a play that depicts age usurping the province of youth into a happy ending. Against all the logic of comedy, the *Amphitruo* ends not just with a romantic rebirth but with the most spectacular birth in the whole corpus. Segal (1987: 171–91) is absolutely right when he points to the lack of coherence between the erotic obsessions that drive the play and Hercules' birth. Forehand (1973) is equally right to draw our attention to the artificiality of the *Casina* ending. Both plays prove that the love of a *senex amator* is fundamentally opposed to the forward-looking love of youth and romantic comedy, and, although the *Casina* entertains the possibility that a *paterfamilias* might be a successful rebel, only a *deus ex machina* can overcome the logic of comedy, which insists that subversive heroism comes only at the cost of admitting that one is constrained.

The radical refashioning of the character of the *uxor dotata* corresponds to that of the *senex amator*; it too exploits an ambivalence in the usual characterization, since the *uxor* usually ends up helping the cause of the young lover, her enemy's enemy. The *Casina* circumvents the negative greed and rigidity of the type by an unusually stark representation of the values associated with sex and food. Throughout the Plautine corpus and throughout the tradition of romantic comedy, there is a well-defined complementarity between the desire for love in the master and the desire for food in the slave or servant.[82] This complementarity itself is a ground of contention between the romantic and farcical strains of comedy. In romantic comedy it is generally skewed to reveal the difference between the animal lusts of the slave and the more refined emotional desires of the master. The more farcical the comedy gets, however, the sillier the young lover is shown to be, and in step with this development, the slave's preference for food is made to seem down-to-earth and sensible when compared to the mad love-sickness of the master. As might be expected, the *Casina* makes use of both of these meanings by equating Lysidamus' failure to achieve his sexual desires with his failure to get any dinner and by minimizing Cleustrata's rebellion through an emphasis on the importance of food to her and her allies.

Perhaps the most well delineated use of food imagery in this play is its association with what Lefèvre has called the "Triummatronat." The triumph of Cleustrata, Pardalisca, and Myrrhina is expressed when they deny food to Lysidamus and Olympio but also through their own extravagant

---

[82] E.g., *Poen* 313, 325, 367; *Am* 664–67, 254 (the latter distinguishes between the slave's cowardice and the master's bravery). Cf. also *Two Gentlemen of Verona* II.1 (spoken by Speed): "Though the chameleon Love can feed on the air, I am one that am nourished by my victuals and would fain have meat."

eating (552, 777–79). This exclusive control over food was foreshadowed in Cleustrata's first lines, which were a command to lock up the storerooms and bring her the key, and is carried to the end of the play where the banquet, which usually takes place on stage to signify the victory of the forces of comedy over the blocking characters, is held out of sight, before the end of the play, and excludes even the one male conspirator (Chalinus). Thus we can say that food here is not only associated with the party of the rebel but specifically with the women who make up this party.

Even more striking, this usual use of food as a marker of slavish trickery is integrated here with the more realistic portrayal of women's control over food, and the surprising excessiveness of the women's eating is compared to the excessiveness of Lysidamus' lust. In the rest of the corpus, only parasites merit the kind of comments aimed at the women's appetites here.[83] Because the role of rebel is given to a wife in this play, and because the theme of female adultery (though for another wife) is prominent, decorum requires Cleustrata to be explicitly distanced from any hint of sexual impropriety. The play accomplishes this by emphasizing her attachment to food even more strongly than is usual for a trickster. Since the complementarity between food and sex is so well established in the tradition, the necessary asexuality of Cleustrata can be established by presenting her as a gourmand.

In fact, the asexuality of all the women in this play is a marked departure from normal comic practice and is particularly meaningful in this context of runaway desires and adultery. In this play, which seems to be positively steeped in sexual tension, none of the women who appear on stage are identified as possible sexual objects, and the one woman who is the sexual object of all the men in the play is kept hidden in the wings. Only the *Captivi* is as scrupulous in avoiding attractive or seductive female characters. Of the three women characters, Cleustrata and Myrrhina are specifically described as deriving their sensual satisfactions from eating, and Pardalisca is shown using even the smallest hint of sexuality between herself and her master to trick him, thus sacrificing sex for a good trick, much as Chalinus defers the hope of freedom for the same end. The three major male characters, on the other hand, play out among themselves all the possible combinations of sexual partnerships.

When we look at the other plays in the corpus, we can see that food is used to define both sides of the comic stereotypes of women, as cynical controllers and as unbridled consumers. Often these two sterotypes are

---

[83] In two of the four plays with *uxores dotatae*, parasites are instrumental in revealing the affair of the husband (*As, Men*), and in one other it is the cook who reveals the husband's secrets (*Mer*). This could be seen as further evidence that the *senex amator*'s runaway sexuality is consistently balanced in the "grammar" of Plautine comedy by women's connection with food.

split between *meretrices* and *matronae*: the former are depicted as schemers able to manipulate others' sensuous desires, while the latter are seen to spend their own and their husbands' money on an unending train of luxury goods and services.[84] In the *Casina*, Cleustrata's trickery and her control over her husband combine these two aspects, yet the focus on her sensuous satisfaction in food as well aligns her more closely with the nonteleological aesthetic of clever slaves. Integral to Cleustrata's ability to exploit the more sympathetic side of her role as dowered wife is her transformation of this connection with food from a symbol of greed into one of rebellion. Perhaps her closest counterpart in the corpus is the *meretrix/matrona* of the *Truculentus*.[85] Like Cleustrata, Phronesium plays her trick by exploiting the most positive aspects of feminine stereotypes, in this case a mother's concern for her child's well-being. The emphasis in the *Truculentus* on food as a marker of control is even more pronounced. Phronesium's hold on all of her lovers is expressed through her extortion of food from them. Her dismissal of the soldier is justified by his bringing her useless things like gold and slaves instead of food (II.6), and her acceptance of Diniarchus is predicated on his slave delivering to her a basket of delicacies (II.7). Finally, the *Truculentus* provides us with an explicit comparison between male and female sexual objects, a comparison that emphasizes the bodily hungers of women:

> procaciores esti' vos, sed illi peiiuriosi;
> illis perit quidquid datur neque ipsis apparet quicquam:
> vos saltem si quid quaeritis, exbibitis et comestis.

> (154–56)

You women are pushier, but boys are faithless; whatever one gives to them disappears, and they have nothing to show for it: you, at least, if you get your hands on anything, you drink it down and eat it up.[86]

This description reinforces the image of women as unbridled but also unsubtle, an image that should be shattered by the elegant stagecraft of Cleustrata and Phronesium. But even these women remain obsessed with food, which testifies both to women's control of food in real life as a marker of their domestic authority and to comedy's structural imperative to diminish the social impact of their successful trickery, just as clever slaves' imaginative talent at playacting reduces their rebellion to child's play.

---

[84] See the remarks on Erotium in the previous chapter and the canonical complaints about women as consumers at *Aul* 167–69, scene III.5; *Mil* 685–700.

[85] Although the evidence is less clear for the *Truculentus*, it seems that it too could be a farcical treatment of a romantic story; cf. the *Epitrepontes* of Menander, which, if twisted to emphasize the role of the *meretrix* rather than the plight of the wife, would look a lot like the *Truculentus*.

[86] My translation of the last part of this quotation owes a debt to Nixon (1934).

The *Menaechmi* and the *Casina* each depict a *paterfamilias* whose authority is under attack by the other members of his household. Neither play allows the romantic plot line of a son's search for love (and money) explicit expression, though each play has a reflex of this traditional paradigm. Although they seem superficially very different, they represent the same essential event: the attempt to reconcile the naturalistic authority of the *paterfamilias* with the farcical authority of the slave and the romantic authority of the lover. In the beginning of each play we are shown a husband rebelling against a dowered wife. This rebellion sets up the initial expectation that he will be the comic hero and she the blocking character. Each husband's authority, however, is soon shown to be beleaguered by threats of disobedience from his dependents. In the *Menaechmi*, this threat is countered by the creation of a super hero, Syracusan Menaechmus, who is both a trickster and an authoritative master. His status as a double, an alter ego, of the beleaguered master allows his personal strength to compensate for his brother's weakness. In the *Casina*, on the other hand, since farce privileges discord over harmony, the *senex*'s failed rebellion can only be supplanted by the *uxor*'s attempt at rebellion. In the *Menaechmi* we are uncertain at times with which brother to sympathize; the *Casina* strains our sympathetic response much further by making the heroism shift between what seem to be the schemer and the blocking character.

Although separated by these different strategies of portraying the threat to the authority of the *paterfamilias*, the *Menaechmi* and the *Casina* are united in their resolutions: to fabricate a character who contains the opposing authorities of master and slave. Again, this solution is less fully worked out in the *Casina* because the threats have been greater and have been situated in a character who is opposed to the *paterfamilias*. In the *Menaechmi* the two brothers' union at the end shows how the farcical and naturalistic authorities might be joined into one. But the *Casina*'s resolution, while granting farcical authority to Lysidamus by portraying him as a slave, undermines his naturalistic authority by emphasizing his groveling. Cleustrata, likewise, has been robbed of the farcical authority she wielded throughout the play, but her naturalistic authority is limited by her assumption of the role of a submissive wife, as Myrrhina advised at the beginning of the play. Thus, just as the *Menaechmi*'s ending shows a great revelation and resolution while the *Casina*'s only emphasizes the lack of progress, the construction of an authoritative figure at the end of the *Menaechmi* corresponds to the destruction or undermining of authority in the *Casina*.

A further difference between the two plays can be traced in the system by which each determines value. The *Menaechmi* is overwhelmingly a play about wealth and money and defines identities and relations economically. Money is strangely absent from the *Casina*, which is ruled instead by a single-minded focus on sexuality.[87] This basic distinction can account for several of the differences between the plays. First, in the *Menaechmi* the Matrona is grouped together with Epidamnian Menaechmus' other dependents by virtue of her economic relation to her husband. This play flattens the distinctions between *matrona* and *meretrix*, between slave and parasite, because its primary focus is the relation of economic dependency. In the *Casina* the transformation of the wife into a clever slave highlights the similarity between these two states not on an economic basis but because of their role in the personal and sexual aspects of Lysidamus' authority. Where the *Menaechmi* shows marriage to be a relation of economic dependency like slavery, the *Casina* shows slavery to be a relation of interpersonal power like marriage. Note that both plays end with the rejection of marriage (the marker of resolution in the romantic paradigm). In the *Menaechmi* this rejection is stated economically by envisioning the sale of the Matrona along with Epidamnian Menaechmus' property; in the *Casina* it is stated erotically when Chalinus complains that neither of his "husbands" fulfilled his duty.

These endings contrast in yet another way. When the *Menaechmi*'s conclusion casts off the particular restrictive marriage we have been shown, it is with the idea of great things to follow. When Chalinus makes his complaint, it merely serves to underline that nothing has happened in this play: there has been no change and will be none in the future. Thus, even though in terms of its story the *Casina* seems to be closer to the romantic paradigm, it is the *Menaechmi* that ends with hopes of rebirth, looking out at rosy vistas, while the *Casina*'s farcical orientation brings only an unending parade of tricks and jokes and song.

---

[87] The only place where money is introduced is in scene II.2, precisely because at that point it is necessary to limit Cleustrata's characterization to that of the typical *uxor dotata*.

Chapter IV

A KIND OF WILD JUSTICE: *PERSA*

> Revenge is a kind of wild justice which the more Man's
> nature runs to, the more ought the law to weed it out.
> —F. Bacon, "Of Revenge"

THE *PERSA* ("*The Persian*") departs in important respects from the patterns observed so far in the *Menaechmi* and *Casina*. In each of the two plays considered in previous chapters, the characters waged a tug-of-war over roles and hierarchies within the household. On the other hand, the plays examined in this chapter and in the next, the *Persa* and *Captivi*, illuminate the tensions of public life and thus will turn my investigation of slavery in Plautus in a new direction. These public tensions center on the nexus of two related oppositions: that between citizen and slave and that between master and slave. The *Persa* and *Captivi* show that these two oppositions neither completely coincide (since sometimes these plays separate the domestic power of the master from the civic power of the citizen) nor are they completely distinct. In parallel, the slave sometimes has the status of an insider to the community, because of his alliance with the young master, and sometimes of an outsider, because of the many ways he differs from freeborn citizens. These two plays, which seem so different in tone and moral outlook, are fundamentally related in their content, which seeks to define the citizen community in a way that reinforces the authority of individual masters and yet maintains citizenship as an independent category.

In another way as well, the *Persa* marks a departure from the two previous plays. In my discussion of the *Menaechmi* and *Casina*, I called attention to the ways that the hero, who performs the functions that comic convention associates with slaves while retaining his character type of master, provides a kind of lens that focuses the plays' dramatic energies and social tensions. This ambiguous hero does not actually resolve either the dramatic or the social conflicts implicit in Plautus' incongruous confections, but he contains within himself enough disparate elements to allow the play to run its course. The *Persa*'s hero, the slave Toxilus, is obviously just this kind of mixed character. One of the most remarked-upon features of this play is its innovation in combining the types of young lover and clever slave into a single character. Unlike the heroes of the *Menaechmi* and *Casina*, however, Toxilus' servile persona is grounded in the representational level of the play, and it is only at the metatheatrical level, because we know the speech and mannerisms of young lovers from other plays, that he looks like a freeborn *adulescens*. This inversion has a fundamental effect on the *Persa*, since Toxilus' identity as slave limits his portrayal of the lover in important ways. Like the cropping out of the romantic elements in the *Casina*, Toxilus' fusion of types can help us to pinpoint the social meanings of both modes of comedy, even if the original impulse has nothing to do with social commentary.[1]

Romantic comedies are based on two fundamental themes: the "oedipal" theme of achieving maturity through shaking off the father's authority and the theme of the apparent contradiction between the erotic desires of youth and the social requirements of the community. Both of these themes, however, rely on the social status of a freeborn young man and do not apply to a slave. In place of a genetic relationship to a father, one that the son will eventually outgrow, the slave's relationship to authority is juridically defined and has no natural trajectory through youth and maturation. The standards of the community that seek to restrict the freeborn lover's choices embody the perceived need to protect the integrity of the citizen group. Far from trying to restrict the slave's choice of love object, such standards operate to exclude the slave from the citizen community altogether. The need to reconcile these two defining aspects of romantic comedy with the features of a slave-lover produces some of the peculiar aspects of the *Persa*.

The first of these necessary adjustments is in the choice of blocking character. The person targeted for trickery by the comic alliance usually is the head of the household, who is both father and master. Neither father nor master can be the object of Toxilus' scheme. Because Toxilus is a slave rather than a freeborn lover, he cannot enact the full meaning of filial rebellion: the crisis of maturation by which the son opposes and eventually transcends his father's authority. Making Toxilus' master the blocking character, on the other hand, would violate the principle of comedy that limits the subversive meaning of slave trickery, by ensuring that such slaves never

---

[1] This fusion clearly blends elements of two different types of comedy. Because of Wilamowitz's (1894) speculation that the original was of pre-Menandrian date (relying on perceived similarities to Aristophanic theater), the debate for the *Persa* has centered on early versus late rather than Greek versus Roman. Webster (1953: 78–82) assumes without argument that the *Persa* is pretty much a transcription of a Greek Middle Comedy. For a full summary of the dating question, see Woytek (1982: introduction). Woytek's own observation is that each of the major characters is blended from two stock types. Although this observation accurately describes the inconsistencies of the characters, it does not go very far towards an explanation either of their genesis or of their effect on other aspects of the play.

act in their own interest.[2] If Toxilus is to be a lover acting in his own interest, he must trick someone other than his own master. Nor can the *Persa*,
using the paradigm of the *Miles Gloriosus*, make the tricking of an unworthy
rival the center of the play. No one, not even a bombastic soldier, could be
less appropriate as the romantic hero than a slave. The *Persa*'s choice to
use the *leno* as blocking character avoids the domestic entanglements connected with the father/master figure and distracts the audience from the
tenuousness of Toxilus' claim to romantic heroism.

The choice of blocking character is of fundamental importance in shaping the outlook of the play. When the *paterfamilias* performs this function,
the overturn that takes place during the play is temporary; tomorrow (or
the close of the play) will bring the father/master back to his rightful place.
On the other hand, when a rival or pimp is the object of trickery, the subversion is permanent. No future days will restore to the braggart soldier
Pyrgopolynices the girl he has lost, nor will the pimp Lycus in the *Poenulus*
ever recoup his losses. This is part of a broader pattern: the subversion of
Plautus' plays coexists with a countervailing conservative impulse, which
knits back together the familial and civic bonds that have been strained in
the course of the play. These comedies create the sense of "all's well that
ends well" either positively, by referring to the imminent reestablishment
of the father's power or the reunion of a family through recognition of
citizen identity, or negatively, by emphasizing the removal of a threat to
the community.[3] Because this play lacks a citizen family to be reunited,
neither of the positive endings will be possible; instead, the *Persa* ends by
punishing a man who tried to sell a female citizen.

The defense of the community that is implicit in such an ending gener-
ates a compensatory emphasis on civic values within the deception itself.
The *Persa*'s deception scheme makes use of the mechanism through which
romantic comedies often resolve the apparent contradiction between the
erotic desires of youth and the social requirements of the community: recognition (*anagnorisis*). This plot mechanism implicitly emphasizes the integrity of the citizen group by sidestepping the threat of Eros to override

---

[2] Bettini (1982: 51–52) sees the slave's conventional lack of self-interest as a reflection of
his social status as "subalterno," and that the compensation for this lack is the slave's primacy
on the metatheatrical level. I would only add that, since theater not only reflects an external
reality but also offers its own vision, depriving the slave of self-interest also keeps the fantasy of that vision within acceptable bounds by refusing the slave's trickery any meaningful
outcome.

[3] Bettini (1982: 60, 80, *passim*) on recognition as a "compensation" for the father's being
tricked; Konstan (1983: 30–31) on the punishment of outsiders establishing a countervailing
force to the theme of subversion. The *Persa* and the *Miles Gloriosus*, the harshest examples of
tricking outsiders, are the only plays in the surviving corpus in which there is neither a father
figure nor a *pseudo-meretrix* recognized as a citizen daughter.

the social and civic boundaries of the community and even more strongly
by showing that this threat was illusory, since the boy was attracted to the
"right" girl all along.[4] Thus the passions of young romance are employed to
reinforce the inherent belongingness of the members of the citizen group.
Obviously, this paradigm can have no place in a play where both lovers are
slaves. Yet the plot device of *anagnorisis* is so important for reinforcing
citizen identity that it produces a displaced version within the deception
trick. Toxilus' lover Lemniselenis herself remains a slave and is not recognized as freeborn, but the trick to extort money out of the pimp and to
punish him takes the form of a trumped-up recognition of a parasite's
daughter.

The accommodations made necessary by Toxilus' status as a slave—the
leno as sole blocking character and the displacement of the recognition
from the representational level (Lemniselenis) to the metatheatrical level
(the parasite's daughter)—produce the peculiar characterization of Toxilus
as defender of morality and explain the curious prominence of ethical values in this farcical play. These accommodations have a stylistic effect as
well, translating motifs usually depicted on the representational level to
the metatheatrical level. In fact, only through the separation of "real" and
"unreal" by means of metatheater can Toxilus be both a subversive slave
and a defender of civic values. The punishment of the pimp Dordalus becomes the basis for a theatrical trick, one that represents a defense of community values. The metatheatrical use of the recognition plot is even more
extreme. In Menandrian comedy, the power of Tyche in the human world
is one of the important philosophical themes.[5] *Anagnorisis* in those plays
expresses the righting of a world gone wrong, the correction of human
ignorance. Here in the *Persa*, this very element is usurped and shown to be
manipulable into a typical slavish trick, a trick that creates misunderstanding rather than dispels it. Thus the unresolved contradiction between
Toxilus' roles as subverter and defender parallels the unresolved contradiction between the subversive connotations of metatheater and the serious
moral content of the "script" Toxilus produces.

That these changes grow out of the contradictions between Toxilus' dramatic function as lover and his persona as slave becomes clearer when we
examine an element of the romantic paradigm that has been maintained.
Unlike the complications caused by his slave status in the themes of maturation and the defense of citizen identity, there is no barrier to Toxilus
enacting one of the other common themes of these romantic plays, the

---

[4] Konstan (1983: 24–25, 110).

[5] The most prominent example is the prologue of the *Aspis*. On the role of Tyche in Menander, see Webster (1974: 21 and 1960: 199). See also Lefèvre (1979) on *Cas*; he suggests
that Plautus translated the effect of Tyche in the original to a metatheatrical trick.

noble bonds of friendship between young men.[6] In the *Persa*, this theme contrasts the true friendship that binds Toxilus and his slave ally Sagaristio with the cynical expressions of affection, gratitude, and faithfulness with which the comic tricksters dupe the pimp. The appearance of this theme within the representational plane, not at a metatheatrical level, adds yet another unexpected juxtaposition of form and content. In this play the slavish trope of metatheater contains serious moral content, while the "honor among thieves" that binds the rebel and his allies appears with all the dignity of *philia*.[7]

We would expect the clever slave as lover to be an unequivocal hero, since lovers and slaves are both usually heroic in comedy. But, because of the implicit social assumptions governing the attributes of each of these characters, this play reveals the irreconcilable differences between the free-born young man as a hero of comedy and a slave in that role. When the *adulescens* is the hero, the comedy focuses on "paradigmatic freedom,"[8] the triumph of such virtues as flexibility and open-mindedness, and an ending that embodies reconciliation. When the slave is the hero, the comedy aims not at presenting a new, more humane vision but at savaging the self-importance implicit in such moral pronouncements and the naturalistic style in which they are presented. The plays that have a slave as hero end with the humiliation of the master, as he is coerced into promising not to punish the slave.[9] These two character types, the lover and the clever slave, are as contradictory and produce as contradictory dramatic situations as do the *paterfamilias* and slave.

In the *Persa*, the presence of competing literary and ethical structures undermines even the conventional associations of style with moral orientation. Because of the need to represent civic values (imposed by having a romantic plot with no family structure to be reconciled), even the metatheatrical trick in this play takes on a moralizing cast. Yet, the heroes are also bolstered by the serious idealizing representation of the friendship between Toxilus and Sagaristio. The character types' personalities are wrenched out of their usual places, and so too are their orientations toward the moral structures of honesty and justice and toward the theatrical structures of naturalism and metatheater. This extreme manipulation of comic conventions accounts for the strange quality of the *Persa*, especially of its

---

[6] This theme is foregrounded in the *Bacchides* and *Mercator*, but it also holds some prominence in the *Epidicus*, *Pseudolus*, and *Trinummus*. For the possibility that the Greek author Philemon might have been particularly attracted to this theme of "the helpful friend," see Anderson (1993: 34–46).

[7] Woytek (1982: introduction, 45–46) notes the translation of the motif of friendship from freeborn citizens to slaves.

[8] Frye (1957: 169).

[9] Consider, e.g., the endings of *Bacchides*, *Mostellaria*, *Pseudolus*.

main character. As a subverter of civic values, Toxilus relies to an unsettling degree on those very values in order to catch his prey; his trick punishes the blocking character not for being narrow-minded and pompous but for being trusting. Nor can he be taken seriously as a defender of civic values, in large part because he is a slave whose very identity is defined by his exclusion from the community of citizens and also because the manner in which he punishes the pimp is so aggressive, cynical, and opposed to reconciliation.[10] That a play riven by such internal contradictions in theme, tone, and moral outlook could be successful with Plautus' audience supports my overall contention that the kind of dramatic consistency we are accustomed to was unimportant for those viewers. Further, the *Persa*'s inconsistencies can help us to refine our understanding of the social forces that drive these comic forms.

THE THREE FACES OF TOXILUS

Although the surprising combination of slave and lover is advertised so prominently in the beginning, it is in fact only the first of three aspects of Toxilus' character. Each of these aspects defines him in opposition to the slave we expect him to be. These oppositions all function on the literary level of comic conventions and on the level of social status. However, these three aspects are merely juxtaposed: they neither develop from one to the next nor do they reverse each other. As I argued for the *Casina*, we should see this play as a series of skits rather than as a teleological development of a single situation from problem to resolution. In fact, the *Persa* privileges the nonteleological aesthetic of farce to such an extent that we will miss much of what happens if we rely on an analysis that integrates meaning over the course of the whole play and subordinates the stylized language to some larger thematic statement. On the level of plot, the *Persa* resists this kind of integrated reading (because the romantic goal of freeing Lemniselenis recedes so abruptly in relation to the revenge plot against Dordalus); in addition, however, the language of this play must be studied carefully at every point in its relation to comic conventions in order to understand the ways that the unusual permutation of the clever slave, which this play makes its focus, is grounded in the same theatrical and social structures as the more familiar slave tricksters. As the following overview of "the three faces of Toxilus" will describe, each of these three movements of the *Persa* makes sense only by setting Toxilus' unusual characterization in the context of familiar comic patterns.

[10] Cf., for example, the father in the *Rudens*, who is introduced as a man who has lost his property by helping others (35–38) and who ends by inviting to dinner even the pimp who owned his daughter.

In the first movement of the play (Acts I and II) Toxilus is the lover, as is established by his prominent use of the language, attitudes and themes consistently associated with young lovers in New Comedy.[11] He opens the play by bewailing the fact that the pimp Dordalus has decreed that Toxilus must find the money to buy his girlfriend, Lemniselenis, today or lose her forever. Furthermore, Toxilus seems more like an *adulescens* because his helpers, Sagaristio and Saturio, are depicted as a clever slave and a parasite, thereby maintaining the expected comic structures around the unexpected portrayal of the slave as lover. From the very first words of the *Persa*, the audience is confronted with an explicit distortion of the canons of comedy. When Toxilus announces,

> qui amans egens ingressus est princeps in Amoris vias
> superavit aerumnis suis aerumnas Hercul<e>i.

(1–2)

The man who, being in love and out of money, first began the journey of Love outdid with his own tribulations the tribulations of Hercules.

we immediately recognize the contradiction between his appearance, marked as that of a slave, and his words, marked as those of a young, free-born lover.[12] There are specific dramatic requirements for negotiating this strange conflation. Although romantic comedy has a clearer goal than do the plays of pure deception, the lover himself is incapable of coming up with the schemes necessary to move the plot forward. Acts I and II will show that this difficulty can be solved only by alternating between the characterizations of helpless lover and clever slave, not by fusing them in any way.[13] This phase ends with his receiving the money to free his beloved, exactly the action that usually brings romantic plots to resolution. However, because the need to move the plot forward has sacrificed Toxilus' qualities as lover to such a great extent, this resolution almost disappears: instead the play swerves towards a plot of trickery and revenge.

In the play's second movement (Acts III and IV) Toxilus and his allies turn their energies toward luring Dordalus into a trap and thus forcing him to pay back money he has just received for Lemniselenis. The trap they set involves convincing Dordalus to buy what seems like an exotic Arabian captive but is really the freeborn daughter (designated in the play only as "the Virgo") of the parasite Saturio, with the slave Sagaristio playing the part of the Persian slave-merchant selling the girl. Since it is a crime to buy freeborn women, the revenge can be achieved by exposing this sale

---

[11] Flury (1968: 93–94).

[12] Slater (1985: 37).

[13] Woytek (1982: introduction, 44) notes that the focus on the clever slave aspect of Toxilus' character eclipses the development of either himself or Lemniselenis as love interests.

to the praetor. In this part of the play, Toxilus takes on the role of a defender of citizen integrity, squaring off against the pimp Dordalus: he defends the civic virtues of *fides* and *amicitia*, and Dordalus' punishment is justified by his crime of trading in freeborn citizen women (749, 845). This role is better integrated with that of the clever slave than was the role of the lover, by making use of the split between the representational and metatheatrical levels of the play. Toxilus defends the principles of faith, trust, and gratitude through a theatrical trick that exploits the appearances of these same civic values. This constitutes a double-switch concerning the normal comic paradigm. The clever slave usually appropriates moral language and ideas as part of his stagecraft aimed at an immoral trick;[14] here, this kind of trick has itself been appropriated as a means of defending citizen values. This conflation of morality and its opposite is complicated by the fact that Toxilus' expression of civic values goes well beyond his parody of them in his trick. His friendship with Sagaristio also forcefully represents the ideals of loyalty, gratitude, and trust in the representational level of the play. This noble friendship is a positive example of the values he is defending but also, like the ideal of *fides*, becomes a weapon in the fight against Dordalus.

The opposition between the role of civic avenger and that of the slave is obvious on the social plane, but it is not so well developed in the literary traditions of comedy. However, an ideal of civic solidarity is implicit in the recognition plots that are so familiar in Plautus. Thus, this movement is also concluded by its proper paradigmatic comic resolution, the Virgo's "recognition" by her father, which simultaneously punishes the pimp and reinforces the differences between the insiders and the outsiders of the community.

The final movement (Act V) presents a version of the usual comic banquet but twisted to emphasize hostility rather than reconciliation. Toxilus appears here as master, a role so clearly opposed to slave on both the literary and social levels as to require no further elucidation. Toxilus uses his own slave Paegnium as an instrument to mock Dordalus, appropriates Lemniselenis as his own freedwoman (and lectures on her duties as such), and declares that it is his birthday they are celebrating[15]—all these actions

---

[14] E.g., Chrysalus' story of bravery in defending his master's money against pirates (*Bac* II.3), Tranio's impersonation of the pious slave in defending his master's family from ghosts (*Mos* II.2); cf. Phronesium's complaint of the emotional difficulty of motherhood (*Truc* II.5).

[15] Cf. Ballio in the *Pseudolus*, esp. 775–78. Dumézil (1977: 124–25) calls attention to this paradox: "C'est certainement pour tirer le plus d'effet possible de cette parodie du droit des maîtres que l'action de la pièce est située le jour où tout maître fête son propre Genius et le fait révérer par ses esclaves: son *dies natalis*. . . . L'esclave illustre sa prétention, son simulacre de liberté en célébrant son jour de naissance dans les formes prescrites aux hommes libres." Note that, unlike Ballio's, Toxilus' announcement of his birthday comes only in the final act, thus coinciding with what has been defined here as his phase of mastery.

establish Toxilus' authority as master at the domestic level in the same way
that his manipulation of the ethical concepts of friendship and faithfulness
established his authority at the civic level. The positioning of this role at
the end of Toxilus' protean performance corresponds to the final scenes of
the *Casina* in which a master appropriated the comic immunity of the slave
to gain for himself the double authority of comedy and real life. Here, a
slave ends the play with a surprising show of mastery in which he celebrates
both his own domestic power and his punishment of the peregrine pimp.

These three aspects of Toxilus' character—lover, civic defender, and
master—and the constantly shifting formal and moral background against
which they take place, will appear most clearly in a linear analysis of the
play. Although this play does not exhibit a constant unidirectional dramatic
structure, the varied literary and social elements in tension at each point
will expose the principles governing this unusual instantiation of the clever
slave. It is the tension of these elements that gives the *Persa* its strange
ambivalence: not completely subversive but far from ethical.

Toxilus as Lover

The play opens with a scene that immediately confronts the audience with
a disorienting blow to comic expectations. Toxilus enters and delivers a
speech on the trials of love; his friend Sagaristio echoes, expounding on
the trials of slavery. The structure of the scene itself activates our expectations of two different opening scene types, that of the argument between
two slaves (as in *Mostellaria, Casina, Amphitruo, Epidicus*) and that of the
young lover asking his slave for help (as in *Curculio, Poenulus, Pseudolus*).
Visually, this opening sets up the expectation of the first type of scene, but
the content turns out to be the latter. The tension between these two types
of scenes integrally relates to the tension produced by the contradictory
characters joined in Toxilus. It is significant that the shock of the lover-
slave continues after the initial identification. Toxilus' speech does not de-
volve into parody, as Sagaristio's will. He maintains the style and tone of
the comic lover, allowing the parodic element to be expressed at the visual
level by the contrast between his words on the one hand and his mask and
costume on the other.[16]

These two opening speeches are metrically and syntactically parallel.[17]
This formal echoing provides a link between speeches that are parallel in
meaning, although they issue from two different comic registers, that of
the lover and that of the clever slave. Both speeches make great use of
the hallmarks of Plautine style, such as alliteration, repetition, and *figurae*

---

[16] Slater (1985: 37).
[17] Woytek (1982: ad loc.), Leo (1913: 123, note 1), Fraenkel (1922: 228 = 1960: 218–19).

etymologicae.[18] But where Toxilus' opening lines have an elevated tone, Sagaristio's speech has the effect of the playful language of comic slaves rather than the melodramatic language of comic lovers. For example, in place of Toxilus' mythological reference to the labors of Hercules, we get from Sagaristio the distinctively slavish trope of the "identification conundrum" at lines 11–12.[19] In content these two speeches invert each other. Toxilus' speech uses the imagery of mythological heroism to express the powerlessness of the impecunious lover, while Sagaristio's uses the exaggerated humility and rectitude associated with good, obedient slaves to exult in his power over his master.[20] Thus, these opening speeches offer a microcosm of the structure of the play as a whole, as they break the rules of comic conventions (when Toxilus voices the lines of a lover without irony), while at the same time forcefully reasserting those same rules (when Sagaristio perfectly instantiates the parodic skill of the clever slave). Furthermore, the inversion between these two speeches introduces some of the key themes of this play, in particular the unexpected alignments between status and power, between *malitia* and *amicitia*, and between style and content.[21]

A further way in which Sagaristio's speech engages the comic tradition is to invoke the paradigm of the master's absence. One of the fundamental premises of comedy is that the master's or father's absence engenders the freedom of slaves and sons to indulge themselves. Thus the specific statement at line 29a that Toxilus' master is out of town sets a trap that is never sprung in this play.[22] This foregrounding of the master's absence gives a

[18] Examples from Toxilus' speech: alliteration (*amans egens ingressus*), repetition (*aerumnis . . . aerumnas*), metaphor (*in Amoris vias*); from Sagaristio's: strong alliteration of *s* throughout the speech, repetition (here in the form of *figurae etymologicae* on *serv*-compounds in 7 and *praesenti/apsenti* in 9).

[19] Of the examples Fraenkel (1922: 23–58 = 1960: 21–54) gives of the identification and transformation conundra, at least three-quarters are spoken by slaves. The *lippus oculus* conundrum is used also at *Bac* 913–15, there spoken by a master in soliloquy after he has just been convinced by his slave how necessary the slave's machinations are. Bettini (1991: ad loc.) notes that *oculus* in comedy is usually a term of endearment, thus adding another source of tension to this strange locution.

[20] For the language of good slaves, cf. *Men* 966–85, *Ps* 1103–13, *Mos* 858–84, *Aul* 587–91. See Fraenkel (1922: 243–45 = 1960: 234–35) on the "catechism of the good slave."

[21] Woytek (1982: on 12) sees the contrast between the two speeches as casting a light of cynicism over the extravagance of Toxilus' love affair by having Sagaristio expound on the problems of "the little man." This is true in some sense, but it does not take into account the richness of the comic tradition in representing the types of lover and slave and their opposing interests.

[22] Woytek (1982: introduction, 19) believes that the emphasis here on Sagaristio's master rather than Toxilus' excites the expectation that Sagaristio will carry out the deception. To put this observation in terms of the analysis developed here: the romantic paradigm at the beginning leads us to believe that Toxilus will be helpless and that Sagaristio will be his clever helper.

sense of crisis and danger, which is necessary for the comic rebellion, but in the end this threat is meaningless. Toxilus' master never returns, and his absence is used to advantage in the deception scheme by cooking up a fake letter from him. In the earliest part of the play, the romantic paradigm is still in force, requiring a fatherlike figure as blocking character. Because of the clash of this figure with Toxilus' status as slave, the only way for this authority figure to align himself with those of other romantic plays is by emphasizing his absence. When the time comes for the father's return, the normal catalyst for confrontation in the "oedipal" plot type of romantic comedy, the play has turned to a different plot line. It then abandons the romantic importance of rebellion against the father for the civic importance of the punishment of the outsider.

After the parallel speeches of lines 1–12, this first scene divides into three parts, each of which emphasizes in a different way this play's contradictory relations to comic conventions: first, a silly, stylized bit of slave fooling; then, the introduction of the twin improbabilities of Toxilus' love affair and his *de facto* freedom; and, finally, a closing part in which Sagaristio declares his friendship for Toxilus and his willingness to help in the hopeless search for money with which to pay for Lemniselenis' freedom. The first of these parts introduces the serious theme of the duties of friendship at line 19,[23] but the two slaves' use of the language of civil and military business to describe Sagaristio's sojourn in the mills is more reminiscent of clever slaves' ironic way of speaking:

> SAG: negotium edepol— TOX: ferreum fortasse?
> SAG: plusculum annum
> fui praeferratus apud molas tribunus vapularis.
> TOX: vetu' iam istaec militiast tua. . . .

(21–23)

SAG: Well, really, business obligations— TOX: Kept you tied up perhaps? SAG: For a little more than a year I was put in chains. . . . I mean, in charge . . . at the mill, as chief of flogging. TOX: Yes, I know you've long distinguished yourself in that department.[24]

The second section focuses on Toxilus' appropriation of the persona of the young lover, in his woes of love and in his invitation for an extravagant

---

[23] Cf. the offers of help to friends spoken by freeborn people at *Aul* 193 and *Ps* 713, both of which use the verb *impero*.

[24] My translation of these lines is looser than usual, since I have tried to offer English puns that echo the effect, if not the semantic content, of the Latin; e.g., Plautus' economical *praeferratus* (which means "tipped with iron" [i.e., manacled] but also puns on *praefectus*), I have had to render with a slip of the tongue on Sagaristio's part.

feast.[25] The final section comes closest to the conventions of the scenes in which a young lover asks his slave to get money for him to free his girlfriend in its emphasis on Toxilus' despair and Sagaristio's pessimism.[26] In a particularly pointed twist on Toxilus' double identity, the usual romantic goal to free the girl redoubles the irony of the lover being a slave. His desire to free Lemniselenis expresses a compassion for her servitude (as well as his sexual desire for her), yet his own servitude is so light a burden on him that he seems hardly to notice that he is a slave.[27] This irony is augmented by language that associates the devotion of a friend with the obedience of a slave. At line 35, Toxilus declares that Sagaristio would buy himself an eternal friend (repeating *sempiternus* from 34a) by finding this money.[28] Sagaristio tartly responds that he could not get that much money if he sold himself (40–41). Although Sagaristio here continues his habit of demystifying the language that Toxilus borrows from the freeborn to express his love, their parting exchange shows a triumph of the ideal of friendship expressed at the beginning of their conversation (19), and Toxilus offers Sagaristio the pleasure of the feast no matter what the outcome of his search (46). Throughout this first scene the ridiculousness of this slave-as-lover has been pointed up by his companion's puncturing of high-flown language and by his own command of the mannerisms of clever slaves, but, strangely, this opening manages nevertheless to sustain Toxilus' identity as a young lover.

[25] In this context Toxilus uses a word group often associated with uppity slaves: *basilice* (29) and *basilico* (31). Cf. *Rud* 431, *Ps* 458; see Fraenkel (1922: 193–96 = 1960: 183–85). Previous commentators believed that the rhetorical question *iam servi hic amant?* (25) was inserted by Plautus to explain Greek proceedings to a Roman audience. But Woytek (1982: ad loc.) offers two more interesting interpretations, either that Sagaristio is offering a sarcastic parody of masters' limited conception of slaves or that it is a metatheatrical joke in which "here" means not "Athens" but "in comedy" and compares *Amph* 16, 151).

[26] Unlike other comedies of this type, where the threat is the sale of the girl to a rival (usually a rich soldier), the *Persa* never makes explicit why this day brings a crisis as to whether Lemniselenis will be freed or live forever in servitude (34–34a). There is no rival and the only explanation can be an unstated arbitrary threat on the part of Dordalus that he will only sell her today. The difficulty is in finding a rival who would still seem to be an outsider even when compared to a slave.

[27] See esp. 34–34a: *haec dies summa hodie | est, mea amica sitne libera an sempiternam servitutem serviat.* ("Today, this very day, is the turning point, as to whether my girlfriend will be free or live forever as a slave"), where the triple alliteration and *figura etymologica* invests her slavery with emotion and compassion. Dumézil (1977: 124) notes the paradox.

[28] Woytek prints *<facere ami>cum* rather than *emere amicum* found in the Codex Turnebi, arguing that the latter is interpolated from *As* 72, 673 and *Trin* 1056. On the contrary, the context here fits so closely with that of the other three instances as to argue for a conventional phrase whose primacy at any one locus cannot be asserted. In all three, it is a question of people trying to win the good favor of a lover by lending him money. Sagaristio's line at 40–41 is comparable to *Ps* 87, underscoring similarity of this scene to scenes of young lover and slave.

In contrast to the double valence of Toxilus' characterization, our uncertainty as to whether to see him as a young man wounded by love or a clever slave playing at such an affliction, in the next scene Saturio the parasite conforms more closely to the consistent cynicism of comic schemers. His entrance monologue explicitly reasserts conventional comic structures, as he distorts civic virtues and principles to serve the purposes of parasitic greed and appetite.[29] The first section of this monologue (53–61) makes use of the venerable language of ancestry and family tradition to claim a nobility for the parasite's "trade."[30] The rest of the monologue from line 62 to almost the end (74) has puzzled commentators because of the abrupt transition and because of the apparent lack of connection between this criticism of *quadruplatores* and Saturio's current situation.[31] What seems to connect the two is an implicit analogy between the private sphere and the public, an analogy that would equate the flattery and humiliating service by which the parasite feeds himself at his master's table with the public informing by which the *quadruplator* makes his living. Although the two spheres are analogous, Saturio's argument is that the self-interest that is permissible in the private realm is shameful in the public. He defines the good and faithful (*fidelem*, 67) citizen as the one who acts not in his own

---

[29] Note the introduction of a nickname at 60, which seems to be canonical in parasites' entrance monologues. Cf. *Men* 77–78, *Capt* 69–70, *St* 174–77. Slater (1985: 40–41) notes that Saturio's fulfillment of the usual function of parasites is "a reassertion of the comic world the audience knows and expects." He cites in support a 1980 APA paper by J. W. Halporn on the *Captivi*. For more on these conventional speeches, see above in chap. 2, notes 9, 30.

[30] The language is formal and dignified with its repetition (*maiorum meum* in 53, *meorum maiorum* in 55; the *avos* compounds in 57), alliteration, and pleonasm (e.g., *veterem atque antiquom* [53]). Woytek (1982: on 53) notes that the four spondaic feet and the ring composition of this section (with the words *quaestum* and *maiorum* returning in 61) contribute to a solemnity of style. But the solemnity of tone is disrupted by the vulgarity of content at line 56, with the neological verb *parasitor* (only here and at *St* 637; the compound form *subparasitor* appears at *Am* 515, 993 and *Mil* 348 and is used for people who are not parasites but are acting like parasites) and with *venter*, the key word for the comic parasite. The progression from ritualistic to parasitic occurs again in lines 57–60. The long list of male ancestors, linked by the repetition of *-avos*, devolves into an analogy of this family to mice, because they live off the stores of others. (This exact line also appears at *Capt* 77, spoken by the parasite Ergasilus. Cf. also *Cur* 587, where the parasite is compared to a weevil in the grain store.)

[31] Woytek (1982: on 62) agrees with Leo (1912: 123–124) in seeing the strangeness of this passage arising from the inexact correspondence between the Greek word *sycophantēs* and the Latin word *parasitus*, the former having been used originally for forensic informers, and only later applied to all kinds of ingratiating behavior intended for self-serving purposes. This explains the origin of this seemingly nonsensical transition, but still we need to explain its effect as it stands in this play. Bettini (1977) is sensitive to the moral irony of the passage (esp. 86) and makes several interesting observations about this and other legislative proposals in the corpus (cf. *Aul* 478–95, *Mer* 823–29, 1015–24, *Trin* 217–21, etc.). In contrast to my perspective, however, he hears the individual voice of Plautus making a serious social comment rather than the voice of the farcical mode making use of moralizing language to differentiate itself from morality.

interest but in the interest of the polity (65–67). The two obvious ironies here reinforce each other: that a parasite would set himself up as an arbiter of good citizenship and that he, the ultimate embodiment of self-interest in comedy, would base his judgments of public morality on selflessness.[32]

Saturio soon admits, however, that, like other parasites, he adheres to any ethical point of view only as a ruse to ensure the satisfaction of his appetites (see 132). In reorienting himself towards his proper sphere of concern, yesterday's leftovers, he uses imagery that both recalls the public/private distinctions above and shows that he has no intention of maintaining them. He inquires into the well-being of the leftovers using the language and imagery of the *salutatio* ritual, in which a client pays homage to his patron (77–79).[33] This relationship is probably the best example of the crossing of public and private realms in Roman culture. Its introduction here further undermines any preliminary confidence we might have had in Saturio's ethical system, by which he proposed to make his own conduct exemplify citizen values. Rather, we see that his rhetorical distinction between public and private was a way of using ethical concepts to the advantage of an unethical emphasis on his own stomach. As I will argue more fully for the *Captivi*'s parasite in the next chapter, Saturio represents a stable baseline of farce amid the flux of ethical and stylistic allegiances of this play.

Toxilus enters from his house and informs the audience that he has come up with a scheme to make the *leno* himself bear the cost of freeing Lemniselenis (81–82). Saturio will be useful to him in this plan, but rather than gaining his alliance by a straightforward invitation to join the fun of rebellion, Toxilus tricks him into joining the comic alliance.[34] His aside to the audience (83–84) establishes a link of sympathy that implicitly places Saturio in the position of a blocking character to be deceived.[35] Toxilus presents himself to Saturio as a typical gullible patron who will be sweet-talked into

[32] Cf. Peniculus' speech on the *comitia* (*Men* 446–59), discussed above in chap. 2.

[33] Cf. *Mil* 709; Fraenkel (1922: 105–6 = 1960: 99), Woytek (1982: on 78). For personification of leftovers, cf. *Cur* 322; for use of the language of *clientela* to express excessive humility, cf. *Cur* 16, where such language is addressed to a door in a *paraclausithuron*.

[34] This strong-armed approach will be used later by Saturio against his daughter in a parallel scene. The underlying pattern of this scene is similar to that at *Cur* 317–25, 366–70, where a parasite is forced to give his news by the simultaneous allurement of food and the threat of withholding it; however, the threat and the requested form of cooperation are both less extreme than in the *Persa*. Both these scenes invert the power relationships shown in *Men* I.1 and *Capt* 129–91, where the parasite is in control and makes use of his own knowledge or ability to flatter to weasel a dinner out of his patron. The *senex* in *Captivi*, however, is not taken in.

[35] Slater (1985: 41) points out that Toxilus' ruse of luring Saturio into his power by pretending to prepare for a lavish feast reverses the usual positions of power in eavesdropping; see also (1985: 48, note 11), where he notes that Dordalus performs a similar "eavesdropping" at lines 549–75 but does not explicitly connect the two scenes.

inviting the parasite. In truth, this meal is nothing other than bait for a trap. Saturio's response to this overheard menu (93–98) continues the themes begun in his monologue. In pronouncing an opinionated judgment on the importance of cooking the pasta *al dente*, he gives this opinion in language loaded with legal and moral connotations.[36] Toxilus at first (99–107) continues to play the patron (cf. 101 to *Men* 137, 139), emphasizing the luxury and correctness of the spread. But from line 108 on, he makes an attempt to steer Saturio's mind away from food and towards the scheme of trickery, though as we will soon see, the feast and Saturio's compliance in the scheme are causally related (139–44). Saturio's best defense against the claims of his patron is an impressive philosophical argument that the very identity of a parasite depends on his inability to get money for himself (120–26).[37]

At line 127 we finally begin to learn about Toxilus' plot. He proposes to sell Saturio's daughter to the pimp Dordalus, who will then be charged with commerce in freeborn women and forfeit his money. Saturio's reaction to the idea of "lending" his daughter (128) momentarily comes up to our standards for fatherhood, but as soon as he realizes that his dinner is at stake (145–46), agrees to allow his daughter to be sold and even offers himself for sale if only he will be sold with a full stomach.[38] Not until the very end of the scene (162–63), after Saturio has agreed and the plans have been laid, does Toxilus reveal that the sale will be temporary. The parasite's parting line leaves us with the strong impression that the girl's fate is of less consequence to him than his own satiety: "Let him have her for himself if I don't immediately take her away from him" (*sibi habeat, si non extemplo ab eo abduxero*, 164).[39]

In this preview of the deception trick, the ostensibly romantic intent of getting money to free Lemniselenis is eclipsed by the emphasis on punish-

---

[36] See esp. *decet* (97); *ius est* . . . (106); is a pun on the legal/moral meaning of *ius* intended at lines 95 and 97? Cf. Cic. *Ver* 1.121 where it is so used, with a neological adjective as here.

[37] Besides continuing the moral language already so consistently a part of his characterization (*nihili, oportet*; cf. 94, 96), the comparison of parasites to cynics (123) anticipates the comic use of philosophy that will characterize his daughter in her great pronouncements on civic ethics. This argument also is consistent with Saturio's problematic status as family man, which has been introduced in his parodic genealogy and will be repeated at lines 390–92 when he offers a book of jokes as a dowry for his daughter. His familial responsibilities are consistently replaced by his "profession" as jokester and sponge. This philosophical argument can also be seen to have metatheatrical force. The mention of the actor's wardrobe (*soccos, pallium*, 124) may give this argument the meaning, "How can I properly play a parasite on a full stomach?"

[38] Note the commonplace of a parasite preferring material satiety to freedom; see esp. *Men* 97. Woytek (1982: on 147).

[39] The sarcasm of this line works at two levels. First, it depends on the audience's expectations for a father's reaction in a situation like this. He must mean it as an oath, expressing his committment to free her as quickly as possible, but his previous lack of concern for his

ing Dordalus as an outsider and exalting Toxilus as an insider. The emphasis on the *leno*'s status as outsider (*sicut istic leno non sex menses Megaribus/ huc est quom commigravit* "it's not six months since this pimp has moved here from Megara," 137–38) is the first indication of the theme of civic integrity, which will shape the latter part of the play.[40] Both Slater and Chiarini have noted how boldly Toxilus and Saturio call attention to the dramatic illusion in this scene.[41] In light of the revelation that Dordalus is a peregrine, when Toxilus refers to the choragus and aediles as the source of the disguises the tricksters will use in their scheme (159–60), he does more than just rupture the dramatic illusion. He points to these civic officials as allies in the comic assault on Dordalus, an identification that will become more meaningful as the specifically civic nature of Toxilus' campaign is made clear. The power of the civic theme in this trick increases when Toxilus chooses this moment to make clear the legal implications of buying freeborn girls (162–63) and uses the technical term (*manu adserere*) for an action to free an unjustly enslaved citizen. This crucial moment foreshadows the transformation of Toxilus' romantic goal into the goal of civic vengeance, through the manipulation of *anagnorisis*.

The external structure of Act II, the actions and motivations depicted, relate to the progress of the romantic plot line, focusing on the need for money to obtain the object of desire and, to a lesser extent than most, on the emotional distress of the lovers at having their love obstructed. However, this framework is filled out by some of the most purely farcical language and slapstick in this or any other Plautine play. The farcical language and dramatic techniques associated with Sophoclidisca and Paegnium nearly overshadow the romantic plot, when Lemniselenis and Toxilus try to use these slaves to deliver their love messages. The joke of the long scene II.2 (183–250) is that the exchange between the two slaves, repetitive in both style and content, contradicts the stated urgency of their errands[42] and even comes close to derailing the romantic plot. At the representational level of the play, slave fooling threatens to delay the happy union of the lovers while, at the metatheatrical level farce threatens to overtake

---

responsibilities as a father creates an ambiguity. Second, Woytek (1982: ad loc.) points out that this kind of oath is usually phrased with oneself as the thing forfeited (cf. 292, 294).

[40] A lacuna has been proposed between lines 136 and 137 (accepted by Ritschl, Schoell, and others but, in my opinion, correctly rejected by Lindsay, Ernout, and Woytek), evidence of the strained fit between the motivations of the romantic plot line and those of the plot line of civic vengeance.

[41] Slater (1985: 41–42), Chiarini (1979: 44–47). Chiarini, in particular, highlights the heroism in their theatrical exuberance and the reversal of values implied in Saturio's pride that his daughter is three times worse than Toxilus would want her to be (153), i.e., three times more capable of theatrical virtuosity.

[42] Chiarini (1979: 58) gives a metatheatrical interpretation: the actors (Sophoclidisca and Paegnium) reversing the instructions of the director (Toxilus) for speed.

romance. The latter half of the act returns to Toxilus and Sagaristio. Again
we see the distinctive blend of a serious treatment of the theme of friendship coupled with a rebellious emphasis on subversion and trickery. But
this scene differs from I.1 in that it moves away from the romantic model
in which Sagaristio is assimilated to a slave dependent of Toxilus and towards a model focused on the punishment of Dordalus, in which Toxilus
and Sagaristio act as equals and allies.

In scene II.1 and the beginning of II.2 Lemniselenis and Toxilus try
to send love letters to each other through their singularly difficult slaves,
Sophoclidisca and Paegnium.[43] The two lovers earnestly worry over the
course of their affair, in contrast to the usual indifference of slaves to romance. On the other hand, Sophoclidisca and Paegnium shine out with
the careless brilliance that everywhere in the comic corpus is the mark of
the trickster. Chiarini (1979: 51–61) is right to interpret this scene and the
following one as a metatheatrical tour de force in which these unruly slaves
demonstrate their skill in the required elements of comic slavery. Yet even
more striking is that these two characters, whose theatrical brilliance is so
extensive, will take no part in the central deception scheme. These scenes
are nonteleological at the level of plot (their refusal to move the romantic
plot forward) and in relation to the dramatic function of characterization.[44]
Scenes II.1 and II.2 cohere with the tone of the play, in the kaleidoscopic
play of malicious insults in patterned language, but their nonteleological
orientation is at odds with the marshaling of comic heroism towards the
defense of civic virtues.

At the beginning of scene II.2 Toxilus speaks in a language used by every
comic master who has ever had to confront the cheekiness of his slave, and
Paegnium responds with the arrogance common to clever slaves.[45] Paegnium shares two qualities with clever slaves in other plays, confidence in
his own abilities and an infuriating ability to deflate the master's authority

---

[43] Both of these slaves bear significant names. The *soph*- root in Sophoclidisca is an obvious
reference to her skill in banter and in metatheater. For Paegnium, it is not only the semantic
aspect of his name (something like "plaything") that is relevant but also the form. His neuter
name here aligns him with the *meretrices* throughout the corpus.

[44] Fraenkel (1922: 402 = 1960: 381) wryly notes that, although it would not be unreasonable
to expect that such a "Clownsunterhaltung" might do something like establish character notes
or echo the primary themes, our search for such dramatic usefulness would be in vain.

[45] Slater (1985: 43). For *verbereum caput*, cf. *scelerum caput* at *Bac* 829, *Mil* 494, *Ps* 446, etc.;
verberea statua at *Capt* 951, *Ps* 911; one of the most common insults from master to slave is
verbero, usually in the vocative, as at *Am* 565, *As* 416 (where a slave is impersonating the
haughty *atriensis*), *Cap* 551, *Mer* 189, *Ps* 1205, etc. *scelus . . . pueri* seems to be a variant of the
more common *scelus viri* (cf. *Cur* 614, *Mil* 1434, and *Truc* 621), perhaps intended to emphasize
that Paegnium is a *puer delicatus*.

through a literal-minded interpretation of his words.[46] Toxilus' sharp rebuke heightens the ever-present irony of his mastery: "I'll pay you a slave's wages for that" (*ob instanc rem ego aliqui te peculiabo*, 192). Paegnium's response to this threat acknowledges its clear sexual signification,[47] and the metaphoric use of the term for the master's financial largesse towards his slave.

> PA: scio fide hercle erili ut soleat inpudicitia opprobrari
> nec subigi queantur umquam ut pro ea fide habeant iudicem.
>
> (193–94)

> PA: I know how likely it is that sexual misconduct will be brought up as a charge against masters' good faith, and how they can never be brought to have anyone as a judge for those promises.

In the long scene of byplay between Paegnium and Sophoclidisca while they should be delivering the lovers' messages, instead the play takes a detour to indulge the gamelike, nonsensical quality of their language and the mock-moralistic content of their jibes at one another. For fifty lines in scene II.2 their interchange takes on an absurd cast, as their exchange of rhyming, punning insults, and arrogant claims of superiority begins to look more like the babble of children than like a scene in a scripted comedy. Their repetitive and highly stylized language stands in sharp contrast to the ethical claims of friendship made in the first act and to their masters' explicit demand for quick action. Each tries to get the other to reveal the content of the lovers' messages. When this exchange of confidences occurs in the final lines of the scene, it is clearly anticlimactic, and the slaves have very little interest in their masters' affairs beyond the opportunity they offer for some slapstick play.[48] The content of their argument consistently

---

[46] E.g., when Toxilus asks him to go so quickly that he will be back home when Toxilus thinks he is at Lemniselenis' house, Paegnium cleverly turns around to head home (190–91). This strategy of being extremely literal minded is a very pointed response on the part of the slave to the masterly ideology. The slave's literal-minded interpretation turns the slave into a computerlike object that responds only to exact commands without the human advantage of being able to understand the intentions behind the commands. Thus literal-mindedness forces masters to make a choice as to whether they want their slaves to be human or not.

[47] Woytek (1982: on 193), Bettini (1991: on 193).

[48] Chiarini (1979: 52) notes that in neither case is the actual transmission of the message to Lemniselenis or Toxilus represented on stage; what is foregrounded instead is "l'aspetto metaforico implicito nell'atto formale della trasmissione dei messaggi. . . ." Slater (1985: 42) calls II.2 "comic relief within comedy. . . ." See also Leo (1913: 120). On the refusal to move the plot forward, Fraenkel's observation on II.4 (1922: 402 = 1960: 380–81) is equally applicable to II.2: "Hier ein gewandter Tänzer wirbelnd auf und niederspringt, ohne dabei den Ort zu wechseln. Das Ganze kommt nicht vorwärts; wenn Plautus mit seinen Späßen aufhört, ist man am gleichen Punkte wie vorher."

returns to the key themes of decorum and, at the end, *fides*. Like Saturio's monologue, which also maintained the usual comic stance of using ethical language to subvert ethics, this scene contrasts with Toxilus' attempt to fuse slavish cleverness with a naturalistic perspective on morality.[49] For example, the use of moral terms (*decet*, 213, 220 and *oportet*, 229) here conform to their use in the farcical mode delineating the usual antimoralism of clever slaves. As Chiarini (1979: 54, 61, *passim*) emphasizes, the farcical characters express their committment to and abilities in the world of theatrical inversion by taking insults as compliments. Sophoclidisca and Paegnium pride themselves on the "virtue" of *malitia*.

The contrast between this celebration of *malitia* in scene II.2 with the opening of Sagaristio's pious prayer of thanksgiving in II.3 could not be stronger. He has returned with the desired money in hand, the result of his master's foolhardy choice to trust Sagaristio to go to Eretria and buy some cattle. The patterned nature of this prayer language demonstrates something that will be important throughout this play: that the playfulness of farcical language and the solemnity of ritual language in Latin are almost too close for comfort. Both registers rely on alliteration, repetition, and pleonasm for their effect.[50] Usually the consistent antimoral orientation of the clever slave maintains the boundaries between the two registers and clearly marks parodic uses of solemn language. The slipperiness of these registers, the ever-present possibility of one transforming into the other, underscores the moral/antimoral ambiguity of this play.

Sagaristio begins by giving thanks to Jupiter that he has been allowed to help his friend. In the atmosphere established so far in this play, in which the bonds of friendship and alliance have been singled out as the basis of morality, this does not sound particularly parodic or malicious. Yet as the monologue proceeds and we learn that it is through tricking his master that Sagaristio is able to help his friend, this sentiment's claim to moral purity becomes more suspect. It is typical of this play that the tension is maintained between these two interpretations; it is resolved neither by truly exalting the honor among thieves nor by undermining it to the point of making it an obvious reversal of the morality of real life. The mention of Sagaristio's scorn for his impending punishment, usually a marker of

---

[49] Formal parallelisms (alliteration and rhyme) appear both within the lines of each character and as devices through which they mirror each other's lines, which are often identical in meaning as well. Examples include: PA: *com*pellabo. SO: *com*morandust. (203); SO: quid agis? PA: feminam scelestam te astans *contra con*tuor. / SO: certe equidem *puerum peiorem* quam te *novi nem*inem. (208–9); PA: quid ais? certumnest *celare quo* iter facias, *pessuma*? / SO: offirmastin *occultare quo* te immittas, *pessume*? (221–22).

[50] Danese (1985: 80–86) gives a detailed formal analysis of the phonic, lexical, and grammatical patterns of this speech. In particular, he emphasizes the way that these patterns link the divine generosity of Jupiter and the human generosity of Sagaristio in helping his friend.

the *malitia* of the comic slave, may seem to tip the balance towards a consistently antimoral stance in the entire passage, but the repetition of the word *amicus* serves to remind us of a transcendent, rather than negative, vision of morality that has been developed so far.[51]

Toxilus' entrance in scene II.5, as he is giving last words of instruction to Sophoclidisca, reinforces the impression he gave at the beginning of scene II.2 with Paegnium. In both conversations, his obvious use of the themes and tone associated with lovers distances him from his slave interlocutor. Here, his assurances for Lemniselenis that he will take care of everything emphasize his emotional and sexual desire rather than his anticipation of the coming trick. After this little moment of romantic angst in which he perfectly sounds all the notes appropriate to the young lover, Toxilus almost immediately reverts to the persona of the scheming slave. Both he and Sagaristio, who seemed the personification of dignity in the preceding scene with Paegnium, repeat the slavish antics with which they began the play.[52] The scene type invoked here is that of the clever slave wringing out of his young master as much humiliation as possible before revealing that all their problems have been solved, the most extreme examples being *Asinaria* III.3, and *Casina* III.6 (this time with a *senex amator* rather than a young lover). The most striking difference between this scene and those in the *Asinaria* and *Casina* is the absence of the topos of having the master call the slave first master, then patron (cf. *As* 650–52, *Cas* 738–39). The reason for this omission is obvious, that Sagaristio is in fact not the slave of Toxilus; nevertheless, the absence of this expected part of the formula further highlights the ways in which Toxilus cannot enact the part of the lover, and it transforms this scene from one depicting the most outrageous forms of the reversal of master-slave hierarchy to one between equals, knowingly joshing each other.[53] In comparison to the *Asinaria*, here in the *Persa* the lack of the reversal motif and the corresponding expansion of the metaphorical joke about the cattle being inside the bag (one line in

[51] The ambiguity of the moral stance presented in Sagaristio's monody is continued into the next scene, where he meets Paegnium. What should be only a brief scene of transition becomes a confrontation between the true *malitia* of the younger slave and Sagaristio's offended dignity. The cynicism and arrogance with which Paegnium responds to Sagaristio's reasonable request that he help him find his master are appalling even within the jaded world of comic etiquette. Having been told that he must be obedient because he was bought and paid for, he now refuses to be obedient unless he is bought and paid for (273).

[52] Note that the structure of I.1 was similar: first, Toxilus gave a canonical lover's speech, and Sagaristio started to recite the catechism of the good slave, before the scene was transformed into typical slave patter.

[53] Sagaristio begins by pronouncing all the required language for a scene in which an uppity slave tortures his master, including *graphice, gloriose,* and *magnufice.* For *graphice,* cf. *Trin* 1024, *Epid* 410, *Ps* 519, 700; see also Fraenkel (1922: 195, note 1 = 1960: 185, note 1). For *magnufice,* cf. *As* 351. Despite the serious textual difficulties in 308, the reading *magnufice* is not in doubt.

the *Asinaria*; nine lines [312–20] devoted to two different metaphors in the *Persa*) are the product of Toxilus' anomalous status as lover and, in turn, have the effect of making this scene one about alliance rather than about the reversal of power.

The importance of this shift for the progress of the play is paramount. By indirectly showing the breakdown of Toxilus' persona as lover, and by emphasizing his alliance with Sagaristio rather than making Sagaristio subordinate to him, this scene prepares us for the shift from a romance plot—in which the erotic goal of the lover is the primary focus of attention and in which the slave is subordinated (logically, if not dramatically) to the young master—to a revenge plot—in which the ties of solidarity between members of the trickster's alliance are the thematic key.

Toxilus as Civic Defender

Act III serves as a hinge between the opening movement, in which the forms of romantic comedy alternated with antimoral farce, and the rest of the second movement, which will champion civic values within a metatheatrical frame. The very fact that the disguise trick is carried out after Toxilus has acquired the use of the money to free Lemniselenis heightens the underlying civic motivation of punishing the pimp rather than freeing the girl. This act establishes the moral themes that will shape the deception scenes and defines the two characters whose surprising and self-contradictory qualities will express the paradoxical nature of this moral vengeance. The Virgo is one of the most tantalizingly strange characters in the whole Plautine corpus: the brilliance of her rhetorical style and deceptive wit is equaled only by her stubborn prudery. Her use of theatrical imaginativeness in the service of antitheatrical moralism complements Toxilus' pious use of the language of friendship and faithfulness to pull off the dirtiest of tricks. The combination of these two polar opposites brings about the downfall of the pimp Dordalus.

Although scene III.1 is not the only place in the corpus where an immoral parent parodies the language of *pietas* in convincing a child to abandon the path of virtue,[54] it is the only example where this cynicism is on the side of the comic hero. Another important difference between this scene and other related scenes is the prominence that is granted to the daughter's argument. Not only is she right by the standards of right-thinking Romans (as are the daughters in the other plays), but she has at her disposal an elegant and astute rhetorical style, a way of speaking that completely upstages her father's theatrical presence as well as undermines his

---

[54] Cf. *As* III.1, *Cist* I.1. In the latter example, the Lena is not Selenium's mother but still an older "advisor."

moral arguments. This scene establishes the character of the Virgo and reveals how her unusual ethical perspective in turn fosters an unusual theatrical perspective.

Saturio manages his entrance here in much the same way as his entrance in I.2, with solemn formulaic language that quickly reveals an antimoral purpose. *Quae res bene vortat . . .* ("May this matter turn out well . . ., " 329) is a prayer formula that is several times associated in Plautus with marriage negotiations, a particularly pointed twist of connotations.[55] Although his command of alliteration, pleonasm, and formulaic language is as impressive as in his first scene, here Saturio's parasitism breaks through much earlier, in the first line in fact, where he puts his stomach on a par with himself and his daughter as recipients of the blessing.[56] The daughter picks up on this personification of his belly to begin her argument (338): "Are you going to sell your daughter for the sake of your belly?" (*tuin ventris caussa filiam vendas tuam?*).[57] Saturio's response continues the contrast between public and private developed in his entrance monologue (see esp. 65–67), and, as earlier at 75–76, he roundly rejects the idea that his hard work should benefit anyone other than himself. The Virgo adeptly counters this argument when she reminds him, in line 344, that the nature of his control over her is the *potestas* of a father, not the *imperium* of a public official.[58]

At line 351, she launches into the real heart of her argument, and her thought becomes as elaborated as her speech has been throughout. Her chief point is that the difference between reality and appearance is meaningless when it comes to *fama*: having a reputation for something is equally bad whether the reputation is deserved or not. In the most pointed contrast to the great comic heroes and their willingness to exploit the gap between appearance and reality, the Virgo staunchly believes that there is no difference between the two, and if she plays a *meretrix*, she will, in some sense, be a *meretrix*. Her train of thought thus also clarifies the analogy she uses at lines 361–63, where she complains that her anxiety at the thought of participating in this ruse is like the anxiety of a slave who has been told to ready himself for a whipping. Besides returning to the complaint that her father is treating her like a slave rather than like a daughter (cf. 341), this analogy is a further example of her point that "thinking makes it so." The slave's punishment lies in the mental anguish of knowing that his master has the power to whip him, whether he exercises that power or not. The

---

[55] Cf. *Aul* 218, *Trin* 500, 572.

[56] Woytek (1982: on 329).

[57] Even this deceptively simple and plaintive line is artfully constructed, with chiastic alliteration of *t* and *v*, and the balancing of "stomach" and "daughter" by the repetition of *tuus*.

[58] Note the heavy alliteration, repetition and other parallelisms through this and the following section: *potestas . . . pater; pater . . . pauperculae; modice et modeste meliust vitam vivere*; repetition of *paupertas* in 347–48; *fit . . . fides*.

importance of this point of view should not be underestimated. It provides the link between her singularly strict moral standards[59] and the brilliance of her performance. As will be shown in the discussion of scene IV.4, her performance derives both its theatrical virtuosity and its convincing quality from the fact that she speaks truthfully, though in veiled language, rather than relying on extravagant stories and lies.[60]

She has good reason to fear being treated like a slave, because her father talks to her in the idiom of master and because her own language carries many of the marks of the comic slave. Saturio twice dismisses her concerns in almost exactly the same authoritative words as those that Syracusan Menaechmus used towards his slave (359, cf. *Men* 250; 369, cf. *Men* 249). Her adoption of the conversational gambits of back-talking slaves can be seen in her over-literal interpretation at lines 369–70, where she pretends to hear *malo* as referring to "a bad man" (with unpleasant implications for her father) rather than to "trouble" or "punishment."[61] We saw above how Paegnium, who embodies many of the rebellious qualities of comic slaves (even though his cleverness may be doubted), used exactly the same technique to annoy his master (191). She follows in Paegnium's footsteps again, when she refuses to allow her father to coach her on her part but assures him that she can handle it, a claim that is more than borne out (*docte calleo* at line 380 has connotations of skill gained from experience; something like "hard boiled" in English.)[62]

Toxilus' verbal battle with Dordalus accounts for the second scene of this act. Though comparable to the shouting match of *Pseudolus* 360–68, which also involves a *leno*, a slave, and a lover, this spate of stylized insults takes on different force here for several reasons. First, it should be noted that the scene here in which the pimp is being paid inverts the dunning *flagitatio* of the *Pseudolus*. In both plays, the *leno* seems to win this exchange of insults, even though he is destined for ruin by the end of the play. Ballio

---

[59] The ethical emphasis on *fama* resurfaces again twice in this scene, at lines 371–72, and 383–84.

[60] The conflicting interpretations of the Virgo hinge on the sincerity of her moral outlook. Chiarini (1979: 114) believes that her performance in III.1 is nothing but an extremely clever impersonation of a moralistic young girl, a sort of "screen test" for her performance as an Arabian captive. Lowe (1989b) focuses on the Plautine tendency towards inconsistent characterization and argues that her morality in III.1 is true to her portrayal in the Greek play, while her acting skill later is a Plautine addition. (Prescott [1916] had made a similar, though less detailed argument.) Slater (1985: 45 and note 3) sees her as univocally moral but confesses that it is unclear how her morality fits in.

[61] Woytek (1982: ad loc.).

[62] Cf. Sophoclidisca's language at 168, 176, 305. The scene ends with a memorable joke, which again recalls the imagery of Saturio's entrance monologue. Just as in the earlier scene he claimed to be the recipient of an ancient patrimony of parasitism (53–61), here he promises to pass this heritage on to his daughter, in the form of a dowry of jokes (390–96).

in the *Pseudolus*, far from denying the *leno*-like qualities attributed to him, actually takes pride in the powerful and consistent performance of his persona. Here, Dordalus is less arrogant and less explicitly theatrical, but he puts forward his claim for respect in the theatrical world through his artfully arranged parallelisms and the impressive breath-control that this speech requires (to which both he [at 417] and Toxilus [at 427] call attention).[63]

Perhaps the most important difference between the two scenes of *flagitatio* is the *Persa*'s moral atmosphere in which the criticism of the *leno* is grounded. Unlike Ballio, who first introduces himself through his impressive *canticum*, an aria of cruelty and greed in which he holds the stage for one hundred lines, Dordalus' entrance leads immediately to this exchange. The result is that the audience sees Ballio as a character, and they see his cruelty and the need to oppose him, before the war of insults begins. The *Persa*, on the other hand, has stressed the complementary themes of friendship and self-interest. When the *leno* enters and begins wondering, in proper legal terminology, whether Toxilus will keep his promise about the money, the interest of the scene focuses on these ethical problems more than on Dordalus as a character. Further, in the *Pseudolus* the scene of *flagitatio* comes at the beginning of the play and establishes the lover's plight of needing money to free his girlfriend. The appearance of a similar scene halfway through the *Persa* reinforces the discontinuity between the romantic plot of Acts I and II and the plot centered on *ludificatio* that will unfold later in the play.

After a tussle between the two combatants, in which the insults they sling back and forth make specific reference to both the social position and the conventional comic attributes of each,[64] Toxilus finally hands the money over, and they set the terms for the manumission of Lemniselenis. It never is made clear why this simple business transaction has taken on the flavor of moral warfare, except that Toxilus says he was angry at Dordalus for not

---

[63] Slater (1985: 45).

[64] Toxilus' insults to Dordalus emphasize the imagery of filth (*lutum*, *caeno*, *sterculinum*, *inpure*, etc.) and of faithlessness (*inhoneste*, *iniure*, *inlex*, etc.), both canonical associations for *lenones* (Chiarini [1979: 119]). For comparable uses of these insults against *lenones*, cf. *Poen* 157–58, 825–26, *Ps* 366, and *Rud* 651–53. Dordalus taxes his opponent with slavery itself, with a litany of servile punishments (*stabulum servitricium*, *suduculum flagri*, *compedium tritor*, *pistrinorum civitas*, *perenniserve*, etc.) and with his unrestrained physical passions (*scortorum liberator*, *lurcho*, *edax*, *furax*, etc.) A surprising element of Dordalus' tirade is the extent to which he makes sarcastic use of the language of citizenry, as Toxilus and Sagaristio did in the opening scene. In a strange phrase that closely echoes Sagaristio's claim at line 22 (*fui praeferratus apud molas tribunus vapularis*), he calls Toxilus *pistrinorum civitas* (420); Woytek (1982: ad loc.) argues that *civitas* should be understood concretely as = *civis* (cf. *servitus* = *servus* [425]). In contrast, Toxilus' only use of civic imagery (*labes popli*, 408) is not sarcastic or parodic at all but straightforwardly expresses moral indignation at the pimp.

trusting him (431–32). Dordalus quite justifiably points out that, based on past experience, he would have been foolish to trust Toxilus.[65] If this play were a simple romantic plot, the payment would constitute resolution rather than the opening of hostilities. Because the original goal of freeing Lemniselenis has been overtaken by Toxilus' desire for vengeance against Dordalus, the play continues and takes as its new goal the punishment of the *leno*.[66]

Act IV amply delivers on the promise of Act III: that Toxilus and his allies will bring off a peculiarly moral and extravagantly theatrical deception. These two mutually contradictory elements continue to shape the language and the action of the play. Sagaristio, disguised as a Persian foreigner, will sell to Dordalus the exotically dressed daughter of Saturio, only to have her father arrive, claim her as freeborn, and drag Dordalus off to the praetor. The moral content of this disguise trick presents itself in the two ways used to take advantage of Dordalus. First, in scene IV.3, Toxilus gains the confidence of Dordalus by repeatedly stressing the concepts of friendship and gratitude. This is a perversion of the genuine commitment to friendship that motivated Sagaristio in daring to offend his master for the chance to help Toxilus. Second, the virtuoso performance of the Virgo is an even more extreme example of this same kind of appropriation. She uses ethical arguments and an unwavering commitment to speak the truth in the service of what is surely one of the most sly and deceptive tricks in the whole corpus of Plautus. As in her scene with her father, her moral purity may set her apart but so too the unparalleled adroitness with which she uses that purity for deceptive ends.

In the opening scene of this act, Toxilus artfully weaves together the habits of thought familiar to the clever slave with those familiar to the good, obedient slave.[67] The message of this monologue is all about care and industriousness in the creation of a good trick.[68] In the context of moral

---

[65] Dordalus' astuteness contrasts implicitly with the stupid credulity of Sagaristio's master (261). Sagaristio claims that he is justified in feeling contempt for anyone so stupid as to trust him with a moneybag, yet the implied respect for the wary does nothing to help Dordalus here.

[66] The rest of the scene prepares for this next phase. Dordalus proves to be quite confident in his judgment, proud that he is not gullible. He boasts of his ability to defend himself verbally (428–30) and of his caution in business dealings (433–36, 442–43). In all three cases, gnomic language draws attention to his show of sagacity. This scene also lays the groundwork for what follows by using the word *credo* prominently (432, 435, 441) to express Dordalus' reluctance to trust.

[67] Chiarini (1979: 124).

[68] Throughout the first six lines (449–54) we might almost be hearing the ghost of good slaves, slaves like Messenio who fervently believe and preach to others the value of sober hard work and inborn moral fiber (453–54). The lines from 455 to 458 tack onto this solemn

debate that the diptych scenes of the third act have established, this is no isolated joke. It is rather emblematic of the degree to which, in the *Persa*, the monkey business of slave scheming is given a serious moral aim. The imagery of Toxilus' monologue continues into scene IV.2, where it advertises the presence of the required elements for slave trickery. He uses words that in this play and elsewhere in the corpus are almost code words for such trickery: *basilice* (462), *lepidus* (463, 466), and *graphice* (464).[69] Equally canonical is the metatheatrical reference to tragic and comic actors (465); Sagaristio claims that this disguise scheme surpasses most theatrical efforts.[70]

Scene IV.3 begins Toxilus' deception with a conversation in which Dordalus claims to be a changed man: he has had a conversion to *fides*. Toxilus, after making sure that Lemniselenis has really been freed, exploits Dordalus' new commitment to trust by showing him a letter, purportedly from his master, which asks Toxilus to help sell a beautiful Arabian captive. Here Toxilus establishes that he will use simulacra of civic values (good faith, friendship, gratitude) to lure the pimp into the trap. In his earlier scene (III.3), Dordalus fulfilled every requirement for the perfect comic pimp, including greed, a quick tongue, and a wariness that advertised his resistance to trickery. Here he expresses his joy at being so reformed from his former untrusting self that he will from this day hence trust everyone and never fear betrayal (476–79). Far from being an obstacle to the lovers, a function he ceased to fulfill as soon as he got the money, Dordalus is now no longer even acting in the pompous manner that usually justifies the punishment of blocking characters. There is a contradiction between the surface motivation for Dordalus' punishment (greed, lack of trust) and the underlying structural motivation, that is, his status as a scapegoat who must be punished for order to be restored. The *leno*'s resolution to reform cannot save him from his fate but only makes him an easier target. Toxilus' trick will make use of the *leno*'s new virtue of trust and his old vice of greed, the only aspect of Dordalus' stereotypical characterization that persists.

Dordalus' readiness to trust and Toxilus' readiness to take advantage of it are fully exploited in their first exchange (482–90), where Dordalus repeats the key word *credo* ("I believe/trust") seven times. The tables have been turned from scene III.3. Dordalus is now exasperated with Toxilus' unwillingness to believe that he has really freed Lemniselenis, and he ex-

sermon the more usual language of the clever slave (see esp. *facete, callide, confido, hodie,* and the imagery of a trap).

[69] On *basilice* and *graphice*, see above, notes 25, 53; for *lepidus*, cf. *Poen* 901, *Mil* 767, *Men* 132, *Ps* 946, *Truc* 964, etc.

[70] Cf. *Poen* 581 for verbal correspondence; the same idea is expressed differently at *Cas* 685–88, 855–61, *Bac* 649–50, *Mos* 1149–51, *Ps* 401–8.

hibits his own trust extravagantly in the litany of *credo* and also in his refusal to allow Toxilus to swear to his present good intentions (490), since asking for an oath would imply lack of faith. Toxilus, for his part, uses a show of his own gratitude for Dordalus' freeing of Lemniselenis (492; see also 495–96) to introduce the "favor" he proposes to do for the *leno*. At the same time, he emphasizes the magnitude of this favor by projecting the enormous gratitude that Dordalus will feel towards him in the future (494). Like the use of *fides* and *credere*, the theme of gratitude transforms the concept of the true friendship between Toxilus and Sagaristio into an instrument of deception.

The letter appeals, however, to the element of Dordalus' characterization as *leno* that has been preserved, the desire to make a profit (*facio lucrum*, 503). As Chiarini has noted, the description of the city from which the captive is supposed to have been taken emphasizes its wealth and venerable antiquity, especially in the name "Chrysopolis" ("City of Gold").[71] Beyond awakening in Dordalus a hunger for the wealth of the East, the letter also establishes Toxilus as a responsible, well-intentioned slave carrying out both his master's orders and the more general demands of etiquette in helping his guest sell his goods.[72] We find out here that the buyer will get no legal title to the girl but rather purchases her at his own risk (*suo periclo*, 524). Thus, as in the deal for Lemniselenis, the problem of trust and faith in business becomes paramount. The letter closes with a triple repetition of *curo* "I take care," (527), lending Toxilus the appearance of a careful factotum for his master. His use of the language of diligence in the monologue that opened this act (449, 451), however, assures us that his care is oriented toward his own interests rather than his master's.

In scene IV.4 the Virgo dazzles Dordalus and even Toxilus with a tour de force impersonation of a remarkably philosophical Arabian captive. The scene begins with a splendidly theatrical enactment of a theme that has been more diffuse up to this point, the relation between the integrity of a city and the morality of its inhabitants. The Virgo delivers an impressive "philosophical" list of ten deadly civic sins (555–58). The connection of these "sins" with the stereotype of the comic pimp would be clear anyway, but Toxilus states it explicitly at 561–62.[73] We have seen no evidence in this play of Dordalus' breaking faith (*peiiurium*); we acknowledge Toxilus' charge only because of the well-defined persona of the *leno*. This list again emphasizes that Dordalus' punishment is not for anything he has done in

[71] Chiarini (1979: 139, 145); see also Slater (1985: 47–48).

[72] The word *curo* at 511 plants this idea (reprised at 523 and in triplicate at 527). The language of the business transaction in lines 524–26 looks back to the acrimonious dealings between Toxilus and Dordalus in scene III.3.

[73] Chiarini (1979: 147).

the course of the play.[74] His punishment is necessary to reestablish the sense of civic order and well-being. The list also implicitly identifies Toxilus, the Virgo, and the others in the deception scheme as defenders of the city, since they are punishing those faults that lead to the city's weakness.

Toxilus' attempt to push Dordalus further into the trap leads to an extended treatment of a curious image of the *leno*'s future success, an image that conflates business success with both erotic and social success (565–73). Toxilus tries to convince Dordalus that the owner of a girl such as this one would have customers of the highest rank bankrupting themselves for his benefit (564–68). This notion expresses the essential tension of the typical Plautine romances, that men of high social status and great wealth are held hostage by *lenones*, the most despised members of the community. Yet Dordalus' addition to this fantasy complicates the vision even more: "but I would forbid that they be let in" (*at ego intro mitti votuero*, 568). This response is nonsensical on the plane of business (why would anyone refuse to admit customers?); it makes sense only if we realize that Dordalus has translated the purely financial success envisioned by Toxilus into an image with both erotic and social meaning.[75] His refusal to admit the potential customers is parallel to the power implied by the beloved's shutting out the lover (a familiar topos from elegiac poetry) and by the haughty patron's refusal to see a client. Toxilus, in turn, spins out a scenario that first picks up on the elegiac imagery, then twists Dordalus' logic in such a way that his increasing restrictions eventually have the opposite effect (569–73). The phrase (*noctu occentabunt*, "they will serenade you by night" 569) makes explicit the parallel of this situation with that of the *paraclausithuron*.[76] But then Toxilus leads Dordalus down a different path by enumerating a series of bars and locks that would, in the image Dordalus had in mind, express the magnitude of his power by symbolizing his exclusiveness. The repetition of *ferreum* (iron, here referring to manacles), however, as a description of how strong these barriers will be, transforms this lock-out into a lock-up, with Dordalus reduced to a chained slave (573) rather than to a powerful, exclusive lover or patron.[77]

---

[74] Wilamowitz (1894: 23), Woytek (1982: introduction, 56).

[75] These meanings may already be implicit in Toxilus' statement at 567: *cum optumis viris rem habebis*, "you will be engaged with the best men." Woytek (1982: ad loc.) dismisses *Bac* 564 and *Mer* 535 as irrelevant, but perhaps the erotic sense that this phrase has in those passages is exactly what provokes Dordalus' fantasy.

[76] Cf. *Cur* 145, *Mer* 408.

[77] Woytek (1982: on 573) notes that Toxilus reduces the *leno* to his own social position. Chiarini (1979: 149) sees the imagined assault of clients against Dordalus' house as reflecting the real assault now being carried out by Toxilus et al. There is yet another irony to this complex comment on social status. The statements that the two men make about the value of the Virgo as a prostitute are predicated on the idea that her "classiness," her quality of being *liberalis*, is what will make her so valuable, i.e., the most desired quality in a slave prostitute is

The dialogue so far makes it clear that Dordalus is already hopelessly entangled in this deception. His attempts throughout the rest of the scene to be a hard-headed businessman, to question the girl about her circumstances, and to negotiate the price only reinforce his doom. His ill-fated negotiations are highlighted by his frequent reference to the friendship, gratitude, and trust that he thinks he shares with Toxilus (in scene IV.3 see 483, 518, 539, 548). The negotiations over price are interrupted by Toxilus' suggestion that Dordalus question the girl first to find out more about her. Dordalus' excessive gratitude for this suggestion (593, 595; see also 598, 603) reveals how far he is from his ideal of business acumen (594) and how absolutely he has been taken in by Toxilus' sham friendship.[78] Toxilus is so sharp that he is able to turn even this dependence to account by pretending to counsel the *leno* to make him a more imposing opponent for the Persian: "I prefer that you approach him yourself, so that he doesn't have a low opinion of you" (*sed ego te malo tamen / eumpse adire, ut ne contemnat te ille*, 602–3).[79] The doubleness of Toxilus' identity is apparent in his simulation of walking the fine line between his duty to his guest in helping to sell his goods and his duty to his new-found friend Dordalus (612–14). This conflict of interest articulates his fragmented identities, since solicitude for the guest is required by his master (612–13), while his "friendship" with Dordalus implies an equality of status. The fact that this conflict is the product of Toxilus' own theatrical creation does not simplify the problem; his double identity as slave and free within his own fiction merely echoes that already attributed to him by Plautus in making him a slave and a lover.

The girl's ability to turn her interrogation into a Socratic dialogue on the nature of slavery should not surprise us by now. What is surprising is the explicitness with which she adopts the language specific to scheming slaves. She refuses to allow herself to be coached in her performance, taking it as a slight to her abilities (608, 610), and makes use of military terminology, including an extended metaphor, enumerating the procedures of going out into battle with good auspices (607–08). Her description of herself and her situation achieves its brilliance through its metaphorical relation to what we know of her real situation. She complained in scene III.1 that her father was treating her like a slave, and she saw her participation in this

---

that she should seem like a freeborn virgin (cf. *Mil* 961–63, 967). This is also explains why the Virgo's reluctance to pretend to be anything other than what she is, far from endangering the trick, ensures its success. See also 645.

[78] Chiarini (1979: 151). Even more extreme later, at 614: DO: *tibi ibidem das, ubi tu tuom amicum adiuvas*, "you do a favor for yourself when you help a friend." Toxilus made a non-ironic use of the same rhetorical pattern at 304 to express his emotional solidarity with Lemniselenis.

[79] An ability he shares with the clever slave Palaestrio, who pushes his master Pyrgopolynices into the trap by means of his pretended concern and helpfulness (*Mil* IV.2, 4).

trick as the equivalent of a slave's whipping. She speaks in this scene of her misfortunes through this veiled language. The parallel of her predicament to slavery emphasizes that her current situation deprives her of her own will to act, makes her subject to others' will through her duty (*officium*, 616) makes her accustomed to misfortune (620–21), and negates her membership in any community (636, 641). The imagery of slavery is restricted to the description of herself; to describe her father, she uses the same imagery of hospitality and gluttony he had used. Her father's use of her as a meal ticket is echoed in her claim to have been born in a kitchen (630–31). Similarly, her description of her father as one who has lost everything he had (644) and who is more "well received" (*acceptior*, 648–49) than anyone else in the city are coded references to his status as parasite.[80]

As soon as Dordalus goes into the house to get the money, Toxilus takes this opportunity to congratulate the girl on the star turn she has performed and to ready Sagaristio for his next scene. As in scene IV.2, which preceded the deception, the language here is clearly that of the theatrical slave trickster, working now as stage manager to organize the finale.[81] In the context of this ethically motivated deception, this language has the effect of emphasizing the confusion of moral and antimoral. By aligning this scene with other slave deceptions that are aimed merely at tricking the father to get some money for the son, the play undermines the ethical vision that might be thought to accompany the punishment of a greedy *leno*.[82] Dordalus returns with the money, and Plautus does not miss a further occasion to paint his greed and stinginess: he has kept back two *nummi* as a deposit against the return of the moneybag (683–85). Nor do Sagaristio and Toxilus miss an opportunity to remind the audience that Dordalus' behavior can be explained in general and in specifics, by reference to his comic stereotype, "not surprising, since he's a *leno*" (*quando lenost, nihil mirum facit*, 688; see also 686–87). Finally, the dirty deed done, Sagaristio is about to take his leave when Toxilus, seemingly insatiable for risk, asks him what his hurry is (693). Again, as when he cut off Dordalus' premature negotiations by advising him to question the girl first, he seems about to ruin a good trick, allowing Dordalus casually to ask for the Persian's name (700). Although Toxilus' fear is made tangible in his attempt to distract the *leno* from this

---

[80] Woytek (1982: ad loc.) argues for an erotic interpretation of *acceptior*.

[81] Slater (1985: 49).

[82] The shifting moral ground affects this short scene in the contrast between the language Toxilus uses to the Virgo and the language he uses to Sagaristio. His praise of the Virgo, and her response to it (673–75), recall the language at the beginning of his monologue in IV.1, where he seemed to be seriously adhering to ideas such as *frugalitas* and *cura* (Chiarini [1979: 167]). But when he begins to remind Sagaristio of his part in the next scene, they revert to the joke, used several times already in this play, of the actor refusing to take advice from the director (cf. 152, 175–76, 183–87, 305, 379–81, 607–10).

possible give-away, Sagaristio's ad lib performance is at least as impressive as the Virgo's is in baptizing herself. He offers a four-line, multisyllabic name (702–5) as the final flourish to his performance. It sums up the renegade attitude of the gang who brought off this trick, by representing an excessive and theatrical response to a problem of their own making.

Saturio's return to save his daughter is amazingly quick and to the point. After more than two hundred lines of text devoted to luring the *leno* into this purchase, the abruptness of this outcome is surprising. Also, in view of Saturio's considerable abilities in argumentation and ornamented language, we might expect these qualities to be more exploited in this key scene. He springs the trap remarkably quickly, pausing only to articulate the *leno*'s (grim) legal position (745–49). The emphasis on law in this brief scene recalls Saturio's surprisingly acute command of civic knowledge throughout the play. Here he plays both prosecutor and judge, assuming that the heinousness of Dordalus' crime will prevent him from getting any witnesses.

> DO: nonne antestaris? SAT: tuan ego caussa, carnufex,
> quoiquam mortali libero auris atteram,
> qui hic commercaris civis homines liberos?
>
> (747–49)

DO: Aren't you going to call a witness? SAT: What free person in the world would I call as witness,[83] for you, you scoundrel, who sell free citizens?

Dordalus is doubly an outsider: no freeborn person would think it worthwhile to testify in this case precisely because his crime has been to sell freeborn citizens. Saturio has come full circle. Like the *quadruplatores* whom he criticized in his first scene, he has become an accuser who reveals a crime against the city. Even more like them, he has done it in his own material interest rather than as a public service.

His daughter's resigned "yes, I'm coming" (*sequor*) with which she leaves the stage, repeating her father's command (752), recalls the resignation with which she allowed herself to join this project (SAT: *sequere hac*, "come this way"—VI: *dicto sum audiens*, "I hear and obey"—[399]). We might have expected that her demonstration of theatrical skill would have placed her permanently in the camp of the clever, but with this obedience, she returns to her ambiguous position of daughter/slave. Unlike Toxilus and Sagaristio, she has not derived any pleasure from her participation and, unlike her father, no material benefit.

---

[83] Lit. "whose ear would I touch": the Roman ceremony for asking someone to serve as a witness in court.

Toxilus as Master

Toxilus opens the fifth and final act with a monody in which Fraenkel recognized long ago the style and language of a triumphal prayer.[84] We are used to hearing slaves boast in the language more proper to military victors, but in the atmosphere of judgment on civic values that has pervaded the *Persa*, we must acknowledge the particular pointedness of a slave rejoicing,

> Hostibu' victis, civibu' salvis, re placida, pacibu' perfectis,
> bello exstincto, re bene gesta, integro exercitu et praesidiis,
> quom bene nos, Iuppiter, iuvisti, dique alii omnes caelipotentes,
> eas vobis gratis habeo atque ago, quia probe sum ultus meum
>   inimicum.

(753–56)

The enemies are conquered, the citizens are safe, our state is at peace, the peace is concluded, the war is over, success secured, with the army and fortifications intact, since you, Jupiter, aided us, and all the other gods powerful in heaven, I declare and avow my thanks to you, since I have so nicely had my vengeance on my enemy.

The form of this prayer recalls Sagaristio's prayer of thanksgiving at 251–56 and again creates the perspective that this band of thieves is bound by a truly moral outlook.[85] Nowhere is the solemn tone disrupted by any reference to tricks (cf. *Bac* 1070). The content emphasizes gratitude to the gods (756) and to friends (757, 762). This monody should be seen as an example of the principle that the most canonical of comic forms can take on new meaning when the context is changed. These slave triumphs conventionally celebrate the victory of youth over age and slaves over masters; here, the triumph celebrates the punishment of a pimp who threatened the civic values of faith and gratitude, as well as the integrity of the citizen identity. By a double switch, the serious civic form that is usually used playfully by a slave to extol his subversion of established values is here used by a slave to extol his defense of these values.

This prayer is a fitting introduction to Act V in which two superficially similar scenes articulate the opposing moralities that have shaped this play. These two banqueting scenes differ in tone and moral perspective, and,

---

[84] Fraenkel (1922: 236–40 = 1960: 228–30) includes both a formal analysis and a comparison to the diction of what we know of triumphal prayers from Livy (XLI.28.8–10). The most famous example of this topos in comedy is at *Bac* 1067–71, where Chrysalus abruptly breaks off his triumphal monody, claiming it has become too common. Fraenkel (1922: 235 = 1960: 227) argues convincingly that this is a metatheatrical comment about comic convention and not a comment on the frequency of triumphs in real life.

[85] Chiarini (1979: 182) "la ricomparsa . . . del linguaggio perbenistico. . . ."

moreover, they relate to two opposed schemes governing the resolution of comedy, that of reconciliation and that of *ludificatio*, an almost ritualized form of ridicule. Comedies that end in reconciliation, such as the *Captivi*, *Cistellaria*, and *Rudens*, are those in which Tyche, the deification of chance, has had the greatest influence in bringing about the resolution. Comedies that focus on the confusions created by slave antics rather than by fate, on the other hand, tend to end with *ludificatio*, as do the *Asinaria* and *Miles Gloriosus*.[86] The difference between these two paradigms demonstrates once again that the struggle over literary conventions in the *Persa* mirrors the struggle over the moral perspective of the play. Beginning with Toxilus' triumphal monody, the first scene of Act V revives the serious atmosphere of true friendship and mutual sacrifice and sets up an expectation that this play will end in reconciliation. The second scene of this act also begins with a long patterned monologue, representing another form very familiar to the audience of comedy, the bitter tirade of the *senex iratus* after he has found out how he has been tricked.[87] From this beginning, the scene becomes progressively more bitter. Just as in Act IV Toxilus, a slave, used the system of civic values to bring down the wealthy pimp, here again he belies his juridical status by using the domestic authority of a master. The most telling instance of his authority also makes it clear that reconciliation will have no part in this ending: far from bending to, or even tolerating, Lemniselenis' attempt to bring the play to a conciliatory conclusion, Toxilus sharply reins her in (835–37) and insists that this play will end in a *ludificatio* (833).

In the first scene the sense of harmony and celebration is expressed by Toxilus' rituals of gratitude (757–62), while he also plays the roles of lover and patron without irony. In the conversation between himself and Lemniselenis, the emphasis is on courtly deference to one another and the mutuality of their affection.[88] Especially in Lemniselenis' final blessing (*bene / ei qui invidet mi et ei qui hoc gaudet*, "let it be well for the one who holds a grudge against me, and for the one who rejoices in this," 776–76a) we seem to be laying the groundwork for a solution that will find the discomfited pimp accepting his loss and sitting down to dinner with his deceivers.

The directions that Toxilus and Lemniselenis give for the arranging of the banquet (769a–772a) remind us of the two invitations issued in Act I,

---

[86] The consistency of this pattern can even be demonstrated in "mixed" endings (those that have elements of both reconcilation and *ludificatio*) such as in *Epidicus* and *Poenulus*. The conciliatory aspects are related to the recognition plot, while the ridiculing aspects are related to the plot line of slave trickery.

[87] For example, the beginning of Dordalus' speech closely parallels that of the father at *Bac* 1087–88.

[88] The parallelism of the language matches Lemniselenis' expression of mutuality at 763: *Toxile mi, qur ego sine te sum, qur tu autem sine med es?* Toxilus expresses the same thought through semantic means at 766a, *mutua fiunt a me*, and again structurally at 775a–76, *ut aman-*

a sincere offer of revelry to Sagaristio (I.1), and to Saturio the promise of payment for services rendered (I.3). Only the first of these will be honored here. Saturio's absence from the banquet underscores Toxilus' assimilation to masters/patrons in other plays. Interestingly, although throughout the corpus parasites are depicted as earning their bread by helping out with tricks or by keeping or revealing secrets, we never see them enjoy these ill-gotten meals. As will be argued more fully in the case of Ergasilus in the next chaper's analysis of the *Captivi*, this segregation reinforces a view of parasites as merely instrumental in the mechanics of the plot. So much more significant then is it that Saturio conforms to this pattern, thus showing Toxilus to be more like freeborn patrons than like a slave confederate of the parasite.[89]

The final scene most explicitly allows Toxilus the authority to impose harsh punishment on Dordalus. He does this in two ways that reveal his authority over his own domestic circle as well as the comic authority he has gained by outwitting the *leno*. First, he encourages Paegnium's *ludificatio*, ordering him to torture Dordalus by making sexual advances to him (804–18). This bizarre interlude is Dordalus' nadir in the play; Paegnium's earlier scene with Sagaristio has already established his status as lowest of the low, and to become the catamite (*cinaedus*, 804) of such a one is the greatest dishonor imaginable. Second and even more brutally, Toxilus recalls Lemniselenis from her attempt to intervene on Dordalus' behalf by reminding her of the debt of gratitude she owes to him for freeing her (834–43).

Dordalus' impersonation of a *senex iratus* is only one of the ways that he tries to reassert his power. His use of the conventional tirade as an entrance monologue momentarily recalls the household structure that has been successfully suppressed for most of the play. At lines 786–87, and again below at line 811, Dordalus reminds Toxilus that the freedom he has exhibited throughout the play should, by the canons of the genre, be defined by contrast to his usual submission to his master. He calls attention to the fact that, unlike most comedies, the slaves' revelry in the *Persa* has not been interrupted by the master's return. Although this reminder impresses us with the strangeness of this closing scene, there is little hope in it for Dordalus. At line 795, he calls Toxilus a wearer-out of goads (*stimulorum tritor*), an insult reminiscent of those he used more successfully in his scene of

---

tem amanti decet. Lemniselenis' deference towards Toxilus here has an erotic connotation (766), though later it will be seen in terms of mastery.

[89] Sagaristio, in keeping with his more consistently slavish persona, is not very charmed by the love fest between Toxilus and Lemniselenis and more eager for the *ludificatio*. Chiarini (1979: 188) gives an ingenious metatheatrical interpretation for the problematic lines 767a–68: that they refer not to a girlfriend for Sagaristio but to Dordalus, and to the promise of the coming comic persecution. We can expand on this observation by noting that the erotic imagery of *ludificatio* here foreshadows Paegnium's form of torture. Woytek (1982: on 767) summarizes the other interpretations.

flagitatio (cf. wearer-out of chains, *compedium tritor*, 420). That scene was the one triumph for Dordalus in the play; moreover, the success of his tirade there was marked by his recitation of the most stereotypical qualities for slaves, focusing on punishment and appetitiveness. Again, this can be seen as an attempt to reduce Toxilus to the stature of a normal comic slave, one who in the final scene would acknowledge that his power ends with the play. Needless to say, this attempt is unsuccessful.

The rest of the scene enacts the struggle between reconciliation and *ludificatio*. Slater is correct in observing that Toxilus does invite Dordalus to sit down.[90] But his sarcastic vocative *homo lepidissume* ("oh, you most charming man," 792, echoing Dordalus' sarcastic greeting of Lemniselenis at 789–90) holds out little hope for the sincerity of this welcome. His rejection of quarrels at line 797 might seem to be looking towards reconciliation; however, the language is closer to a warning (*iurgium hinc auferas, si sapias*, "You'll take that quarreling away from here, if you know what's good for you").[91] Toxilus' intent to extend his authority through the final scene is highlighted by the contrast with Lemniselenis' assumption that the usual norms of comedy will operate:

> . . . LEM: stultitiast,
> quoi bene esse licet, eum praevorti
> litibu'. posterius istaec te
> magi' par agerest.

(798–801)

. . . LEM: It's silly for anyone who can be at ease to get involved in quarrels. Far better for you to take care of all that later.

She believes that this revelry will heal the wounds of the previous deception, but that later (*posterius*) there will be a time when a realistic hierarchy reasserts itself and Toxilus will have to pay for his tricks.

This assumption is countered not verbally but by the humiliation of Dordalus through Paegnium's sexual advances. Dordalus understands from the very beginning the specific theatrical status of his punishment (*ludos me facitis, intellego*, 803). Throughout the next lines there is a string of the clichés of comic ridicule (*elude, basilice, facete, inridere, lubidost, delude, ut lubet*). This language underscores the authority of the comic rebels to punish Dordalus. However, here the punishment is more explicitly degrading

---

[90] Slater (1985: 52–54) follows Segal (1987: 87–90) in seeing this final scene unambiguously as an offer of revelry on the part of the comic rebels, an offer that is refused by the ill-natured agelast.

[91] The closest parallel is in the language of a master to his slave at *Poen* 1035–36; at *Rud* 1398–99, in keeping with the conciliatory emphasis of that ending, Daemones upbraids Gripus for using such language to the pimp. Cf. also *Mos* 1173, *Aul* 401, *Men* 121, *Mil* 476.

than those imposed on other blocking characters. Rather than just being forced to accede to the comic view of the world and join in the revelry (cf. *Pseudolus, Bacchides*), Dordalus is threatened with being subordinated sexually to a character who was not even involved in the deception scheme. The *puer delicatus* Paegnium, who has consistently scorned any morality, even claims to be the instrument of divine justice:

> DO: ego pol vos eradicabo. PA: at te ille, qui supra nos habitat,
> qui tibi male volt maleque faciet.

> (819–20)

> DO: By god, I'll wipe out the lot of you. PA: On the contrary, he who lives above us, who wishes you ill and will treat you ill, is going to wipe you out.

Lines 834–42 are the site of the sharpest battle between conciliation and *ludificatio*, and it is also the point where Toxilus' domestic mastery is made most explicit. Seemingly oblivious to the ironies, Toxilus shows his complete integration with the worldview of masters towards their slaves. He defines slaves as commodities (834, 842; cf. Paegnium's reflection of this ideology at 273) and masters as protectors (836–37); he nimbly uses the twin weapons of threat of punishment (835) and the expectation of gratitude (840) to enforce the desired behavior. His scornful tirade includes a description of freed slaves that depends on a view that slavish natures can never sufficiently encompass the liberal value of gratitude:

> sed ita pars libertinorum est: nisi patrono qui advorsatust,
> nec sati' liber sibi videtur nec sati' frugi nec sat honestus,
> ni id ecfecit, ni ei male dixit, ni grato ingratus repertust.

> (838–40)

> But that's how freedmen are: if they haven't opposed their patrons, they don't seem to themselves to be quite free, nor quite worthy, nor quite respectable, if they haven't done this, if they haven't cursed their patrons and been found ungrateful to those who deserve their gratitude.

His iron-fisted treatment of Lemniselenis is shocking not just because it relies on master-class ideology but also because Lemniselenis has consistently been referred to as Dordalus' freedwoman, not Toxilus' (see 82, 474–75, 484, 491, 737, 789; even at 849, Lemniselenis addresses Dordalus as *patrone mi*). His appropriation of her as his own freedwoman underscores the turn that he has taken from rebel to established master. Her response is exactly as it should be, combining submissiveness and gratitude (841) with a willingness to join in the *malitia* (843).[92]

---

[92] Toxilus' description of what Lemniselenis' behavior should be precisely echoes the words of the Virgo: *te mihi dicto audientem . . .* (836); cf. 399.

Appropriate to the strange conflation of moral perspectives that has shaped this play, it ends with a coda of the themes of high-minded civic values and low-down ridicule. While Dordalus is being hit, pinched, and generally abused, we are reminded that his crime was selling freeborn girls (845). Dordalus himself ruefully describes his punishment in terms of gratitude (853). Toxilus' final line makes explicit the scapegoat effect of the *leno*'s permanent punishment: "Dear spectators, good-bye. The pimp's had it" (*mei spectatores, bene valete. leno periit*).[93]

THE LIMITS OF FARCE

The *Persa* is an extreme example of farce, or, more precisely, it is an attempt to make farce self-sufficient, not just a reaction to the naturalistic mode. Granting Toxilus the roles of both clever slave and lover can be seen as a way of trying to write clever slave comedy without the legitimizing framework of a young man in love as the impetus for the slave's tricks.[94] But the outcome of this farcical coup is not as subversive as one might expect, to judge from the rebellious impulse farce brings to other plays. Unless Plautus were prepared to write a play that presents a real, meaningful challenge to his audience's sense of social order, a play in which a slave rebels against the real constraints of his servitude, he must aim Toxilus' rebellious pursuit of his love affair against a pimp, who is a blight on the citizen community rather than against any legitimate household authority.

This is not to claim, however, that Plautine comedy in general or the *Persa* in particular is merely a rehearsal of master-class truisms about the fundamental passivity of slaves. First of all, even though Toxilus' rebellion has been circumscribed in this way, the very desire to heroize clever slaves testifies both to masters' acknowledgment of slaves' potential to resist (and so the desire to see that resistance enacted but shown to be meaningless) and, further, to masters' need to experience, vicariously through comic slaves, a rebellion against their own superiors. There is yet another way in which farce, and especially the rebellion of subordinates, even as it is domesticated in response to master-class decorum, can still retain elements of genuine subversion.

In the *Persa* the main body of the play is a farcical rebellion that has been made to accommodate some of the key thematic elements of naturalistic comedy, specifically by honoring friendship and defending the integrity of

---

[93] Chiarini (1979: 203) "il 'sacrificio rituale' è compiuto. . . ."

[94] See the final section of chap. 2 on the *adulescens* as an important bridge between the two modes. Even though the *adulescens* is greatly overshadowed by his slave in most clever slave comedies (*Ps, Mos, Epid*), his vestigial presence is an important guarantee of a "real" world (i.e., a world of *kaloikagathoi*) outside this fantasy world in which slaves hold the power.

the citizen community. But within this general framework are two extremely odd characters, Paegnium and the Virgo, who attempt to rebel against Toxilus' rebellion. Even though they operate on completely different principles, they are structurally similar in being subordinates to characters who are themselves labeled (both in this play and in the system of comic convention) rebels, namely a clever slave and a parasite. An even more intriguing similarity is that both Paegnium and the Virgo question theatricality itself, the cardinal virtue of the farcical aesthetic. These two characters represent a view that runs contrary to the overall momentum of the play, revealing the limits of farce by critiquing the emptiness of the rebellion farce offers.

Because the *Persa* shows Toxilus and Saturio to have the authority of a master and a father respectively, as well as the farcical authority of a clever slave and parasite, Paegnium and the Virgo are in the unusual position of being dependents of the characters engaged in rebellion.[95] Their duty to those who hold power over them requires them to be mischievous tricksters. Just as the Virgo bows to filial duty in performing a theatrical deception, Paegnium carries out a bold *ludificatio* in the final scene under the direction of his master. Paegnium's seemingly greater pleasure in fulfilling his master's orders should not obscure the similarity between these two characters. Both perform under orders actions that everywhere else in the corpus are marked as rebellious, independent, and carnivalesque. Paegnium provides us with the clearest statement of the paradoxical position he shares with the Virgo:

> servam operam, linguam liberam eru' iussit med habere.
>
> (280a)

My master has ordered me to be a slave in my work and free in my speech.

Both his servile obedience and his uppity back talk are required by his master.[96]

But the overall farcical emphasis of this play makes every hierarchical relationship a site for potential rebellion; as a result, Paegnium and the Virgo oppose their farcical authority figures by appropriating elements of

[95] The previous discussion of Lemniselenis in the final act shows that she too is in this strange position, though her simultaneous identification as Toxilus' beloved blunts the edge of her subordination. We might also compare the situation of Olympio and Chalinus in the *Casina*, though in that play because the tricksters are characters who normally function as blocking characters (a *senex amator* and an *uxor dotata*), the logic of the two slaves' being subordinated to rebels is not pushed as far as it is in the *Persa*.

[96] The Virgo does not have any single statement so lapidary, but throughout her scene with her father, she continually presses the paradox that her filial duty is leading her into *malitia*; e.g., *necessitate me mala ut fiam facis* (382).

the naturalistic mode. Although they both seem to have a flair for the repertoire of the clever slave (back talk, extravagant metaphor), Paegnium and
the Virgo are actually closer in type to good, obedient slaves. The quality
that the Virgo and Paegnium most obviously share with good slaves, but
not with clever slaves, is self-interest. One of the central features of the
clever slave, the one that permanently separates him from any society based
on the values of the freeborn, is his refusal to act teleologically to bring
about his own manumission. Despite all his apparently subversive power,
the clever slave never seeks to break the bonds of his servitude.[97] It is this
that separates him from the character of the good slave who longs for freedom, like Messenio in the *Menaechmi*, and from all freeborn characters.
The combination of the willingness to deceive with the desire for freedom,
if made more explicit and central than it is the *Persa*, would present to
masters a frightening specter: a slave whose trickery might operate in the
terms valued in the real world rather than just in the terms of the fantasy
world of comedy.

Unlike tricksters throughout the corpus, Paegnium and the Virgo enjoy
deception or even revelry not for its own sake but only as a means towards
fulfilling their obligations. Both hope to rise in the world through fulfilling
these obligations—to rise, that is, not in the farcical world, in which Tranio,
Chrysalus, and Pseudolus hope to rise by being acknowledged as accomplished tricksters, but in a world that shares the values of real life. Through
manumission for Paegnium and a citizen marriage for the Virgo, they hope
to shake off the authorities who compel their participation in these comic
revels. The value farce places on artifice serves to point out that social
categories are constructed rather than natural. However, by reintroducing
reality as a gauge of value, Paegnium and the Virgo reveal that farce's usual
critique of real-life social hierarchies contents itself with merely registering
their lack of natural justification but does nothing to challenge the fact of
social inequities. These two strange rebels may not get much further than
the usual farcical rebels in escaping their subordination, but they are radical
in voicing their dissatisfaction with the hermetically closed world of farce.

The Virgo's moral position and her antipathy to playacting shine
through clearly in scene III.1. Paegnium, instead of adhering to naturalistic
morality, uses the real experience of slavery to disrupt the assumptions of
the fantasy world of farce. Paegnium's confrontation with Sagaristio (who,
in this whole company of slaves, most closely preserves the characteristics
of more usual clever slaves) highlights his distance from the normal comic

---

[97] The sole exception is Epidicus. I can offer no explanation for this exception, but I find
intriguing the persistent language of sacrifice in this play (see Duckworth [1940: on 185] on
the recurrence of *exentero*) and its possible connection with the bizarre power structure of the
final scene where Epidicus gets his freedom by refusing to allow his master to undo his bonds.

paradigm. His rudeness provokes a reaction of offended propriety from Sagaristio, who clearly feels that his age and greater cleverness call for certain deference from the younger and less clever slave. This reminds us that comic slaves in other plays, although they have no desire for money or freedom, do champion their rights to a recognition of their boldness and artistry. The farcical authority of the trickster produces its own hierarchy of cleverness, parallel to the hierarchies on which the naturalistic authority of the master rests. We can see that Paegnium's back talk to Sagaristio is more than just cheekiness (which in fact would align him with the clever) it is a hard-headed, realistic critique of the worldview of the clever slave. This confrontation of ideologies is made clearest at line 286. Paegnium declares that his sexual service to his master is not for nothing (*gratiis*, as he claims Sagaristio's is) but is a down payment towards his freedom: "For boldly I believe that I will be free, while you never bother hoping that you will be" (*nam ego me confido liberum fore, tu te numquam speras*). The impatience of real slaves with the reign of the carnival king who is content to remain a slave breaks through into comedy.

The similarity between Paegnium and the Virgo also rests on a use of sexuality that inverts the norms of the comic society. Paegnium is a *puer delicatus*, the master's sexual pet. Everywhere in Plautine comedy, these boys are degraded and abused by the master class and even more so by their fellow slaves.[98] Paegnium creates a *puer delicatus* who may be distasteful and crude; however, he is anything but powerless. Like the *meretrices* whose name form he shares, Paegnium is able to make a commodity out of submission. But Paegnium's character combines elements that are usually mutually exclusive for *meretrices*. These women fall into two categories: either they are sincerely sweet and tender and end up freed by their boyfriends or recognized as freeborn, or they are already freed and independent but adept at using the appearances of tenderness for their own gain. Paegnium cuts across these categories, as he cuts across the categories that define male slaves. Paegnium's confidence in achieving freedom is out of step with the maliciousness of his character, whether measured by the norm of male clever slaves or of *meretrices*.

The Virgo, on the other hand, belongs to the character type of the *pseudo-meretrix*, the girl whose sexual integrity embodies the integrity of the citizen identity. For most young men in comedy, their identity as a citizen is either never in doubt or else is always capable of being corrected (see *Captivi, Poenulus, Menaechmi*). The citizen identity of young women, on the other hand, is negotiated through their sexual status. The promiscuous, commercial sexuality of the *meretrix* effectively defines her as a noncitizen, while the exclusive, procreative sexuality of citizen women ensures

[98] See *Ps* III.1, *Mos* 885–903; see Lilja (1982: 59, 62–64).

their place in the community by ensuring their reliability as the mothers of citizen children. The crisis of the girl at the point of becoming a prostitute, and therefore lost forever as a possible citizen wife and mother, creates the dramatic urgency of recognition plays. Because women's belonging to the community depends on the exclusiveness of their sexuality, the imminent loss of this exclusiveness is connected (on the thematic plane) with their rescue and recognition.

This generic structure forms the background against which the Virgo's recognition hoax is played. At lines 383–84, the Virgo warns her father that this recognition, unlike most comic recognitions, may make her unmarriageable by showing her to be outside the group of legitimate wives because of the shamefulness of this disguise trick. Here we see the link between her status as *pseudo-meretrix* and her refusal to indulge in the revels of comedy. Most *pseudo-meretrices* are freed from their mistaken identity through the operation of Tyche, the divine force that reveals the errors of human perception. But because the Virgo assumes the role of *meretrix* not through mistaken identity or misfortune but because of the trickery of a band of slavish rogues, her recognition, instead of proving her to be marriageable, may have just the opposite effect and take her out of the pool of citizen wives. It is precisely the theatrical manipulation of the operation of Tyche that the Virgo finds shameful. Her sense of *officium* requires her to obey her father. However, like Paegnium, she has the trick of turning passivity to her own advantage. By maintaining her own persona and refusing to accede to the deceptive tactics of the others, she is able to maintain her honor and her citizen identity as well.

Finally, the theme of trust and risk taking provides another example of how the farcical perspective is subtly challenged by the Virgo and Paegnium. One of the ways that Toxilus' deception works its magic on Dordalus is by playing on the need for *fides*, the necessity for members of the community to trust each other even where absolute empirical evidence is lacking. Especially in this play, where the true bond of friendship between Toxilus and Sagaristio has been contrasted with the simulacrum of friendship the clever slave offers the pimp, we can see that the faith that Toxilus asks of Dordalus is a dupe's version of the risk taking that is a cardinal virtue for the comic trickster.[99] The deception scheme of the *Persa* offers some clear examples of this kind of risk taking: when Toxilus stops Dordalus from prematurely negotiating a price by reminding him that he ought to question the girl first (591–603), and when he detains Sagaristio, who is about

---

[99] Chiarini forcefully equates the desire to take risks with the theatrical aesthetic (1979: 91 [on 63]): "Amor del rischio, dell'avventura, e amore del'arte, del teatro, sono in Plauto una cosa sola. . . ." See also 166 (on 665).

to make good his escape (693).[100] Like cleverness, the willingness to take risks supports a farcical hierarchy, privileging the members of the comic alliance (fearless, clever) over everyone else (cautious, unimaginative).

The band of tricksters clearly distinguish between their honorable risk taking and the sanctimonious professions of *fides* they sling around in the deception trick. But, just as with the rejection of nonteleological deception and playfulness, the ideal of risk taking for the party of comedy is challenged by the canny self-interest of both the Virgo and Paegnium. The Virgo's argument against her father insists on the real consequences of theatrical performance, as it counters the tricksters' underlying assumption that risk taking is the highest calling:

> SAT: quid? metuis ne te vendam? VI: non metuo, pater.
> verum insimulari nolo. . . .
>
> (357–58)

SAT: What? Are you afraid I'm really selling you? VI: No, Father, I'm not afraid, but I don't want an accusation to come from this.

She specifically makes the point that fear is not the only reason why someone might not be interested in playing these dress-up games, thus undermining the sacred value of risk taking. As noted above in the discussion of this scene, the Virgo's attachment to *fama*, to reputation in others' eyes, makes her take appearances very seriously; from the idealizing perspective she represents in this play, the idea that one can play with appearances without consequence seems a childish illusion.

Paegnium's assault on this value, as might be expected, is more explicit in its reference to the gap between the fantasy world of comic slaves and the harsh realities of slavery. At lines 193–94 and 243–44, he rejects an offer of faith as hollow.

> PA: scio fide hercle erili ut soleat inpudicitia opprobrari
> nec subigi queantur umquam ut pro ea fide habeant iudicem.
>
> (193–94)

PA: I know how likely it is that sexual misconduct will be brought up as a charge against masters' good faith and how they can never be brought to have anyone as a judge for those promises.

> <SOPH> fide data credamus. PA: novi: omnes sunt lenae levifidae,
> neque tippulae levius pondust quam fides lenonia.
>
> (243–44)

---

[100] The riskiness of the trick is emphasized by Toxilus' expression of fear at 624–26 and by his attempt to deflect Dordalus' question at 700.

<SOPH> Let's trust each other, once we've given our word. PA: I know: all madams are weightless in their words, nor is even a mosquito lighter than a madam's promise.

The first of these rejections is based on the glaring differences between comedy, where slaves can force their masters' hands, and real life, in which the master's promise to the slave is only as binding as the master wishes it to be. In the second, Paegnium makes use of his metatheatrical "experience" of pimps and bawds. Its relation to the principles of comedy is less confrontational. But the combination of the two has the striking effect of equating *fides erilis* and *fides lenonia*. Paegnium matches the frequent statement that comic pimps are faithless with a more radical observation on the faithlessness of real masters.

Paegnium also specifically reverses the language that comic slaves use to exalt their risk taking. *Confido* and the related word *confidentia* are often used to denote a clever slave's high hopes that his trick will succeed, despite the great odds against him.[101] Within the *Persa*, these words express the grandiosity of Toxilus' project.[102] Paegnium's use of these words, however, like his rebelliousness and his use of sexuality, is aimed at the real-world goal of manumission. The exchange with Sagaristio at lines 284–86 is again illustrative:

> SAG: video ego te: iam incubitatus es. PA: ita sum. quid id attinet ad te?
> at non sum, ita ut tu, gratiis. SAG: confidens. PA: sum hercle vero.
> nam ego me confido liberum fore, tu te numquam speras.

> SAG: Now I see what you are: been brought to bed already, haven't you?
> PA: So I have. What's it to you? But unlike you, I don't do it for free.
> SAG: Aren't you a bold one! PA: Yes, indeed I am. For boldly I believe that I
> will be free, while you never bother hoping that you will be.

Sagaristio mistakenly accounts for Paegnium's arrogance as that of the clever slave. Paegnium implicitly corrects him, by showing that his confidence is in his manumission, not the success of a deception scheme.[103]

Farce is essentially a reactive mode. Unlike naturalistic theater, it emphasizes its ability to "parse" its social and dramatic surroundings rather than the ability to create a world of its own. (To put this in the Bakhtinian terms I used in the general introduction, farce accepts dialogism as fundamental,

---

[101] Cf. *Mil* 189a, 465, 941, *St* 454, *Mos* 38; *As* 547. In connection with the preceding argument, note the etymological connection between *fides* and *confido*. These related words are usually firmly associated with naturalistic values and farcical trickery respectively.

[102] At line 39, Sagaristio describes his friend's attempt to raise money to free his girlfriend as *confidentia*, and at line 456 Toxilus confidently anticipates the success of his scheme.

[103] A similar pattern is observable at lines 230–32: Sophoclidisca teases Paegnium with the usual fate of masters' pets, and Paegnium retorts that his *confidentia* will ensure his freedom.

while naturalistic theater makes the effort to appear monologic.) In a play so dominated by farce as the *Persa* is, the farcical aesthetic and worldview themselves become grist for the mill. Paegnium and the Virgo represent two very different types of this self-critique. Paegnium's hard-headed appraisal of Toxilus and his gang continues the reactive logic of farce, cleverly exploding others' pretensions to meaning but not offering any system of value to replace them. Just as the *Persa* has shown the limits of farce as a freestanding mode, we cannot envision Paegnium's perspective, both more genuinely subversive and more reactive, ever taking center stage. The Virgo, on the other hand, critiques farce not by moving further into its dialogic maelstrom but by taking a step back towards the naturalistic mode. Unlike Paegnium, she does create a positive moral vision and is not content merely to point out the emptiness of playacting. In the *Persa*, her spectacularly high-minded performance may ripple the surface but cannot fundamentally change the course of the play. In the next chapter, I will argue that the possibilities of such a "theater of truth" as the Virgo creates, a theater that allows the naturalistic perspective powerfully to challenge farce, are fully realized in the character of Tyndarus in the *Captivi*.

The *Persa* embodies a confrontation between two dramatic modes (the naturalistic and the farcical) and two moral outlooks (one that preserves the ethical standards of real life and one that inverts them). Yet these two confrontations do not neatly align with one another. In each phase of this play, fantastic comic forms are juxtaposed to naturalistic ethical content. The well-known divisibility of form and content in Plautine comedy is often used as a weapon to expose the pretensions of moralizing blocking characters. The *Persa* offers the strange spectacle of this theatrical self-consciousness, and the *malitia* that usually accompanies it, in the service of restoring civic order by punishing the transgressions of a greedy pimp.[104]

A brief look back at the *Casina* will clarify the *Persa*'s more radical integration of the perspectives of farce and real life. The *Casina* is the farcical reformulation of a romantic comedy; it displaces freeborn characters from

---

[104] Chiarini's (1979) analysis of the *Persa* is valuable, both for its many acute observations and for its emphasis on the comic worldview. Although we overlap at some points, Chiarini sees the process of comedy as one of univocal opposition (he notes that Plautus overturns both comic conventions and social/historical reality [1979: 215]) and emphasizes the carnivalesque aspect of rebellion. He acknowledges the ways in which Toxilus uses civic values in the deception scheme, but he does not acknowledge the ways that this scheme and the whole action of the play embody a real defense of these values. In keeping with Chiarini's vision of the consistency of comedy's *malitia*, his treatment of the characters of Saturio, the Virgo, and Paegnium tends to flatten out the differences among them and between them and Toxilus and Sagaristio. My view of comedy emphasizes that even within the play naturalistic values are championed alongside *malitia*. Finally, I cannot agree with either the premises or the conclusion of Chiarini's specific argument (1979: 219–29) that the *Persa* is a response to the excessiveness of the triumphal *ludi* of 186 B.C.E.

their usual dramatic and moral positions into the dramatic and moral position of comic slaves. The characters' rejection of the ethics of real life parallels the play's rejection of the teleology of romance. In the *Persa*, on the other hand, we have slaves taking on the dramatic and moral positions of freeborn people. Toxilus' defense of civic values is at odds with the play's preservation of the forms and, at times, the values of comic rebellion. This conflict is not resolved; rather, the tension between dramatic styles and between moral perspectives animates the entire play. We are never sure whether Toxilus is a crook or a hero, whether he believes in the value of *fides* or not, and whether his control over Lemniselenis and Paegnium is real or just part of the joke.

Plautine comedy creates its characteristic complexity precisely by refusing to stabilize the interaction between subversive fantasy and naturalistic mimesis. The generic resolutions that articulate the relation of comedy to real life offer the best example of this complexity. The *Casina*, formed in reaction to the "oedipal" theme of romantic comedy, undermines the normal dramatic meaning of marriage as a resolution by displacing it into the burlesque deception trick. Likewise, the *Persa*, informed by the civic identity theme of romantic comedy, performs a similar operation on *anagnorisis*, the canonical resolution for this theme. The farcical theatricality of each play has the effect of devouring the usual marker of resolution. These resolutions define the border between fantasy and real life. In their absence— or, more precisely, with their transformation from naturalistic events into deception tricks—this border goes unmarked. This is not merely an entropy towards artifice and away from any realistic perspective. The *Persa* has shown how the dramatic devices of farce and metatheater can become containers of naturalistic values. In the next chapter, an analysis of the *Captivi* will show how an idealizing dramatic form can absorb farce and metatheater and turn them to its own purposes.

Chapter V

TRUTH IS THE BEST DISGUISE:
CAPTIVI

IN THE *CAPTIVI* ("*The Prisoners*")we immediately recognize the familiar elements of Plautine comedy: disguise tricks, a clever slave, a hungry parasite. But the didactic tone of this play and its concern with the emotional and philosophical problem of identity mark a gulf between it and much of the rest of the corpus.[1] Neither its skillful use of the stock elements of farcical comedy nor its transformation of those elements into carriers of ethical precepts should be allowed exclusively to define this complex play.[2]

As can easily be seen in the high-minded self-descriptions in the prologue and epilogue, the *Captivi*'s philosophical agenda engages polemically both the substance and the style of farce. In substance, this play champions a kind of essentialism, a belief that personal and moral qualities are defined not by experience or conscious choice but by an unalterable divine dispensation. This belief in a stable, fixed character conflicts in obvious ways with the worldview of farce, which assumes that the social world is constantly in flux and that it is influenced more by human agency than by the unseen hand of Fate. Thus, the *Captivi*'s preference for essentialism as a way of understanding human life is both reinforced by and, in a sense, determined by the literary style of naturalism, which conceals the action of the poet behind the cover of Tyche (Chance).

The fundamental philosophical issue for the leading characters in the *Captivi* is the difficulty of maintaining fixed moral standards, standards that are not conditioned by time or circumstances. The consistent maintenance of such standards is fostered by and in turn supports the belief that morality and character are inborn qualities. The central tension of the play sur-

---

[1] Of course, not all the rest of the corpus; the *Trinummus*, *Rudens*, and other plays are aligned on the *Captivi* side of the gulf.

[2] Much of the scholarship on the *Captivi* has centered on the problem of its similarity to or difference from the rest of the corpus. The best of this work has brought forward important observations, even though grounded in this rather one-sided methodology. For example, Segal (1987: 191–214) ignores the difference between moral and antimoral goals of the tricks (209), and he dismisses the importance of the distinction between fantasy and realism (199). In general, such Procrustean arguments, both pro and con, on the place of the *Captivi* within the Plautine corpus are probably the result of our impoverished view of the Plautine tradition (that it consists solely of farce). See also Leach (1969b), Gosling (1983), Viljoen (1963).

rounds Tyndarus, a freeborn young man whose experience of being kidnapped and raised as a slave has not diminished the noble aspects of his
character and who indissolubly adheres to the highest moral standards,
even when that adherence endangers his life. The continual confusion of
the appearances of slave and freeborn is merely a superficial confusion, one
that affords satisfaction precisely because the characters' identities remain
constant.

Although Tyndarus maintains his freeborn qualities, the play shows several characters to be pessimistic about the stability of virtue and good character. This pessimism emerges most clearly in the assumption that it is all
too human to act with merely selfish and short-term goals in mind.

> tum denique homines nostra intellegimus bona,
> quom quae in potestate habuimus ea amisimus.
>
> (Ergasilus, at 142–43)

Only then do we mortals understand our good fortune, when we have lost all
that we held in our power.

> nam fere maxuma pars morem hunc homines habent: quod sibi volunt,
>   dum id impetrant, boni sunt;
>   sed id ubi iam penes sése habent,
>   ex bonis pessumi et fraudulentissumi
>   fiunt.
>
> (Tyndarus, at 232–36)[3]

This is how most people act: when they want something, they are well behaved
until they get it; but once they've gotten their hands on it, they turn from
upstanding folk into the most evil and treacherous types.

> mos est oblivisci hominibus
> neque novisse quoiius nihili sit faciunda gratia.
>
> (Stalagmus, at 985–86)

People generally forget and fail to recognize someone whose goodwill is not
worth cultivating.

Although these three moralizing generalizations are all quite different,
they each assume the moral laziness of humanity. They implicitly contrast
an abiding sense of right and wrong with a pragmatic, localized view of
one's position and prospects. Despite the difference in the specific moral
failings at which each of these generalizations takes aim, they are unified
in focusing on short-term contingent behavior as the underlying problem
(as opposed to behavior that is governed by immovable rules or inborn

---

[3] Cf. 432–41, esp. the contrast between *fides fluxa* and *in perpetuom amicum*.

standards). There is a consistent opposition throughout the play between the kind of good behavior that is merely useful or convenient, expressed most fully in the precepts of the Lorarius (195–209), and that which is morally motivated, to which one adheres even in the face of great danger, as does Tyndarus in defending his deception of his master (682–743).

The *Captivi* is, above all, a philosophical play, interested in replacing this pessimism about consistent moral standards with a firm belief in essential moral character. But the literary choices used to make this argument complicate these philosophical propositions. When slavery is used to illustrate the proposition of essentialism, the result reveals the logic governing the master's conception of the institution. Slavery is the crucible that tests the content of Tyndarus' character. But it also functions to reinforce the unexamined assumption that links principled moral behavior with the freeborn and short-sighted, contingent moral behavior with slaves, by locating this latter type of morality in two minor characters presented as "real" slaves (the Lorarius and Stalagmus).[4] Further, the choice to represent these philosophical problems in the context of a slave tricking his master introduces a comparison between the morality of this play and the amoral antics of the farcical plays in the corpus. The asymptotic relation of this play to the amoral schemings of slaves like Tranio and Pseudolus exemplifies the polemical relation of the naturalistic mode and the farcical mode within the corpus of Plautus.

The social logic of slavery intrudes on the purely philosophical question of identity in two major ways. First, the *Captivi* bases its characterization of Tyndarus, who must be perceived as appearing a slave while "really" being free, on the unspoken distinction between slaves by condition and slaves by nature. Second, Tyndarus' deception scheme, in which he disobeys his present master (Hegio) for the benefit of his former master (Philocrates), draws on the paradoxical expectations masters have for the human and commodified aspects of their slaves.

The notion of testing a person's stable identity through the crucible of slavery is meaningful only if the culture admits the possibility of a slave exhibiting the desired moral qualities. If masters can look at slaves and divide them into those of strong character, who successfully resist the degradation of slavery, and those of weak character, who succumb, then slavery could be a test of character. However, the unstated distinction between slaves by nature and slaves by condition excuses masters from ever having

---

[4] By "real" slaves I mean those whose status is unquestioned and who are perceived within the play and by the audience as properly accounted for by the label "slave," without the ironic gap between label and substance that is opened up (within the play) when Philocrates and (for the audience) when Tyndarus are called "slaves." This is similar to the category of "slave by nature" that will be discussed below.

to recognize nobility in a "real" slave.[5] Those slaves who act "slavishly," who do not sufficiently overcome their humiliating status as property by cultivating a sense of honor, are true slaves, slaves by nature. Those, on the other hand, who can manage to separate their sense of self and of honor from their degrading treatment are merely slaves by condition. The fantasy on which the *Captivi* and most other recognition comedies rests is that these slaves by condition maintain their freeborn qualities and will always eventually be recognized as free. This distinction is clearly reflected among literary slaves: for most slaves in comedy (both obedient slaves and tricksters), we have no idea how they became slaves, whether by birth, capture, or judgment. They live in a timeless element where both past and future are without substance. Only for slaves that we already know to be freeborn, or who will be recognized as such in the course of the play, can the genesis of their slavery be represented.[6] Since we know from the prologue that Tyndarus is freeborn, we perceive him throughout the play in the ironic position of someone whose outward status does not match his identity. Thus his nobility is interpreted in terms of his "real" identity, not in terms of his situation of slavery. Although this play has often been seen to present the perspective that slavery is an accident that can happen to anyone, our perception throughout that Tyndarus is not "really" a slave diminishes the potential impact of such a presentation.[7]

Second, the paradoxical nature of the *instrumentum vocale*, a slave treated like an object but required to respond like a person, further constrains the free expression of philosophical ideas through the image of slavery. The plot of the *Captivi* centers on the problem of a slave's loyalty and thus reveals a fundamental contradiction in slaveholding ideology. The ideal

[5] I am arguing not that Roman masters actively made use of Aristotle's categories of slaves (*Pol* 1254b16–1255b15) but that the distinction Aristotle points out is one made subliminally, almost instinctively, in a culture that has to come to grips with the logical problems of slavery.

[6] E.g., *Cist* 133–42, *Cur* 490–91, *Epid* 107–8, *Rud* 106. The operation of Tyche in bringing about this recognition is extremely important in philosophical/ethical terms in being a guarantor of the "truth" and in literary terms, since recognition comedy uses Tyche to focus on the time of redemption, thus washing away the implications of all that time when things were awry (when Tyndarus was a slave and Stalagmus was prospering in his evil). Note that because of the prologue's revelations, the audience never experiences a time of considering Tyndarus as a "real" slave.

[7] Dumézil (1977: 123–24), in pursuit of a completely different argument, notices the difference in tone between Hegio's language to Philocrates when he believes that Philocrates is not only his own captive but also a slave in his native country ("esclave par nature, si l'on peut dire") and when he knows Philocrates to be freeborn at the end (when he speaks of Philocrates' *genius*). This leads one to observe the difference between the peremptory tone of Hegio's questioning of Philocrates (whom he believes to be a "real" slave) and his more polite tone to Tyndarus (whom he sees as merely a temporary slave). This underscores again that the accident of slavery through warfare is different in the minds of a slaveholding society from the permanent state of servitude. The knowledge of one's own susceptibility to such an accident does not necessarily inspire fellow feeling with the once and future slave.

slave in the master's mind would exhibit the human qualities of loyalty, judgment, and flexibility but somehow be bereft of the corollary qualities of self-respect, independence, and unpredictability. On the other hand, the ideal slave is like a commodity in his fungibility and can be considered a socially inert object. If slaves were like other goods (other *res mancupi*; see 954), their transference from one owner to another would not present a problem. But since masters themselves desire slaves to have an emotional attachment of loyalty, or even of love, for their masters, the instant shift of obedience from one to another would imply a lack of this humane quality (see 715–20).

This problem of the "slave of two masters" illustrates these fundamental inconsistencies in the image of the ideal slave.[8] Because Tyndarus has been wrongly enslaved twice (first, as a child, kidnapped and sold to the family of Philocrates, then captured in war along with this master and sold to his real father, Hegio), he is the perfect moral center around which to build a play that seeks to exalt slave loyalty while ignoring the implications of such loyalty for slave subjectivity. Tyndarus, who might seem so threatening because of his skill at deception, is rather reassuring, since competition for slaves' loyalty is a less frightening prospect than the possibility that they may have no loyalty at all.[9] At the same time, his free birth acts as an assurance that the audience need not seriously entertain the idea that slaves are capable of the human qualities that subtend the kind of ethical behavior Tyndarus shows here.

Like the social logic that allows masters to carry on their mastery, even though it is based on contradictory propositions, there is a literary logic that prevents these inconsistencies from marring the experience of the play.[10] Tyndarus' double identity as both slave and free[11] allows him to embody a harmonious resolution of the tensions of a slave society and to quiet

---

[8] Konstan (1983: 57–72) also sees the play as a variation on the usual theme of a slave's twin loyalties to young and old masters. He, however, emphasizes the conflict between a parochial city-state ethos and a universalizing ethos, so that the dilemma is between the bonds of loyalty among those of the same city (Tyndarus and Philocrates) and the bonds of humanity, which transcend local identities. He writes (64): "Citizenship and slavery appear as mere accidents, and therefore ought not to affect the criteria of right conduct. What would be lauded in the free man—the rescue of his compatriot—cannot be held blameworthy in the slave." In this analysis, Konstan glosses over the distinction I see as most central, that between slaves by nature and slaves by condition. It is only Tyndarus' secret identity as free (secret, that is, to everyone but the audience) that brings to the fore the injustice of his treatment, and, once acknowledged, this acknowledgment does not necessarily extend to all slaves.

[9] See now Thalmann (1996: 127–28).

[10] Konstan (1983: 69): "Thus the moral issue is deflected or sidestepped, after the fashion of comedy, where a general contradiction in values tends to be resolved by an arbitrary or contingent circumstance which serves for the given instance but fails to meet the problem as such."

[11] In some ways so similar to that of Toxilus, yet here established in the representational plane of the play, not at the level of generic conventions as for Toxilus.

the rumblings of thoughts that would be disquieting if followed to their logical extreme.[12] His ultimate identity as freeborn permits the audience to skirt the implications of his honorable actions undertaken while everyone believes him to be a slave. But his full enactment of the persona of a slave offers the comforting image of a truly loyal slave.[13]

A further reinforcement of this harmonious vision comes in the person of the two apparently "real" slaves in the play, the Lorarius and Stalagmus. Neither of these slaves can attain the perfection of slavery that Tyndarus, a freeborn young man, achieves. The Lorarius demonstrates the flimsy moral quality of even those slaves who are obedient and desirous of freedom ("good slaves" in the comic typology, like Messenio of the *Menaechmi*). His ethical philosophy rests completely on giving in to the circumstances: he is a good slave because that is most likely to get him freed, but he would not hesitate to run away if he had the opportunity. It is hard to think of Tyndarus' kidnapper Stalagmus in any terms other than just an undifferentiated vision of human evil. But again, his unrepentant back talk is more a sign of moral laziness than of any more imaginative evildoing.[14] Stalagmus' surly explanation of himself is the seamier side of the Lorarius' advice: take what you can get whenever you can get it. He neither expects principled behavior from others (985–86) nor exhibits it himself.

The social issues surrounding the ideal slave, as presented in the *Captivi*, have specific counterparts in the more farcical comedies. The comic slaves of, for example, *Mostellaria*, *Bacchides*, and *Pseudolus* also embody a contradiction between slavery and freedom. But the resourcefulness of the tricksters there in eluding their masters' strictures only reinforces their servile outlook. Like the Saturnalia, which implicitly defines slavery by contrast, the slave's deceptive trickery in these plays emphasizes a permanent subordination to his master.[15] Furthermore, in terms of the qualities of the ideal slave, far from combining obedience with a sense of honor, the typical clever slave combines disobedience with a lack of real self-interest or self-respect (as measured in real-world terms like the desire for freedom). The quality of nobility, which makes Tyndarus dangerous yet ultimately flatters the master class by demonstrating slaves' love for masters, is utterly lacking in clever slaves. They are not dangerous, since their fooling never changes

[12] Thalmann (1996: 130).

[13] Thalmann's (1996) analysis of the play emphasizes its ability to maintain simultaneously two contradictory "versions" of slavery: the benevolent version and the suspicious version, roughly equivalent to my contention that this play allows masters to see slaves as both similar to themselves and fundamentally different.

[14] It is probably his utter indifference to any moral standards that makes both Ketterer (1986a: 131, note 32) and Konstan (1983: 69) compare Stalagmus to the more interesting and well-developed villain Ballio, in the *Pseudolus*.

[15] This is one of the fundamental insights of Segal's book; see esp. (1987: 164–69).

their subordination, yet they are frightening in their incommensurability with regard to master-class ideals and values.

The paradox of the slave of two masters appears in other comedies in the conflict between son and father, both of whom have the status of master to the slave.[16] Like the conflict between Tyndarus' former master (Philocrates) and his current one (Hegio), this conflict of old and young masters should be easily resolvable through the legal principles of slavery. Just as Hegio should reasonably be able to expect Tyndarus' obedience no matter how long he served Philocrates, fathers in comedy clearly have right on their side when they forbid their slaves to foster their sons' rebellion. But this clarity is lost when one acknowledges the master's desire that the slave's emotions support his obligations, that his heart and mind be consistent with his actions. In the *Captivi*, the conflict of loyalties reassures masters of the emotional content of the slave's obedience. In other plays of trickery, however, the clever slave's desire to help the young master against the old grows out of not emotional attachment but the desire for play and disruption. Just as the clever slave's playful appropriation of a type of "freedom" has nothing to do with a noble resentment of servitude, his preference for one master over another has nothing to do with loyalty. The *Captivi*'s construction of a slave hero whose resentment of servitude can coexist with the greatest loyalty is a triumphant reversal of the farcical ethic/aesthetic.

The superficial similarities of Tyndarus' and Philocrates' trick with the disguise schemes of other plays serves as a defining aspect of the play. Precisely by closely paralleling the progress of amoral deception comedies in a play suffused with morality, the plot of the *Captivi* both declares its identity squarely within the Plautine tradition and yet polemically substitutes ethics for antics, and freeborn characters for slaves. As we saw the Virgo do in the *Persa*, the two young men in the *Captivi* construct a deception scheme that relies for its convincing quality on the truthfulness of their claims. The major difference between these two instances of a "theater of truth" is that in the *Persa*, because of the metatheatrical nature of the scheme, the Virgo is aware of her own use of truth in deception. In the *Captivi*, on the other hand, the truthfulness of Tyndarus' pose as freeborn is established outside the dramatic frame, in the prologue. Only the audience knows how right Tyndarus is when he distinguishes himself from those who were born into slavery (629).

In the *Persa*, the competition between a naturalistic comedy of manners and a fantastic comedy of rebellion takes place on the playing field of fan-

---

[16] Dumont (1966: 193–94) adds another example, comparing the situation of Palaestrio in the *Miles Gloriosus* to that of Tyndarus here. Both serve their former masters at the expense of their current masters.

tasy. Toxilus' performance of the role of the young lover immediately established that the stylistic conventions of the comedy of reversal would be in the ascendant. Further, the unreconcilable contradiction between a young lover and a clever slave relies on the audience's knowledge of both these theatrical types and of the canonical relationship between them. Thus the interaction between the two modes of comedy in the *Persa* takes place in the idiom of the farcical mode, that is, the division of content from style: playful rebellion in the language of civic piety, and serious punishment of civic offenders making use of metatheater. The *Captivi* demonstrates the opposite strategy, how naturalistic didactic comedy can absorb and contain the subversive energy of farce. In keeping with naturalistic comedy's greater emphasis on characterization and maintenance of consistent motivation, the *Captivi* makes use of a single character to embody antimoral rebellion. The relation of the parasite Ergasilus to the rest of the play is tenuous, in both dramatic and logical terms.[17] Of his six scenes, four are monologues, and the other two are dialogues with Hegio. This dramatic segregation is paralleled in the content of his first two monologues (I.1 and III.1), in which he mourns his loneliness and alienation. His only "useful" scene is IV.2 where he brings tidings that lead up to the play's dénouement, but even there his announcement does more to delay the dénouement than to expedite it. His lack of organic connection to the rest of the play emphasizes the gap between his values and those of the other characters. His desire for food, verbal play, the reliable give-and-take of the patron-client relationship make him seem like a stranger to this play of high moral purpose and to the war-torn city in which it is set. He is in fact an interloper not because of his ethnicity or civic status but because of his comic pedigree. As he implies in the opening monologue in which he compares himself to a *meretrix* by punning on the two meanings of *invocatus* (while a meretrix may be "invoked" by name in a game of dice, Ergasilus is "uninvited" to such festivities), he and the farcical world he represents are both necessary markers of the *Captivi*'s generic status and yet unwelcome in this play of masters. He is "invoked" as the retainer of the comic world and "uninvited" in the context of moral and philosophical debate.

The *Captivi*'s polemical inclusion of a parasite is just one example of the ways that this play is intimately connected to the fundamental structures of the more playful and rebellious deception comedies, though it uses these structures for such antithetical ends. The skeleton of the *Captivi* is a triangular relation between Tynadrus and his two masters. When Tyndarus and Philocrates (the man he believes to be his legitimate master, being ignorant of his own free birth) are captured and sold as war captives, they both believe that their first duty is set free Philocrates, since Tyndarus' enslave-

---

[17] Prescott (1920) gives an overview of these "inorganic roles."

ment in war is trivial in comparison to his (putative) slavery by birth. This goal, of course, places them in direct opposition to their new master Hegio; they do not know that Hegio has bought them only in hopes of effecting a trade for his other son, Philopolemus, who is being held as a war captive in Elis (Philocrates' native city). Thus the play sets up the usual form of deception comedy, where a slave (Tyndarus) and an *adulescens* (Philocrates) try to trick an older man in position of authority over them (Hegio).

The triangular relation between the three main characters is worked out through a complex layering of three different plot types, allowing this play to satisfy the competing claims of literary wit and wisdom, as well as the competing claims of ethical subversion and stability. These three plot types are usually associated with three different sub-genres of comedy—romantic comedy, comedy of humors, and trickster comedy. They can be distinguished most clearly by the function that Hegio performs in each. In the romantic plot type (cf. *Mostellaria*, *Epidicus*), he is the father who must be tricked in order for the son to get a girl. This plot type, which is strongest at the beginning of the play, gives prominence to Tyndarus' agility as a trickster, but has no way to accommodate the necessary resolution of the *Captivi*, in which Tyndarus is recognized as Hegio's son and set free from his bondage. The other two plot types focus attention on this resolution and so position Tyndarus not as a clever slave but as a *pseudo-meretrix* character, whose recognition and liberation form the play's dénouement. In the misanthrope plot type, Hegio is the central character, the correction of whose irrational "humors" forms the basis for the action. Konstan notes (1983: 67) that in the later part of the play, after Hegio swears he will never trust anyone again, the focus of the play switches towards a plot in which "social relationships are re-established with the secessionist by means of outside gestures of generosity and good faith." In this plot type, of which we may use the *Aulularia* as an example, Philocrates has the function of the daughter's suitor,[18] a young man whose interests force Hegio to reexamine his own selfish reactions. Tyndarus takes the role normally fulfilled by the beloved girl. Thus, Tyndarus functions in this plot type not as a subject, a schemer, but rather as an object, both as a victim of Hegio's misanthropy and as the vulnerable loved one whom Philocrates must rescue.[19] The third plot type, that of deception, is different from the second only in emphasis. If instead of seeing Hegio as the father of a marriageable daughter we see him as a *leno* (or slave dealer; see 27–28, 98–101) whose control over the *pseudo-meretrix* is as unsanctioned as it is unromantic, then the interest of the plot shifts away from a correction of his humors and

---

[18] Comparable to Lyconides in the *Aulularia*.

[19] Contra Bettini (1982: 88–89), who sees the play as organized around the abstract "freedom" as the object of desire.

toward the triumph implied in the lover's successful struggles to free his beloved. In this plot type (cf. *Curculio, Poenulus*), as in the second, Philocrates plays the part of the young lover, and Tyndarus is both feminized and objectified as a heroine.[20]

Konstan's analysis of the *Asinaria* (1983: 47–56) and my own of the *Casina* have shown how a play can shift plot types partway through. But the *Captivi* presents a new model: a play that maintains three different plot types almost throughout its entire length. The subliminal presence of all three plot types allows the play to avoid stark alignments of sympathy that any individual plot type would create by designating one or two characters as heroes and others as blocking characters. Various situations or speeches can be isolated as belonging to one type or another. For example, Hegio's speech at lines 751–65, after he discovers how Tyndarus has deceived him, clearly fits the misanthrope mode (scene II.3 puts Hegio into a situation almost identical to that of the *leno* Dordalus in *Persa* IV.4). But the shifts among plot types are so numerous and so quick, and so many situations can be seen as belonging to more than one depending on the emphasis, that the borders between them are almost indistinguishable. This juggling act endows the *Captivi* with an unusual balance among the characters, a balance of both the audience's sympathy and their moral approbation. Precisely because all the major characters can lay claim to a certain nobility and liberality, it is essential that neither the schemers nor the person schemed against lose our sympathetic interest. This is exactly the opposite situation from that which prevailed in the *Persa*, where neither the trickster nor the blocking character was unambiguously sympathetic. In place of the moral ambivalence that permeated that play, the *Captivi*'s balanced sympathies suffuse the play with irony at every level.[21]

If this were a typical play of intrigues, Hegio would simply be a pompous, self-righteous father or a greedy *leno*. On the contrary, we find a remarkably nuanced depiction. Unlike the fathers in, for example, *Mostellaria* or *Pseudolus*, Hegio is only too aware of his own fallibility:

> qui cavet ne decipiatur vix cavet quom etiam cavet;
> etiam quom cavisse ratus est saepe is cautor captus est.

(255–56)

---

[20] Abel (1955: 47–48) sees the tragic element of this play made concrete in Tyndarus' assimilation to heroines such as Antigone and Iphigenia, as well as Ion.

[21] The purported seriousness of the *Captivi* (prologue, 55–58) also helps to maintain this tension by diminishing the audience's complacency as to the moral implications of this disguise trick. Usually, even when we see a father being tricked, we do not really worry that all moral standards will be overturned, because we interpret this trickery in fantasy terms; here our assurance that the ramifications of the trick will be wiped away, as they usually are, is missing.

One who takes care lest he be deceived hardly can be careful enough even while he's taking care; even when he thinks he's taken care, often is the careful man captured.

This does not, however, prevent him from crowing when he thinks he has won (III.2) or worrying about his reputation when he thinks he has lost (781–87), as do those other more usual blocking characters. Even more than this, Hegio's disdain for money sets him apart from all other blocking characters (fathers, *lenones*, and misanthropes):

> non ego omnino lucrum omne esse utile homini existumo:
> scio ego, multos iam lucrum lutulentos homines reddidit;
> est etiam ubi profecto damnum praestet facere quam lucrum.
> odi ego aurum: multa multis saepe suasit perperam.

> (325–28)

I really do not think that all profit is useful to a man: I know, indeed, profit has made many a man filthy; In fact, there are times when it is better to incur expense than to make a profit. I hate gold: often has it steered many far wrong.

When we remember the key role that the word *lucrum* played in defining Dordalus' crimes against the community, this is indeed a striking statement for a blocking character to make. In fact, in his preferring the outlay of money to the intake, he almost sounds like a trickster; but this illusion is rapidly dissipated in the final line, where it becomes clear that his preference is based on moral standards. The final way in which Hegio differentiates himself from most blocking characters has already been seen in these two quotations. His skill in stylized language (including alliteration, repetition, and *figurae etymologicae*) is one of the most important factors in overcoming the antipathetic stereotyping of older men. In the Plautine world where the ability to pun and play is tantamount to membership in an elite, Hegio's skill gives him a genial personality and even prevents our discounting him as possible hero.

The structure of the play further minimizes our desire to see Hegio bested as are other *senes*. Although his anger at Tyndarus in Act III leads him to an extreme act of punishment and to an agelastic rejection of all better feelings, we are able to perceive this reaction from his own point of view, because his noble motivations have already been developed in the first two acts. Hegio's prominence early in the play, especially his firm but genial mastery, grants us an unusual insight into him and sympathy for him.[22] We have an interior as well as exterior perspective on this blocking

---

[22] Cf. *Casina*, another play where the *senex* plays an unusual role with respect to comic conventions; here the closeness of the balance of sympathy between Hegio and the tricksters is expressed through their silent presence during the prologue and his being granted the first speaking scene (besides the segregated Ergasilus' monologue).

character. Furthermore, the subliminal presence of the misanthrope plot type helps to focus attention on Hegio as a point of interest in himself, not just as an obstacle to the young men. The ending of the play, however, does not require a change of heart from him, as this plot type alone would lead us to expect. Because of the crossing with other plot types, and because of the healing presence of Stalagmus as a scapegoat, the justification of Hegio's punishment of Tyndarus is never pursued.

Philocrates throughout the play functions as an *adulescens*, but with varying relations to the other characters. In keeping with Hegio's role as old master in the beginning of the play, Philocrates functions as his son, trying to trick him. This identification specifically relies on the presence of the slave "between" the two characters, since it is only through the "slave of two masters" theme that Philocrates can seem like a son of the household rather than an outsider. The tenuousness of Philocrates' assimilation to a son of Hegio keeps alive the underlying possibility that Hegio is playing the role of the *leno*. That is, if Philocrates were not in the position of a son toward Hegio, the scheme would be like those permanent (and implicitly justified) punishments of pimps and rivals rather than like the alwaysforgiven, always-reversible tricks against fathers. This tension is central to the moral sensitivity of the play; by keeping alive both possibilities—that the trick is a permanent one against an outsider and that it is a temporary rift in the *paterfamilias'* on-going authority—the play is able to maintain sympathy both for the schemers and for the deceived, as well as maintain suspense as to the outcome.

Both of the identities Philocrates oscillates between (rebellious son and lover) are sanctioned by the rules of comedy. Unlike Hegio, whose doubleness treads a fine line of positive and negative, Philocrates' dual characterization only affects his relation to the other characters, not his claim to the audience's sympathy. As a lover, he most closely parallels the *adulescentes* in *Rudens, Cistellaria* and *Aulularia*. Like those young men who desire marriage rather than just a meretricious tryst, Philocrates is striving to get for Tyndarus a lifelong freedom. Like the use of marriage as a dramatic resolution, the freeing of Tyndarus will carry with it the symbolism of rebirth and confidence in the future. Again, this goal secures for Philocrates a consistent orientation to morality and the audience's sympathy.

This consistency underscores the inherently justified nature of this deception scheme (like those against rivals and pimps but here even more so, since the pleasure Tyndarus and Philocrates take in the deception is downplayed). Nowhere is the propriety of his underhanded means of escaping from Hegio's power questioned, and this propriety gives us a benchmark against which to align the moral universe of this play. Philocrates' deceptiveness in freeing himself is no less noble than his steadfastness in freeing Hegio's son Philopolemus in Elis and returning for Tyndarus. In all these actions, he is bound by the code of his station in society, a code that requires honesty and faithfulness in carrying out obligations but that equally requires that one not submit oneself to the degradation of slavery. Thus Philocrates' imperative to free himself, and his right to endanger his slave in doing so, are as unambiguous as his imperative to fulfill his promises to Hegio (in ransoming his son) and Tyndarus (in manumitting him for his service).

Of the three major characters, Tyndarus' position in the three plot types requires him to combine the most antithetical elements: he must be both slave and freeborn, both the male rescuer and the female rescued, both subject and object. Beyond the importance of his kaleidoscopic persona in this play, this multiplicity also reveals some of the rules governing the distribution of character functions in the corpus as a whole. For example, the novelty of Tyndarus functioning both as actor in the deception scheme and as the object of desire, whose suitability is acknowledged in the recognition scene, makes us realize that nowhere in the corpus do women take part in deception schemes for their own benefit.[23] This is true even for women who are not in the end recognized as freeborn (see *Asinaria, Mostellaria, Pseudolus*). There is no shortage of women playing roles in deception schemes, most prominently in *Epidicus, Miles Gloriosus*, and *Persa*, but in every case these schemes are designed to free a woman other than the one doing the acting. This observation shows that Plautine comedy finds the deceptiveness and agency required for a good disguise scheme difficult to reconcile with the passivity common to all love objects in the corpus, whether *pseudo-meretrices* or genuine *meretrices*.[24]

The double identity of Tyndarus as slave and kidnapped freeborn child influences the combination of the plot types in important ways. As we have

---

[23] Except *Truculentus*, but in that play there is no question of the boy getting the girl but rather of the girl getting the money. On the segregation of "upper-class women" from disguise tricks, see now Rei (1998).

[24] This dovetails with another observation on the roles of women in the corpus: there seems to be a clear-cut division between independent *meretrices* (i.e., without a *leno*, like Erotium [*Men*], the Bacchis sisters [*Bac*], or Phronesium [*Truc*]) and *meretrices* in someone else's power. These latter are a sort of female equivalent of the *adulescentes*: attractive, but rather bland and dumb. It has been noted above (in chap. 2) that the latter type can be all sweetness since the blocking/withholding function is being performed by another character, while the independent *meretrices* must be both enticing and rebarbative for the tension of the plot to work. I would add here the speculation that the young women who are not independent are vestigial *pseudo-meretrices*, since they maintain all the attributes that would be appropriate if they were to be discovered as freeborn. This is especially true in the *Asinaria* and *Mostellaria*, where they are depicted as wholesome and truly in love with the young men. It is as if Plautus retained the characterization of a *pseudo-meretrix* but did not bother to have her recognized as freeborn in the end.

seen in the *Casina* and elsewhere, the romantic plot paradigm envisions change taking place over the course of the play, so that the end opens out onto a new life, especially symbolized in marriage. Farce, on the other hand, shapes the play so that the end brings us back to the beginning, with a vision of time as circular rather than linear. These two paradigms coincide partially, though not completely, with the dichotomy between the permanence of the overturn when the blocking character is an outsider (*leno* or rival) and the temporariness in the case of the blocking character being the *paterfamilias*. The plot types maintained simultaneously in the *Captivi* contradict each other on exactly this question of the possibility of permanent change. The two identities united in Tyndarus together embody the same contradiction. Within the illusion of the play, Tyndarus is a slave, and his trickery is expected to have either no permanent results or permanent results only for his young master. But the audience knows all along that he is really freeborn and therefore expects a "romantic" resolution, centered on the recognition of his true identity, a resolution that will permanently change the prospects of all the characters. This second expectation is not disappointed.[25] Like the marriages with which other plays close, Tyndarus' recognition by his father and his punishment of his kidnapper, the slave Stalagmus, both depend on and externalize his status as citizen.

THE THEATER OF TRUTH

One of the important dramatic effects of the *Captivi*'s decided preference for naturalism over farce is that the linear progress of the play appears almost seamless, with each scene contributing to the coherent development of the plot and themes. This in itself is not too surprising (it defines the

---

[25] Dumont (1984: 507–8) has shown how the *Captivi* makes use of the language and symbolism of marriage to express its resolution, as do the canonical romantic comedies, e.g., *Aulularia, Cistellaria,* and *Rudens.* We need not agree, however, with Dumont's belief that this similarity with romantic comedies signifies a romantic relationship between Tyndarus and Philocrates. Greek New Comedy and its Roman descendant are unified in the centrality they grant heterosexuality. Nowhere in these two genres do we see depicted the idealized presentation of male homosexuality so common in art and literature of classical Athens. In Roman comedy, male homosexuality appears only as a basis for insult (see Lilja [1982] and examples there). A further bar to Dumont's literal interpretation of the marriage motif in the *Captivi* is that the noble love between two young men that we see at the end would in fact have started as a relationship between a young man and his same-age slave, a situation almost impossible to idealize under the norms of elite male homosexuality in classical Greek society. Rather, we should see the use of marriage imagery metatheatrically as appropriating for the realm of citizen identity and masterful authority the privatized, emotional depiction of harmony implicit in marriage.

later Western dramatic ideal of the Well-Made Play), but it stands in sharp contrast to many Plautine comedies, including the three examined in the previous chapters of this study. In the analyses of the *Menaechmi, Casina*, and *Persa*, I segregated the various forces at work, dividing each play into movements to articulate the shifts between diverse aesthetic and dramatic regimes. Although the *Captivi* exhibits nothing like the grand swerves that characterize those other plays, there are reasons to look at this play, too, in terms of four movements. The most important reason is connected to the least important character: Ergasilus. The way that the *Captivi* treats Ergasilus is key to understanding the polemical position it takes up towards farce as a whole; instead of treating Ergasilus as merely a comic counterpoint to the "real" plot, my analysis will use this character as an index to this dialogic strategy shaping the play. By separating the two extended interactions between Ergasilus and Hegio into separate movements, I am seeking to call attention to this character's broader literary function. In fact, once we see that the first (Act I) and third (Act IV) movements center on patter between the *paterfamilias* and his social inferior, it also becomes clear that these movements serve by contrast to frame the second (Acts II and III) and fourth (Act V) movements, which center on intra-elite and familial bonds.

The first movement offers the necessary exposition of the plot through scenes that show Hegio as the perfect master, balancing humanity with a clear-eyed view of the world. The second movement focuses on the disguise trick Tyndarus and Philocrates use to outwit Hegio: they exchange identities, Tyndarus pretending to be the master and Philocrates pretending to be the slave. Completely taken in by this ruse, Hegio gladly sends Philocrates home to Elis, thinking that he is sending a slave to negotiate an exchange of Philocrates for this own captive son Philopolemus but in fact releasing his most valuable prisoner. Philocrates' departure leaves Tyndarus in a precarious position: he must hope that his imposture will hold up and that Philocrates will return, as promised, to ransom him. Unfortunately, there is among Hegio's captives another young man from Elis, Aristophontes, who recognizes Tyndarus and reveals his true identity. Hegio is so angry when he discovers the truth that he sends Tyndarus to the mines, virtually a death sentence for a slave. It is at this point of crisis that Ergasilus comes on stage from the port, announcing that Philocrates has just arrived from Elis, bringing with him not only Hegio's son Philopolemus but, amazingly, the very slave (Stalagmus) who kidnapped Tyndarus twenty years ago. Ergasilus' expansion of this announcement into a guessing game and Hegio's attempt to ferret out the news make up the entire third movement. The fourth and final movement delivers the expected

finale: discovery of Tyndarus' true parentage and punishment for the unrepentant Stalagmus.

Parasite and Patron, Part 1

The play opens with a parasite's autobiographical monologue, much like
that with which Peniculus opens the *Menaechmi*.[26] Like Peniculus, Ergasilus
reveals the tricks of the parasitic trade by exalting rather than by concealing
submission as the basis of his profession. But a striking difference between
the two monologues results from the varying degrees of success each parasite can claim. Peniculus is at the top of his form; as he boasts of the generosity of his patron, he also offers advice to masters on keeping their slaves,
thus further testifying to his success in joining the dining circles of the elite.
Ergasilus, on the other hand, is the picture of frustration and dejection. He
explains the taunting nickname ("Scortum") that the youth of the city have
given him, he tells of the hardship of trying to find a meal when all the
elite are at their country houses, and he laments the loss of his most generous patron, Philopolemus. The *Menaechmi* charted the course of Peniculus'
increasing alienation, as his ethic of loyalty in exchange for food lost
ground to the ethic of authority based on identity. In the *Captivi*, we are
immediately introduced to a world already inimical to the parasite's brand
of sensuality and self-interest. On the representational plane and on the
plane of dramatic conventions, Ergasilus is alienated from the community.
His monologues at I.1 and III.1 go further than merely describing his inability to crack the tough shell that encases the social life of the *kaloikagathoi*; by repeating the theme of exclusion, these monologues emphasize his
loneliness.[27]

The specific arguments and imagery of I.1 make concrete this clash between the values of the parasite and the values that will shape this play. His
introduction of himself through a scurrilous nickname is not remarkable
in itself, but the choice of nickname and his explanation of it draw attention
to his difficult situation.[28] The similarities between a *meretrix* and a parasite
are so obvious as to make this witticism distinctively witless. If the youth
of the city call him "Scortum," it is hard to believe that is it for any reason
more arcane than that he shares with the *meretrix* the habit of making a

---

[26] The resemblance is so strong that Lindsay (1900: ad loc.) posits that Plautus used Peniculus' monologue as a model when setting out to add this figure of comic relief to the Greek
play on which the *Captivi* is based.

[27] Not only is he inorganic to the plot, but he also has no position of knowledge, sympathy,
or interest with either the trick or the punishment of the tricksters.

[28] This nickname, like that of Saturio (*durus caput*, *Per* 60), calls attention to the parasite's
seemingly insatiable appetite for enduring abuse.

living through submission, including sexual submission.[29] In fact, what is ingenious here is not the *bon mot* that Ergasilus ascribes to the young men but rather his own tortuous attempt to explain it though a pun on *invocatus*.[30] The pun on *invocatus* substitutes a more palatable form of derision for parasites (that their hunger and buffoonery set them apart from the elite), clothed in the language of social niceties, for the balder acknowledgment of their degraded status as sexual objects.[31] Ergasilus' position in relation to the play as a whole is evident in the microcosm of this one joke: while he is absolutely degraded as meretricious, he refuses to see his treatment as anything other than benign jesting at his childlike appetitiveness and willingness to please.

The rest of this opening monologue conforms to this same pattern. Ergasilus uses the language commonly associated with parasites but to describe his failure rather than his success. Especially common in these parasite monologues is the animal imagery (77, 80–87; cf. *Per* 58, *St* 168–70, and the pun of Curculio's name [=weevil]), through which they emphasize both their appetites and their dependence. The parasite's usual gambit of applying aristocratic language to his lowly profession (e.g., *Per* 53–61, *St* 171–73) here takes a slightly different turn. In keeping with Ergasilus' dire straits, and with his name, which draws on a Greek root to form something like "Working Boy," the emphasis is on the "hard work" of parasitism (esp. 78–79, 88–90).[32] The colossus of the vaunting parasite that we have seen in other plays is here reduced to a shadow of his former glory.[33]

Continuing the parallels with the opening scenes of the *Menaechmi*, scene I.2 introduces the master of the household in relation to two dependents. However, the contrast with Epidamnian Menaechmus' heated upbraiding of his wife and gullible acceptance of his parasite's flattery is remarkable. Hegio presents himself as both firm and humane, a master who understands his dependents' point of view but will not let them take advantage of him. With both the Lorarius and Ergasilus, Hegio is witty and engaged but singularly resistant to the charms that are so effective for slaves

[29] See Woytek's (1982: ad loc.) interpretation of *Per* 649, for evidence of sexual submission by parasites to their patrons.

[30] Note at lines 71–72 that he admits to the knowledge that he is giving the nickname a more positive interpretation than the young men themselves would give.

[31] The pun has the same result for *meretrices*: it emphasizes their status as objects of love, or at least lust, over their status as paid servants.

[32] Cf. Peniculus' reversal of the *otium/negotium* concept (*Men* 451–54): he complains that public business should be transacted by men of leisure (i.e., those with money), because busy people like himself have dinner invitations to find.

[33] Lowe (1989a) argues that the depiction of parasites centered on extravagant descriptions of food is derived from Atellan farce, while the depiction centered on the parasite's "flattery, his wit, and his willingness to endure uncomplainingly every kind of deprivation, ill-treatment, abuse, ridicule and humiliation" is specific to Greek New Comedy and Terence.

and parasites in other plays. Hegio further separates himself from other masters in his acknowledgment of the possibility of slaves running away and his iron will to prevent such a destruction of his authority. His opening speech epitomizes his humane yet unshakable mastery. He asks the Lorarius to replace the captives' heavy shackles with lighter ones and to allow them the freedom to walk around, but he immediately follows this with the opinion that slaves cannot be trusted not to run away:

> liber captivos avi' ferae consimilis est:
> semel fugiendi si data est occasio,
> satis est, numquam postilla possis prendere.
>
> (116–18)

A free captive is like a wild bird:[34] if ever the opportunity for escape is given, that's it, you'll never be able to catch him again.

The degree of understanding that Hegio exhibits concerning the opposed interests of masters and slaves and his unapologetic protection of his own interests make him uniquely challenging as a blocking character. Most blocking characters fall prey to their opponents precisely by underestimating the strength of the opposition and their own vulnerability to the temptation of riches or a good reputation. They understand neither their slaves nor themselves. Hegio announces in his very first words that he is free from both of these weaknesses.[35]

The figure of the Lorarius is surprising at first glance.[36] He is in fact the only clear example in this play of the type of the good slave. What should surprise us about him is that he disappears after the next scene and has no part in the rest of the play. For example, in the *Menaechmi* Messenio's loyalty and frankness with his master provided a necessary and significant counterpoint to the greed of the other dependent characters. By analogy, we might expect that the Lorarius' bold expression of his desire for free-

---

[34] There is some controversy as to whether to interpret *liber captivos* to mean "a free man taken prisoner" or "a captive who is allowed some liberty." We need not resolve the ambiguity but rather acknowledge that it is precisely the ambiguous nature of the word *liber* that is used as a pivot around which the categories of slaves are organized. Leach (1969b: 282) follows the former interpretation, incidentally corroborating my argument that a distinction is maintained between slaves by nature and slaves by condition (paraphrasing Hegio's advice to keep an eye on them: "As he explains to his *lorarius*, these captives are not ordinary slaves who may bask in the security of good-keeping, but free men that cannot be contented in servitude.").

[35] See the end of this chapter for a comparison of Hegio's presentation in these scenes with that of Daemones in the *Rud*.

[36] Usually characters of this name are merely silent bouncers used for stage business; cf. *Men* V.7, *Rud* III.5, and below *Cap* 657–59. See Lowe (1991: 31), and the definition of *lorarius* in Aulus Gellius 10.3.19.

dom, coupled with his obedience, would make him a perfect foil for the two young men who pretend to be honorable while effecting their escape. Instead, the Lorarius is brought on stage here to establish the fullness and stability of Hegio's mastery (cf. Syracusan Menaechmus) and in scene II.1 to establish by contrast the obsession with honor that guides the actions of Tyndarus and Philocrates.

When the Lorarius is dismissed to carry out his orders and Ergasilus gets Hegio's attention, the more humane side of the *senex* emerges, but his firm grasp on his household continues. This scene shows that, by taking the parasite's ingratiating expressions of sympathy at face value, Hegio is able to prevent Ergasilus' flattery from having the desired effect. When Ergasilus bewails the loss of Philopolemus, we know from his monologue that it is the loss of a meal ticket that awakens his tearful grief, not the young man's predicament in itself (see 103). Hegio resolutely interprets this outpouring as genuine (even elevating Ergasilus to the status of an *amicus* rather than *cliens*, 141, 151). But this interpretation does not have the effect expected (by Ergasilus and by the audience) of making Hegio more vulnerable to sponging. On the contrary, precisely because Hegio sees (or pretends to see?) Ergasilus as an equal rather than a dependent, he refuses to play the part of a patron.[37] Rather than exalt himself and his riches by extolling the sumptuousness of the banquet to be put before his parasite, Hegio offers a simple, rustic meal clearly designed for nutritive, not festive, purposes.

The strength of Hegio's mastery lies in its complexity. Unlike many other Plautine characters, especially *senes*, he seems capable of an empathetic understanding of others' points of view and attitudes, without slipping into undignified fooling. This ability to assimilate to other characters without losing his own identity shines through in this scene with Hegio's quick verbal wit. With the Lorarius he is able to voice his determination to prevent slave escapes in jingling puns and extended metaphors (note the multiple zeugma of *do* in 121–22 [a joint effort between the Lorarius and Hegio] and the extension of the wild-bird simile in 124). The remarkable exhibition of verbal gymnastics in which he enumerates the legions of Ergasilus' "army of eating" (*edendi exercitus*, 160–64) is even more virtuoso.[38] The real virtuosity, however, lies not in his glib loquacity, but in the fact

---

[37] Segal (1987: 197) sees in this scene an example of role reversal, with Ergasilus mourning the loss of Philopolemus, and Hegio telling him to "cheer up."

[38] Fraenkel (1922: 111 = 1960: 105) on 152–66, esp. the Roman elements of military imagery, *provincia*, personification, Italian geographical names, and the contrast between *imperator* and *privatus*. The repetition between 152 and 167 marks the beginning and end of Plautine insertion. On this speech and this scene as an example of a "reverse comic foil" (i.e., a person of high status making a joke, using a person of low status as a straight-man), see Hough (1942). See also the play on *fundum* and *profundum* at 181–82.

that he uses this glib loquacity not to promise a lavish banquet to a parasite but to refuse it. Other *senes* show verbal skills at times, and some use a language even closer to that of clever slaves. But Hegio is unique in his ability to make use of this style to express authority.

Deceit without Dishonor

Act II introduces into this rather unusual play the normal elements we expect in Plautine comedy: a gullible *senex*, a young man eager to trick him, and a clever, theatrical slave. The circumstances depicted in Act I, however, and the specific characterizations of these three roles bring these scenes into the realm of irony rather than farce. The irony operates at three levels. First, within the illusion of the play, Tyndarus and Philocrates enjoy the kind of smug superiority common to all tricksters in the corpus. Second, the audience recognizes the irony of Tyndarus' pretense of social nobility echoing his true status. And, last, because of the strongly defined structures of the genre, this deception scheme ironically makes use of the forms of playful rebellion for serious purposes, that is, liberating a freeborn person from slavery.

The central themes of honor in slavery and the difference between slaves by nature and slaves by condition shape scene II.1, in which we first encounter Philocrates and Tyndarus.[39] First in the contrast between the Lorarius and these young men and then in the conversation between them, the dialogue at every point seeks to distance them from other fictive slaves, both obedient and rebellious.[40] The Lorarius' advice superficially adheres to an acceptable moral philosophy of taking one's fate with equanimity. But as he continues, it becomes clear that he is arguing not for Stoic perseverance but for an amoral flexibility. In opposition to a fixed identity based on internal emotional and mental states, he argues for accepting what circumstances may make of one. If circumstances have made you a slave, don't try to rebel (195–99); if the master does something *indigna*, it's easier to consider it *digna* than to fight it (200); if the master is stupid enough to put you in a situation where escape is easy, escape (209). Even though his words are cloaked in the language of piety (*si di inmortales id voluerunt*, "if the immortal gods have willed it," 195) and duty (*ei vos morigerari mos bonust*, "it's best to adapt yourself to it," 198), his argument is really that of the path of least resistance.[41]

---

[39] There is a question of whether the two captives, who were visible behind the Prologus at the beginning of the play (1–2), remain on stage during the first act. No solution is entirely without its problems; for an overview of the question, see Lowe (1991).

[40] Also note that throughout this act, both Tyndarus and Philocrates are implicitly treated as slaves by condition; see esp. 197 (*domi fuistis, credo, liberi*), 261–62.

[41] Ketterer (1986a: 114) observes the difference between the Lorarius' "calm and rather flippant" attitude towards slavery and that of the two young men: "To them it is a real dis-

The Lorarius' moral perspective here highlights the unbending honor that will motivate Philocrates and Tyndarus and shows how different they are from comic good slaves as well as from clever slaves. The conversation that begins scene II.1 reveals the weaknesses in the moral code even of good slaves elsewhere in the corpus. Like Messenio (*Menaechmi*), the slave of Lyconides (*Aulularia*), Phaniscus (*Mostellaria*), and others, the Lorarius obeys his master just because it is easier and more likely to result in his manumission. This observation on the flaccid and timorous loyalty of good slaves, of course, also explains the contempt in which energetic clever slaves hold them and explains the heroism of the latter. The actions of Philocrates and Tyndarus are both more rebellious than those of good slaves and more honorable than those of clever slaves. The usual good slaves guard their masters' interests to avoid punishment;[42] Tyndarus does it with a certainty that it will bring him punishment. Thus these two freeborn young men, but especially Tyndarus, combine the energy and enterprise of clever slaves with the virtuousness of good slaves, transcending—and discrediting—both comic stereotypes.

At 206–6a, Tyndarus, with a sense of offended dignity, replies to the Lorarius' protection of his master's interest by claiming, "We know what our duty is, if he should let us be unbound" (*scimu' nos / nostrum officium quod est, si solutos sinat*). On the face of it, he is speaking honorably: that it is beneath him to be sneaky. But in light of the disguise scheme already underway, *officium* here could just as well refer to Philocrates' duty as a free man to escape the degradation of slavery, and Tyndarus' duty as his slave to help him. This is the essential problem that the honorable slave presents for his keepers: will his sense of honor require his obedience or his rebellion?[43] It is also through this insistence on escaping from Hegio's mastery that Tyndarus and Philocrates most run the risk of resembling the negative stereotype of untrustworthy slaves.

The final section of this conversation introduces a new theme, as Tyndarus reminds Philocrates of the debt Philocrates will owe him (231–36), since he is risking his life to ensure his master's escape. This reminder is phrased in language that resonates with the great concern expressed

---

grace." Lowe (1991: 37–38) dismisses any such meaning of the Lorarius' unusual speaking role and attributes it instead to Plautus' desire to bolster the element of "slave punishment and thug comedy in general," of which the Lorarius is a reliable marker. Thalmann (1996: 123–24) remarks on the Lorarius' "demystified view of slavery."

[42] As the Lorarius does at 203–5, in insisting that the master's interest in keeping his slaves from running away is more important than the slaves' shame at being bound.

[43] Ketterer (1986a: 115) notes that the chains represent the dishonor of slavery for the free, but "at the same time there is the underlying irony that flight is exactly what they have in mind, and if they fool Hegio later, they do not fool a fellow slave who understands their intention exactly."

throughout the play that morality remain stable in all circumstances. Philocrates' answer to Tyndarus' plea continues to develop the paradox of his
position. He assures Tyndarus that he understands and values the latter's
willingness to risk his life, and he also beseeches him to remember and play
his part well. The doubleness of his response—gratitude and yet still a
request—parallels the doubleness of his identity. He makes use both of
his new status as Tyndarus' *conservus* (241–44) and of his former status as
Tyndarus' master (245, 247) to gain his requested assurance of Tyndarus'
committment to his plan for escape. This is a rare glimpse of Philocrates'
position towards his slave; it reminds us that when a slave has two masters,
both are vulnerable to his bifurcated loyalties. Like the master who does
not know whether to maintain his slaves' loyalty by treating them like objects or like people, Philocrates is uncertain as to whether to rely on Tyndarus' humanity to a fellow slave or his obedience to his master.

The unexpected juxtaposition in Hegio of the verbal dexterity of the
clever slave and the assured authority of the ideal master continues into his
questioning of the captives. When he returns to the stage at the beginning
of scene II.2, he expresses his caution by playfully repeating forms of the
verb *caveo* ("to be wary," 255–56; quoted above pp. 176–77). Again, as in
scene I.2, his use of such patterned language to express authority and rea-
sonableness sets him apart from other blocking characters. In fact in these
lines, he shows that he understands that blocking characters are usually
trapped precisely by their complacency, and he acknowledges that no caution can absolutely protect one. The dramatic problem in this and the next
scene is how to show Philocrates and Tyndarus effective in their trickery
without losing either their claim to a naturalistic virtue (i.e., not in the
topsy-turvy terms in which slaves and young men usually claim virtue) or
Hegio's claim to respect. In other plays where a positive morality is preserved, Tyche does the trickery, thus obviating the need for any human
impulse to deceive. Here it is accomplished in two ways. First, the assistance of Tyche is called upon not to effect the actual trick but to provide
an ironic meaning to Tyndarus' words. Because the audience knows from
the prologue that Tyndarus is in fact freeborn and that his father desires
his ransom from slavery, in the assertions he makes in order to play the part
of Philocrates, his deceptiveness is layered over with irony.[44] For example:

> [sc. fortuna] me qui liber fueram servom fecit, e summo infumum; . . .
>
> (305)

> [chance] made me, once a free man, a slave, changing me from the highest
> estate to the lowest . . .

---

[44] Abel (1955: 48–49), Leach (1969b: 271); see also 299.

>   tam ego fui ante liber quom gnatus tuos, . . .
>
>   (310)
>
> I was previously as free as your own son was . . .

>   quam tu filium tuom tam pater me meu' desiderat.
>
>   (316)
>
> As much as you long for your son does my father long for me.

>   ego patri meo esse fateor summas divitias domi
>   meque summo genere gnatum.
>
>   (318–19)
>
> I admit that my father is very wealthy and that I was born a gentleman.

The usual opprobrium that a realistic morality would attach to tricksters is here deflected by the concentration on the problem of *agnoia* (lack of knowledge) and on the emotional desires so displaced.

The second way that the deception is distanced from the malice of other comic deceptions is by making each of the three major characters in scenes II.2 and II.3 point to the gap between his stock character and the attributes of his individual character and situation.[45] For Hegio, the difference between himself and other blocking characters lies in the degree of interiority he is granted. It is odd that Philocrates and Tyndarus' deception retains the normal emphasis on money as a motivation for the blocking character, even though we know that Hegio's real motive has nothing to do with money and everything to do with Philocrates' identity as elite. Hegio's questioning on finances in this scene continues the danger in which he has already placed himself by taking on the business of dealing in slaves (see 27–28, 98–101; see also 324–28). His ability to maintain his difference from other money-hungry blocking characters depends on his ability to make his concern with money and riches seem motivated by his underlying desire to free his son.

Philocrates and Tyndarus have a more complex relationship to comic convention than does Hegio. They are both at the crossing point between *adulescens* and *servus*, and the juxtaposition of realistic and fictional standards for their behavior adds further complexity.[46] In playing at being a

---

[45] Leach's (1969b) interpretation of the whole play is that its ironies are based on each side taking the other for its stereotype and not acknowledging how it may be divergent, e.g., Tyndarus and Philocrates treat Hegio like a normal money-hungry *senex* and thus miss the opportunity to gain their freedom honestly by simply being exchanged for Hegio's son. In this interpretation, Ergasilus functions as an external index to the ironies of the central plot.

[46] This complexity perhaps explains why, as Hough (1942: 117) notes with surprise, Plautus does not make much use of the "reverse comic foil" motif in this scene, which would seem to be the perfect place for it.

slave, Philocrates chooses the part of a clever (fictive) slave, that is, a slave who is in complete control of the situation.[47] But unlike clever slaves in other plays, his authority is not a momentary breach of the usual hierarchy but is intended as an instrument in his permanent escape from slavery. Thus he shares with Syracusan Menaechmus and with Lysidamus in the *Casina* a strategy that appropriates farcical forms for goals that are valued in the naturalistic realm. Tyndarus, on the other hand, reverses this relationship between farcical and naturalistic worldviews: within the frame of a deception trick worthy of Pseudolus, he achieves his ends through his nobility and moral strength. This nobility is evinced in his impersonation of a freeborn young man, as we see here in II.2 and II.3, and even more so in his moral argumentation when the trick is up in the third act. Tyndarus' sacrifice of himself for his master is a strange permutation of the clever slave's inability to trick for his own advantage. Tyndarus' actions show that slave's concentration on the success of the trick itself as his only compensation could be the result of high-minded selflessness rather than of short-sighted playfulness. It is precisely the extreme closeness of these two different rejections of concrete goals, and the danger that each might be taken for the other, that creates the vibrant moral tension surrounding slave trickery in the corpus.

The third act begins with an unusual string of three monologues (though only the first is performed by a character alone on stage). That each of these characters chooses to confide in the audience emphasizes the disjunction in their relationships to each other.[48] It is also striking evidence of the high degree of interiority granted to all the characters in this play, in contrast to the many Plautine characters whom we see only from the outside. Ergasilus expands on the woes he describes in his first scene by offering an elaborate scenario of the haughtiness with which the young men brush off his services. Hegio's monologue is one of triumph. His experience with his fellow citizens is exactly the opposite of Ergasilus'; they surround him and detain him with their congratulations on the impending return of his son. While Tyndarus' speech is superficially similar to those of other clever slaves whose tricks are about to fail, it also introduces themes that prepare for his distinctively moral defense of his trickery later in this act (III.5).

In Ergasilus' first monologue (I.1), we got the impression that the difficulty of finding a meal lay merely in the absence of his potential patrons.

---

[47] In this scene, while Philocrates is talking to Hegio, Tyndarus has three asides (266–69, 274–76, 284) that resemble those of "stage-managing" clever slaves. Fraenkel (1922: 74, 213–14 = 1960: 69, 204–5) finds these asides to be distinctively Plautine, both because of the imagery (cf. *Bac* 1125–28, *Mil* 768, *Per* 829) and because of the unusual length of the first one.

[48] Leach may not observe this for these particular speeches, but it is in keeping with her general sense of the play and the characters.

Here, the difficulty is made more specific and more hostile in a richly described scene of elite young men revolting against the very principles on which Ergasilus' trade depends. The point of parasitism in comedy is an exchange of the patron's material wealth for the parasite's flattery, jokes, and work as a go-between. In a world undermined by war, the young men of the city have decided that they do not need flattery or jokes (470–73) and that they can do their own shopping and negotiating with *lenones* (474–76). The most revealing moment of this monologue is the one in which Ergasilus narrates a scene of one-sided conversation, a scene that mirrors his own segregation to unanswered monologues within the play:

> "salvete" inquam. "quo imus una?" inquam: [ad prandium] atque illi tacent.
> "quis ait 'hoc' aut quis profitetur?" inquam. quasi muti silent,
> neque me rident. "ubi cenamus?" inquam. atque illi abnuont.
>
> (479–81)

> "Hi," I say. "Where are we going?" I say; and they are silent. "Who says 'my place' or volunteers to host?" I say. They keep mum, as if they've all gone dumb, and they don't even smile at me. "Where are we eating?" I say. And they just shake their heads.

Ergasilus is singularly unsuccessful and powerless (as Peniculus is at the end of his play). His response to this situation is a gloss on the figure of the parasite elsewhere in the corpus. Like other parasites, Ergasilus seeks to use the system of civic values to his own advantage.[49] But Ergasilus' legislative proposal that the law protect the "rights" of parasites to a good meal is unusually bald and therefore unlikely to succeed. Where Saturio's *Persa* was clothed in the appearance of concern for civic values, Ergasilus' proposal lays bare its self-interest and its difference from the operative moral system.[50] Further, his reaction expands the original identification of his services as work, an identification expressed in his name as well. Like his first monologue, this one makes use of all the conventional attributes of the parasite but in a context of frustration and defeat rather than arrogant success.

Even a superficial glance at the Plautine corpus is enough to tell us that characters who celebrate their success before the end of the play are being groomed for failure.[51] Hegio's monologue at III.2 recalls, among others, that of Dordalus (*Per* 470–79) in which he congratulates himself for having done the city a favor and narrates his conversion to trust. This similarity is further evidence that Hegio is here marked out as the blocking character.

[49] Cf. Peniculus' advice to masters and his suggestions for reforming the *contio* (*Men* I.1, III.1), Saturio's legislative proposal (*Per* I.2).

[50] Fraenkel (1922: 246 = 1960: 237) on Ergasilus' utopian law.

[51] Cf. *Cas* II.3, *Cur* 371–83, *Epid* 410–24, *Mil* 1374–77.

In fact, even though it seems to show him in a positive light, the consistency with which speeches like this are preludes to disaster for the speaker takes Hegio dangerously close to an assimilation with money-hungry *lenones* and foolish *senes*. If it were not for the opening scenes, which showed him from his own point of view, this monologue and the following scenes in which Tyndarus' deception is exposed would make him seem like every other angry old man and would undermine the moral foundation of the play.

Tyndarus' monologue is a tour de force of the kind of sound play and figures of speech that make clever slaves' speech so appealing.[52] However, in comparison to other similar speeches (e.g., *Epid* 81–103, *Mos* 348–62, *Ps* 394–414, 574–93), there is a surprising emphasis on the lack of cover, the lack of artifice, the lack of disguise left to him (esp. 520–25).[53] In other slaves' monologues, this would fit with the general tendency to magnify the obstacles they must overcome: the more dire the situation, the greater the heroism. In similar passages, the emphasis is either on the dangers the slave anticipates (especially the gory details of his own physical punishment; see *Epidicus*, *Mostellaria*) or on his confidence in being able to come up with a successful scheme despite the gloomy prospects (*Pseudolus*). Tyndarus' monologue does neither of these things but focuses rather on the ineffectiveness of all possible tricks and the lack of cover for his deeds:

> nec subdolis mendaciis mihi usquam mantellum est meis,
> nec sycophantiis nec fucis ullum mantellum obviam est,
> neque deprecatio perfidiis meis nec malefactis fuga est,
> nec confidentiae usquam hospitium est nec devorticulum dolis.
>
> (520–23)

Nowhere now is there any cover for my tricky lies, nor can I find any cover for my pretenses and disguises, nor can I explain away my deceptions or escape my misdeeds, nor is there any safe hiding place for my brash behavior, nor any asylum for my tricks.

If these words were spoken by Pseudolus or Tranio, we probably would not give them another thought. But in the context already fully established in this play, a context that forcefully presents the possibility of a theater of truth rather than of falsehood, we must hear these words with a different tone. At the level of the deception within the play, in which Tyndarus seeks

---

[52] E.g., the personification of *spes*, *opes*, and *auxilia* (517), the alliteration of *s* throughout lines 517–18. Pasquali's (1927) argument indirectly supports my interpretation. He argues that through Plautine expansion, not contamination, an originally noble and morally serious speech was riddled (esp. at 522, 523) with expressions more suitable to a "servo briccone." Petrone (1983: 59) argues that this monologue has not been subjected to parody or trivialization; its tragic tone is preserved even though it is out of place in this context.

[53] Leach (1969b: 280) sees the difference between Tyndarus and other schemers as the former's unusual ineptitude at scheming.

less to lie than to tell misleading truths, and at the level of irony in which the audience realizes how truthful Tyndarus' impersonation of a freeborn young man is, the power of truth far outstrips the power of falsehood. Just as Tyndarus is using the form of a sneaky deception to achieve a noble purpose, he is reordering the relationship between fantasy and reality that shapes the comic outlook. In the *Captivi*, we are asked to applaud the stability and consistency of essential truths rather than the ephemeral brilliance of a series of shifting appearances.

The clash between Tyndarus and his fellow Elean prisoner Aristophontes functions as the dénouement of the inner play, when Aristophontes reveals to Hegio the true identities of the two captives. This scene crystallizes several of the important themes of the play: the difference between slaves by nature and slaves by condition, the use of clever trickery for moralizing purposes, and the integration of slave trickery into the moral standards of everyday life, rather than a fantasy world.[54] The first of these themes is clear in the rhetorical strategy of Tyndarus. He tries to counter Aristophontes' claim that he is a slave by understanding him to be stating the obvious: of course, he is a slave to Hegio, having been captured in war (574–76, 591, 627). Tyndarus tries to erase Aristophontes' knowledge of his identity by collapsing the categories of a slave by nature and a slave by condition:

<HEG> nam ille quidem, quem tu hunc memoras esse, hodie hinc abiit Alidem
ad patrem huiius. AR. quem patrem, qui servos est? TY. et tu quidem
servos et liber fuisti, et ego me confido fore. . . .[55]

(573–75)

<HEG> For that man [Tyndarus], whom you claim this man is, left here today to go to this man's [Philocrates'] father at Elis. AR: What father can he have, being a slave? TY: You too have been both a slave and a free man, as I trust I will be.

Aristophontes has such a hard time making his point because all three characters assume that being a war captive is different from "really" being a slave. This implicit assumption is in tension with Aristophontes' explicit statement that their common experience of slavery binds him to Tyndarus (543–44). In the same way that in scene II.1 Philocrates made a claim to

---

[54] Konstan (1983: 58) notes that this scene functions as a "recognition scene" at the level of the characters' knowledge within the play, thus implicitly underscoring the gap between the characters' knowledge and that of the audience, for whom only the last scene offers real recognition.

[55] See also lines 591, 627, 629 and Aristophontes' resistance to this collapsing of categories at lines 577, 580. (At line 626, Aristophontes swears on pain of losing his freedom—as if he hasn't already!)

Tyndarus' loyalty based both on their common servitude and on his former mastery, here Aristophontes asserts his equality in slavery with Tyndarus and yet also insists on the difference between himself and the "real" slave he believes Tyndarus to be.[56]

These scenes continue the pattern we have observed in previous scenes, by using the forms associated with amoral or antimoral trickery for morally justified ends. In particular, the aggressive defense of his actions that Tyndarus gives in scene III.5 actually shares language with Pseudolus (cf. *Ps* 460–61).

> TY: decet innocentem servolum atque innoxium
> confidentem esse, suom apud erum potissumum.[57]
>
>   (665–66)

> TY: An innocent and harmless little slave ought to have faith in himself, especially before his own master.

Unlike Pseudolus, whose defense rests on an utter disregard for propriety and morality, Tyndarus is arguing for a higher morality that compels his obedience to Philocrates rather than to Hegio. Through line 680, he sounds like the cheekiest of slaves, haughtily challenging Hegio to punish him for his obvious misdeeds. The joke of this scene, however, is that, where other tricksters challenge their masters out of disrespect, Tyndarus' challenge is rooted in an excess of respect for his former master. At line 682, the tone of Tyndarus' defense changes abruptly to one of serious ethical debate, in which he claims that the horrors of death count for little against the horror of having shirked his responsibility to Philocrates. The strong resemblance between this scene and others in the corpus where a slave defies his master to punish him for his trickery deepens the cruel irony that, unlike those other slaves who are truly acting out of disobedience and disrespect, Tyndarus will indeed suffer the consequences of his scheming.[58]

Third, this scene shows how Tyndarus places his clever trickery in a context of real, not farcical, morality. In other plays tricksters who are not slaves try to wiggle out of difficult situations by pretending the people accusing them are crazy (Mercury in *Amphitruo* I.1, Syracusan Menaechmus in *Menaechmi* IV.2 and V.2, and the *senex amator* in *Mercator* IV.4).[59]

---

[56] Leach (1969b: 272): "To Aristophontes, all slaves are capable of unscrupulous deception; it is outrageous for any slave to pose as free." Even Leach here writes of Aristophontes as if he, too, were not a slave.

[57] See in the previous chapter the comments on the double-edged use of *confidentia*. Cf. also Chrysalus' language in the *Bacchides*, where seeming to get caught is part of his trick.

[58] Ketterer (1986a: 117) and Segal (1987: 155) observe that this is the only instance in the corpus of a clever slave actually being punished.

[59] Fraenkel (1922: 77–78 = 1960: 72–73) compares this mad scene to that in the *Menaechmi* and notes that the situation that is real in the *Menaechmi* (mistaken identities) is precisely

Slave tricksters, on the other hand, when caught, boldly admit to all their wrongdoings.[60] Tyndarus does both; first he tries to discredit Aristophontes' testimony, then he boldly owns up to his deeds. As he has done for other elements in the repertoire of the clever slave, Tyndarus reverses the moral orientation of this boldness. As noted above, his arrogance rests on his fundamental belief that he has done the right thing. His first reaction, though, helps to preserve the naturalism of the play and the moralism of its viewpoint. In the plays that are based on the fantasy of a slave's authority, the difference between the points of view of master and slave does not need to be explained away as one person having a skewed perception of the situation; the difference in perception does not matter, because the slave is immune to punishment anyway. Here in the *Captivi*, the realistic morality links up with a naturalistic worldview in which actions have consequences, and slaves cannot merely intimidate their masters.

Parasite and Patron, Part 2

Act IV is completely taken up with an extended version of the running-slave scene. Ergasilus first exults to himself that the news of Philopolemus' homecoming that he bears will bring him peace and plenty forever, then he extorts from Hegio the kind of fooling indulgence that he has wanted all along, in exchange for his promise of good news. Although this scene is in many ways an apex for Ergasilus, a satisfaction of the desires that have been frustrated so far, it also completes his demeaning segregation to the margins of this world. The satisfaction that Ergasilus is granted here requires an alienation both from his proper attributes as parasite and from the attributes of a clever slave, the other comic hero whom he might seem to emulate. Further, as Leach has observed (1969b: 292), his satisfaction is asocial, animalistic, and lacking in the festivity that should mark a comic banquet.

Ergasilus' prayer that opens this act is a good indicator of his assimilation to the comic paradigm and of the differences with which that paradigm is used here. Clearly this prayer fits the type of prayers of thanksgiving, usually given by clever slaves after they have succeeded in their schemes (cf. *Per* II.3, V.1, *Ps* 905–7).[61] But immediately we are struck with the difference here: Ergasilus is rejoicing not over his own success at scheming but at the twist of luck that has put him in possession of news useful to Hegio. Once

---

what is faked here. He further supposes that the mythological references in both mad scenes are distinctively Plautine.

[60] E.g., *Bac* IV.6, *Epid* V.2, *Mos* V.1, *Per* V.2, *Ps* V.2.

[61] On the language and stylization of this prayer, see Danese (1985: 86–88), Fraenkel (1922: 185–86, 247–48 = 1960: 175–76, 237–38). Fraenkel explicitly states that these prayers are usually associated with the success of schemes and compares *Per* 251–56, 753–62.

again, as we have seen as so many points in this play, Tyche plays the role
that is designated for human cleverness (either that of the clever slave or
that of the poet himself) in other plays. Ergasilus' celebratory pleasure is
misplaced in yet another way, in reference to the comic paradigm: rather
than rejoicing over having gotten the better of his opponents, he is glad at
the prospect of being accepted among them. He further distances himself
from clever slaves because his reward of a meal comes not from the cynical
cleverness of wheedling it out of his patrons but from his willingness to
assimilate himself to their interests and to take pleasure in the master's
pleasure.[62]

When we look more closely at the language of this prayer, we see further
evidence of a shift away from the perspective of the triumphant clever slave.
Ergasilus conflates the realistic and farcical world views by seeming to celebrate his good fortune and independence (*nec quoiquam homini supplicare
nunc certum est mihi; / nam vel prodesse amico possum vel inimicum perdere*,
"now I have decided not to supplicate anyone, for I am capable of benefit-
ting a friend or ruining an enemy," 772–73), but he openly acknowledges
that this "independence" consists of a lifelong meal ticket at Hegio's house
and requires that he transform himself into the likeness of a slave (778–
80).[63] His rejoicing is yet another example of Ergasilus' failure to fit with
the prevailing context throughout the play: his joy is in being an insider,
an heir (775), a sharer in the household, but he fails to see that the role
designated for him in the household is a demeaning one.

At lines 778–79, Ergasilus explicitly says that his performance in the
following scene will be that of the comic slave (*ut comici servi solent*). The
scene that follows treads a thin line between two scene types, the running-
slave scene, and the scene of a clever slave milking every bit of his master's
anxiety before revealing that all their problems are solved.[64] In fact, these
two types of scenes are related and differ only in the degree of malice or
independence attributed to the slave. This quality can be measured both
by the explicitness with which the slave admits that he is holding out only
to torture his master (*Asinaria* III.3 is a high point in this respect) and by
our judgment of how clever the slave is (the nonentity slave at *Mercator*,
lines 111–19, as low point). Our subjective perception of these qualities

---

[62] This is always inherently ambiguous for parasites. Is their getting a meal from their
patrons a victory for their astuteness or a defeat in their dependency?

[63] The mixture of the naturalistic and farcical is echoed at a smaller level in the list of
things he gives thanks for. He mentions things that have value in the naturalistic worldview
(*laudem, lucrum, gaudium*) alongside those that are meaningful only in terms of comic revelry
(*ludum, iocum, festivitatem*, etc.). Ketterer (1986a: 117) notes the irony of Ergasilus' use of the
imagery of freedom for his dependency.

[64] For running-slave scene, cf. *Mer* 111–19, *St* 274–87, etc. For second scene type, cf. *As*
III.3, *Cas* III.6.

makes the difference between a slave who cruelly toys with his master and a slave who just too stupid to get the message out without being frazzled. A good example of the double perspective inherent in these monologues is that the clever Pardalisca in the *Casina* appropriates the appearance of a running slave when she wants her master to believe that she is warning him for his own good (*Cas* III.5).[65]

It is within these boundaries that Ergasilus' development of the running-slave monologue takes place. These limitations do not completely strip Ergasilus of the comic authority he seeks through this transformation (his power over Hegio is comparable to that of the greatest slave-master reversals; see 857) but rather add an ambiguity as to whether this authority is to be taken at face value or winked at from the patronizing perspective of the master. In other comedies that are more univocally oriented towards a farcical perspective—the perspective that values food, rebellion, and hyperbole—Ergasilus' performance would be unquestionably heroic. But in the presence of the strongly drawn morality of the *Captivi*, this judgment is less certain. Hegio's responses throughout this scene underscore the ambiguity of Ergasilus' authority. By consistently equating Ergasilus' authoritative voice with his full stomach, and by reminding the audience that this satiety obviously came at someone else's expense, Hegio keeps Ergasilus in the place of a childlike dependent (see 805–6, 811–12, 837).

Hegio's performance in this scene reprises that of his earlier encounter with the parasite (I.2). Although he is somewhat less indulgent of Ergasilus' jokes, he still combines a willingness to listen to farcical fooling with a firm control over his own resources. He jokes along with Ergasilus but, as in the earlier scene, also reminds him that there will be no elaborate feasting in exchange for this gaiety (852–55). His difference from other open-handed patrons is maintained even when he does agree to provide Ergasilus with the meal of his dreams (894–97). This provision is markedly different from the rewards parasites receive elsewhere, because it is in response to the good news rather than in exchange for flattery or other services and because it consists of handing over the keys to the larder rather than inviting Ergasilus to join in a communal meal. This authoritative treatment establishes that Ergasilus is considered to be a dependent of the household not a free "worker" paid for services rendered. Leach's (1969b: 292) description of this segregation cannot be improved upon: "In his voracity, Ergasilus is reduced to the purely animalistic aspect of his role. Our last image of him, seen through the eyes of Hegio's kitchen boy, is as a dangerous, ravening wolf. Laughable as it may be, there is an unsettling quality

---

[65] The scene at *Cur* II.3 is similar to Ergasilus' in its ambiguity; we know that Curculio wants to help the young man, but it is also clear that he wants to assure himself of the reward before he spills the news.

in this picture of solitary gratification that extends to the remainder of the play." In pushing Ergasilus and his bodily hunger to the margins, the *Captivi* has irrevocably committed itself to a world free of both his faults and his virtues.

The most striking aspect of the fourth act is that it is utterly unnecessary. Certainly if we understand the *Captivi* to have as its central and identifying theme the deep moral issues surrounding the essence of character, this entire act is dispensable and even mars the unity of the play. To describe it as "comic relief" merely begs the question: why would the one of the central events of the play be announced in a throwaway scene? Nor can it have functioned merely as a "covering scene" to produce a more realistic temporal structure. No attempted verisimilitude would be satisfied to send Philocrates to Elis, have him free Philopolemus, find Stalagmus, and return in the space of less than 450 lines. It is only when we recognize the full scope of the *Captivi*'s agenda that the expansiveness of this act, and the very presence of Ergasilus as a character at all, makes sense. In order for the *Captivi* to place itself in the corpus, it must not only make a case for meaningful, naturalistic, moral comedy. It must also implicitly discredit the form of comedy against which it is defined: the nonteleological, farcical, and antimoral comedy that centers on an aesthetic quite close to that of the permanently hungry Ergasilus. Yet it is part of the moralizing aesthetic to preserve the appearance of naturalism and to avoid the kind of overt metatheatricalism that such a literary polemic would seem to require. In depicting Ergasilus throughout the play as a charming but ineffective schemer, and in finally relegating him to the indelicate pleasures of the kitchen rather than to the sociable pleasures of the dining room, this play has succeeded in brushing off his worldview as naive and inconsequential.

Recognition = Resolution

Three events occur in the fifth act, collectively resolving all the various themes and plot lines: Philocrates brings back Philopolemus, the bad slave Stalagmus functions as scapegoat for all the crimes that have taken place, and Tyndarus is recognized as Hegio's son. And yet, in a very real way, there is no resolution at all, merely a confluence of circumstances that obliterates the problems raised in the earlier acts.[66] Romantic comedies never answer the question of whether the youth's passion would have been indulged if it did not happen to conform to his parents' wishes (when the girl of his dreams turns out to be the girl next door). The *Captivi*'s evasions

---

[66] See note 10 above, Konstan's comment on the tendency of comedy to rely on contingent resolutions.

are analogous. Here the problems of slaves' obedience, of the possibility of a noble slave, and of a stable, unified identity are washed away without leaving a trace.

The problem of the conflict between Tyndarus' duties to Philocrates and to Hegio is forgotten in the rejoicing over Philopolemus' safe return. Superficially this seems like the *Epidicus*, where the clever slave gains pardon for his scheming because it results in the master's recovery of his daughter. But it is important to realize that Philocrates' return does not vindicate Tyndarus' disobedience but merely serves to commute his sentence. Hegio does not regret his punishment of Tyndarus as unjust but fears that he has offended his fellow master Philocrates by the harsh treatment of his slave. Hegio agrees to free Tyndarus without any payment in return for Philocrates' honor in upholding his obligations, as he explains to Philocrates: (see also 947–48).[67]

> quod bene fecisti referetur gratia id quod postulas;
> et id et aliud quod me orabis impetrabis. atque te
> nolim suscensere quod ego iratus ei feci male.
>
> (941–43)

In return for your good deed what you ask will be given to you as a favor; both this request and any other you make will be honored. But I don't want you to get mad because I treated him [Tyndarus] badly when I was angry.

Although Hegio is not motivated by any desire to acknowledge Tyndarus' heroism, Philocrates, on the other hand, does feel deeply the sacrifice that Tyndarus has made for him (939–40, 945–46), and he plans to discharge his obligation to him in the way that is proper for masters to reward slaves, by manumitting him. Thus in this resolution (the only one in this act that does not rely on Tyche) both Hegio and Philocrates conceive of their obligations to each other and to Tyndarus as defined by the status of each person. Until Tyndarus is known to be freeborn, there is no question of his misfortunes being anything more than what a loyal slave would do for his master, nor anything more than could be recompensed by his manumission.

The return of the evil slave Stalagmus is extremely important in producing the harmony of opposites that characterizes this ending. He functions as a scapegoat for both Hegio's harshness and Tyndarus' trickiness, allowing us to forget the possible negative judgments for each of them. As

---

[67] Konstan (1983: 68, 70) also sees that Hegio's opinion of Tyndarus does not improve until he finds out that Tyndarus is his son; the difference between Konstan's argument and mine, here and throughout, is that he places greatest emphasis on Tyndarus' status as an outsider to Hegio, while I see his status as slave as more important, especially in the context of a deception comedy.

the earlier kidnapper of Tyndarus, he allows for the improper authority
that has mistreated Tyndarus to be situated in himself rather than in Hegio.
The risk that Hegio ran of seeming excessive in his authority (pointed to
in the earlier descriptions of him as a slave dealer) is decisively averted.
Stalagmus' assimilation to Tyndarus goes beyond the obvious fact that they
are both slaves. As Hegio realizes at lines 759–63, Tyndarus' act in endangering Hegio's plan to get Philopolemus back is a replication of Stalagmus'
earlier crime. Konstan rightly points out that the transferral of chains from
Tyndarus to his kidnapper also serves to indicate that Stalagmus is acting
as a foil for Tyndarus.[68] The dual function of Stalagmus allows for the
solution of the problem posed by opposed interests. Both Hegio's harshness in defending his own interests and Tyndarus' disobedience in defending the interests of Philocrates are expiated in the punishment of Stalagmus. The same effect can be seen as a positive defense of each character:
Hegio's firm mastery in punishing disobedience and Tyndarus' noble loyalty are thus justified.

Obviously the most dramatically and thematically significant event in
this final act is the recognition that Tyndarus is not only freeborn but even
Hegio's son. All through the play, we have been confronted with the question of whether a slave can be noble; the question vanishes when we realize
Tyndarus' true identity. As Konstan (1983: 70) observes, "The extraordinary coincidence that the noble slave and stranger in [Hegio's] house is his
kin permits a fortuitous harmony of sympathy and judgment." This ending
leaves open both possibilities: that there exists such a thing as a noble slave
and that Tyndarus' nobility is a sign of his freeborn state, a sign that en-
dured even the degradation of slavery. Even though a choice between these
two possibilities is strictly evaded, our knowledge from the prologue of
Tyndarus' free birth leads us to see him in the ironic position of a slave by
condition throughout the play and thus obviates the spectacle of nobility
in a slave. We never really see him as a slave, so we never have to confront
the possibility that slaves can be noble. Also left open is the question of
whether his nobility is the result of his free birth or of the humane treatment by his master. We are told specifically that he was raised "chastely
and honorably" (*bene pudiceque*, 992), as are the *pseudo-meretrices* in other
plays.[69] This line specifically associates the ending of this play with the
more common romantic paradigm, in which a marriage symbolizes that all
wrongs have been righted and gestures towards a sunny future. But, again,

[68] Konstan (1983: 70); see also Ketterer (1986a: 117), who observes that this transfer does
not take place within the play, with the result that the play ends with Tyndarus still wearing
his heavy chains ("symbols of what has suffered from his father on behalf of his former master,
not of a slave who has been freed"). Further, he argues that the contrast between Tyndarus'
heavy chains and Stalagmus' light ones underscores the justification for vengeance.

[69] Cf. *Cur* 698, 700; *Poen* 1221.

we cannot take without reservation this evidence that his master's treatment was responsible for Tyndarus' nobility. If there were an unambiguous assumption in the play that masters' treatment determined the virtue of their slaves, Hegio would certainly have to defend himself on the charge of producing bad slaves.[70] Of course, there is no such assumption; on this point as on so many others, the ending produces a situation that avoids a choice between alternatives.

Perhaps the most important agent in this final act is an invisible one: the influence of Tyche (or, more broadly, the sense of divine order and justice) is perhaps the most fundamental difference between the tone of this play and the cynicism that permeates the ending of the *Persa*. That final act, far from comfortably "resolving" all the moral issues that had arisen, on the contrary goes to the extreme in diminishing the moral certainty we had left. Part of the moral authority of the ending of the *Captivi* lies in its disembodied agency. Precisely by invoking the principle of divine justice or Providence, the play claims for its sleight-of-hand the authority of justice.

IN DIALOGUE WITH FARCE

As compelling as the *Captivi* may be in its own right, with its vision of an underlying order to human life, at least part of its dramatic force comes from its subtle handling of the farcical elements of Plautine comedy. This play is able to claim for its hero(es) the rakish charm that attaches to devil-may-care tricksters, while simultaneously discrediting farce's cynical moral perspective. I would like to conclude my analysis of the *Captivi* by looking at two dramatic patterns that can help us get a more detailed understanding of the relationship between this play and the farcical mode so prominent in other Plautine plays: first, the ways that Ergasilus and Hegio define an assault on farce that focuses on money and work; second, through a brief comparison with the *Rudens*, how irony works in both plays to support a moral vision and to gloss over lapses in social and literary logic.

The peculiar aspects of Ergasilus' presentation in this play are a focal point for exploring the polemical relations between the *Captivi* and the farcical side of Plautine comedy. Like the choice to make the central action in this moralizing play mirror the slavish deceptions of the amoral comedies, the choice to include Ergasilus forces us to consider the *Captivi* not as an aberration of Plautine comedy, but as thoroughly embedded in this tradition.

Parasites, like *senes amatores* and *uxores dotatae*, occupy an ambiguous position in the comic society. Like the two figures of the older generation, parasites can be seen as either supporters or obstacles to the schemes so

---

[70] Most notably Stalagmus, but even Tyndarus' disobedience (if he had not been discovered to be freeborn) and the Lorarius' opportunism do not acquit Hegio's mastery.

dear to slaves and young men. The ambiguity of *senes amatores* and *uxores dotatae* is structural in nature, and these two characters often balance each other out. The old man in love tries to usurp youth's erotic power, while the greedy older woman indirectly helps the young by punishing her husband the interloper. The parasite's ambiguity, however, rests instead on his personal qualities. The venality of this character type, his willingness to say anything or praise anyone for a meal, is the first defining characteristic. Thus, he is sometimes allied with the tricksters in their plot (*Curculio, Persa*), sometimes with the blocking character (*Pseudolus, Asinaria*), and sometimes seen to change sides during the play (*Menaechmi*); this flexibility is the literary extension of his untrustworthy nature. On the other hand, the clever slave is always consistent in his antimoral orientation. This consistency looks almost high minded when compared to the opportunism of the parasite.

The second defining characteristic of the comic parasite is his utter conventionality. We may recognize a family resemblance among Pseudolus, Tranio, Chrysalus, and other clever slaves, but each also has distinctive traits and concerns. The several parasites in the corpus are so similar as almost to merge into a single character. While clever slaves are united by a common style of speaking and acting, the substance of their performance, the stories they tell, and disguises they wear must vary with the details of each plot. Parasites' connection with the specifics of each plot is so tenuous, and their abiding interest in eating is so predominant, that their common style of speaking is always trained on this all-important subject.[71] The parasite is a prisoner of conventionality to a greater degree than other character types, even considering the thoroughly conventional nature of farce.[72]

These twin characteristics of venality and conventionality make the parasite a useful figure through which naturalistic comedy can poke fun at the weaknesses of farce. The troubles Ergasilus describes throughout his first two monologues can be seen as the plight of farcical comedy defending itself when judged on the charges of superficiality and acquisitiveness.[73] The association of the parasite with the comic poet is made obliquely elsewhere, on the basis of their common need to make a buck through getting

---

[71] Curculio is an exception, since he has the function of a trickster in orchestrating the disguise scheme.

[72] E.g., compare the structural and substantive similarities in the parasite's canonical introduction of himself at *Cap* I.1, *Men* I.1, *Per* I.2, *St* I.3. Even Curculio, who alone among major parasites does not have one of these monologues, manages to get in his nickname joke during the deception scheme (413–16).

[73] See Horace's critique of Plautus as a poet who composed with one eye on the till: *gestit enim nummum in loculos demittere, post hoc / securus cadat an recto stet fabula talo* ("He's itching to get the money into the till, after that he doesn't care whether the play stands or falls," *Ep.* 2.1.175–76).

laughs; both parasites and comic poets make pleasure their business.[74] Seen from the perspective of a naturalistic, moralizing comedy, the usual antics of Plautine farce would indeed incur the sort of reproach leveled at parasites: farce produces nothing useful but lives second-hand off the leisure of others.[75]

While naturalistic comedy represents the parasite as the genius of farcical comedy, farce itself obviously puts forward the clever slave as its emblematic hero. As noted above, the clever slave's consistency and his willingness to risk all for what he values (a good time) confer a sort of nobility on his silly enterprise. His refusal to do anything useful results not from a lowbrow concentration on his stomach but from the exalted aesthetic pleasure he derives from the art of trickery. The differences in outlook between the *Captivi* and amoral farce are demonstrated by this competitive use of parasites and clever slaves to represent the spirit of farcical comedy. This competition is clearest in the fourth act, where Ergasilus claims to be taking on the role of the comic slave (778). Although his performance is witty and amusing, it replicates only the language of the clever slave. The fulfillment of the clever slave's function—to upset the complacency and self-righteousness of the master through extravagantly theatrical stratagems—is conspicuously absent.

Further, we should recall Ergasilus' opening lines in which he compared himself to a *meretrix*, ingeniously avoiding the most obvious bases of comparison. The character type of the *meretrix*, like that of the clever slave, is also missing from the *Captivi*'s representation of farcical values. She has not exactly been banished but rather reduced to certain qualities that can be equated with the personality of the foolish yet benign Ergasilus. In the rest of the corpus, *meretrices* differ from parasites in being more clever and manipulative and in that the object of their scheming is the ultrarational goal of piling up money, rather than the animalistic obsession with food. While these qualities may not be admirable, they are certainly more potent than Ergasilus' begging and cringing. Thus his nickname serves to taunt him with meretricious greed, but nowhere in this play do we see the seductive power of comic *meretrices*, a power that shows farce to be more subtle (and more successful) than its embodiment in Ergasilus would indicate.

---

[74] E.g., Saturio's joke book at *Per* 392 (see Chiarini [1979: 112]), Gelasimus' jokes at *St* III.2 (see Petrone [1977: 54–58]), etc. See also Petrone (1983: 7) on parasites as "internal playwrights."

[75] This connection is clearest in the monologue that opens the third act. Lindsay (1900: ad loc.) has interpreted *ridiculos* at 470 and 477 as a simple variant for *parasitos*. Yet it is clear from the context of this passage that what is being disputed is the value of jokes in exchange for dinner. Like the young men Ergasilus describes, the *Captivi* prefers the world of freeborn young men, and uses them to fill the roles which in other plays are performed by parasites and clever slaves.

In fact, the problem of work and its relation to money is central to the conflict of worldviews throughout this play. An excessive financial self-interest is the charge hurled by each mode of comedy against the other. Naturalistic comedy's worldview critiques the farcical worldview by heightening the self-seeking attitude of Ergasilus and by revealing his devotion to the good life to be more an occupation than a desire for laughs and leisure. At the same time, Ergasilus is less successful than other parasites. Because Hegio is wiser and more frugal than other potential patrons, Ergasilus' charm is ineffective and falls on deaf ears. The only way that Ergasilus is able finally to get his feast is by being the bearer of glad tidings. This depiction of the parasite as powerless is much more damning than any charge of commercialism or self-interest could possibly be. Comic parasites, and in fact the whole world of scheming comic characters, freely admit to their roguish self-interest, even wearing it with pride as a mark of their distance from any moralizing perspective.[76] But to show these characters as feeble bumblers, whose much-vaunted wit cannot even put a dinner on the table—that is a truly stinging criticism.

As in other plays, where the greed of the *senex* provides a foil for the clever slave's utter lack of interest in money, even here in the *Captivi*, Ergasilus' description of his hostile foes is couched in the language of commercialism and stinginess. In his most extensive description of the fate of a parasite in this moralistic world (III.1), Ergasilus emphasizes how his own values of appetite and good humor are stymied by the young men's stinginess and somberness. This opposition is clear in the terms he chooses to describe himself and the young men: he is a *ridiculus* trying unsuccessfully to fit in with *Lacones*. Towards the end of this monologue he specifically ascribes their close-fistedness to their commercial outlook. At line 484 and again at line 489, he claims that their refusal of his services is a collusive pact among them to save money, on the model of the agreements of the oil merchants of the Velabrum. Thus he deflects the charge of commercialism from himself to those who refuse to indulge him.

These mutual accusations of greed and commercialism should be seen in the context of the problem of money in the *Captivi* as a whole. While the proper attitude towards money is at issue in the conflict between farcical and naturalistic perspectives, even within the naturalistic perspective, there are the twin pitfalls of prodigality and stinginess. Philocrates and Tyndarus design the original disguise trick by assuming that greed is a motivation for all *senes*. It remains unclear, but one of the better explanations of why the young men choose to exchange identities is that they wish to save Philocrates' father the expense of an extorted ransom, not knowing that Hegio only wants to exchange Philocrates for his son Philopolemus.[77]

[76] See Chiarini's (1979: 61, 69, *passim*) description of *malitia*.
[77] Leach (1969b: 270), Abel (1955: 50), Viljoen (1963: 48–49), Lindsay (1900: on 321–23).

Thus they assume that Hegio is motivated by greed, and Philocrates also gratuitously depicts his own father as a miser. This is another example of the confluence of two worldviews: in the farcical worldview, all *senes* are stingy, and it is possible to think of one so stingy as to refuse to ransom his own son. But in the moral worldview of naturalizing comedy, money is merely a means to an end, and it is inconceivable that a father would refuse to ransom his son out of a desire to save money (his ability to spend the money if he wishes is never seriously in doubt). The belief that Philocrates' father will refuse to ransom him unless petitioned by his own slave provides the essential link in the plot. Thus although Hegio has transcended the greed of most *senes*, he still believes that other *senes* fit the stereotypes and so is easily persuaded to allow "Tyndarus" to be the messenger on this mission. The assumption that all *senes* are greedy motivates the actions both of the schemers and of the target of their scheme.

Further, it must be questioned whether Hegio really has transcended this stereotypical characteristic of comic old men. Although he is never really in danger of being stingy or greedy, his consciousness of money as the means and marker of his morality serves not to transcend but to transform the associations of money for *senes*. In other Plautine plays, carefulness with money is seen only as narrow-minded greed, a quality associated especially with *senes*, *lenones*, and moneylenders. The *Menaechmi* offers us the glimpse of another possibility, one that will be fully developed here in the *Captivi*.[78] Just as Syracusan Menaechmus gives an example of a mastery that relies on true discipline and authority, rather than on open-handed bribery, Hegio shows that a consciousness of cost can be the marker of the *paterfamilias'* moderation in all things. In particular, his relationship with Ergasilus reveals a break with comic canons. In scene I.2, he shows himself more capable of light-hearted banter than most other patrons, yet he resists the connection between jollity and providing the parasite with a lavish dinner. The positive evaluation of Hegio's strategy here is that he wishes to replace the degradation of dependency with a less lavish but more sincere offer of charity. This evaluation could be ironized from another perspective, however, to show that Hegio is proposing a hand-out to be measured only by his own generosity, in place of a relationship of give-and-take that puts the parasite in the position of being paid for his work.[79] Throughout the play, Hegio's consciousness of the cost of things—right down to the meaningless repetition of the price paid for Tyndarus twenty years ago—can be seen in both of these ways.

We can get a clearer view of the particular dialogic strategies of the *Captivi* by comparing it to the *Rudens*, another play of mistaken identity

[78] See also the *Trinummus*.

[79] The question of whether dependency should be seen as a rational exchange or as paternalistic charity should remind us of the conflict that animated the *Menaechmi*.

that focuses as much on the father's loss as on the child's. Like Hegio in this play, Daemones there is portrayed as both authoritative to his slave Sceparnio and humane to the wanderer. Furthermore, we know already from the prologue of that play (33–38) that Daemones has lost his financial security in the course of helping others, much as Hegio has almost bankrupted himself while trying to free his son. The characterization of the *senex* in a positive and sympathetic light in both plays derails an audience's initial expectations for a plot of deception and makes it clear that what we will see is more a comedy of chance, the kind of drama that gives full weight to the action of Tyche and the power of irony.

These close resemblances between the initial situations of the *Captivi* and *Rudens* provide a good way of gauging the effect of the deception scheme in the former. Because its premises are so close to those of a play that steers clear of human trickery, relying exclusively on the guiding hand of Tyche, the *Captivi*'s absorption of the farcical paradigm is even more striking. Specifically, *Rudens* is a good example of a play based on the contrast between divine justice and human *agnoia*. The prologue by the star Arcturus explicitly describes the gods as arbiters of human behavior, who punish the dishonest, the greedy, and the hypocritical (9–30). The human characters in the play are clearly divided into good and evil; Daemones never has to defend his own interests as harshly as does Hegio, nor does the pimp Labrax ever have anything like the just cause of Philocrates and Tyndarus. Unlike the shifting plot types that characterize the *Captivi*, constantly reorienting our judgments of the main characters, the *Rudens* offers a simpler and more univocal view of the good being rewarded and the evil being punished. The *Captivi*'s overall structure replicates the *Rudens'* vindication of divine justice, but in addition to *agnoia* as the source of human problems, it emphasizes the opposed interests of Hegio and the captives. Although the *Captivi* on the grand scale is as didactic as the *Rudens*,[80] its incorporation of the deception paradigm requires it to distance itself more polemically from the antimoral orientation of farce.

The relationship between the *Rudens* and the more farcical side of the Plautine corpus, and its difference from that of the *Captivi*, can be seen in the difference between the characters Gripus and Ergasilus. As has been argued above for Ergasilus, Gripus is distinguished from the other characters of the play by his short-sighted, self-seeking behavior. Like Ergasilus, Gripus doesn't care if "god's in his heaven and all's right with the world," as long as he gets a good meal. Both characters are also tangentially, but not substantively, involved with the recognition scenes of their respective plays. Two important features nevertheless show the differences between Ergasilus and Gripus. First of all, Gripus is not a parasite, that convention-

---

[80] See esp. 313–15, where Tyndarus sounds almost exactly like Arcturus.

alized emblem of farce, but a fisherman. No matter how easily we recognize his characteristics as farcical, because of his lack of a clear comic pedigree he can still stand as a character rather than a symbol. Second, in the *Captivi* we noted the striking segregation of Ergasilus from all dramatic structure, with the exception of his retarding presence in Act IV. Gripus, on the other hand, is the center of a genuine subplot, one that echoes important elements of the main plot and crosses with the main plot at the dénouement. These differences between the two comic characters do not show that Gripus is represented in any way that is more respectable or less condescending than that in which Ergasilus is represented. Rather, they show that Gripus' presence in the play is motivated by the play's structural and thematic design. Ergasilus' presence in the *Captivi* is only tenuously connected with the structure and themes of the play and much more so with the dialogic stance of the *Captivi* towards the farcical deception comedies from which it must distance itself.

Finally, the difference between the two plays crystallizes in their endings. The *Rudens*, a play of *agnoia* in which the correction of mistaken impressions clarifies everything, ends on a note of complete reconciliation. The reunion of father and daughter is joyous, the coming wedding is happily anticipated, and even Gripus and Labrax resolve their greedy struggle (with Daemones' almost godlike intercession), as everyone sits down to a festive meal. The final scenes of the *Captivi*, concentrated as they are on vengeance and punishment rather than conciliation, are far different. This concentration even pushes out the happiness at the restoration of the family that we expect here.[81] Because of the structure of the deception scheme that has shaped the *Captivi*, a structure that requires not just ignorance but hostility on the part of the opposed parties, this play has committed itself to an ending like those where the master agrees to forego punishment of the slave while still being unreconciled to the breaching of his authority.[82] In other words, the opposed parties at the end of such a play remain opposed. Neither group is unambiguously labeled "right" or "wrong" precisely because the whole point of farce is to subvert such labeling.[83] Although the *Captivi* throughout has so brilliantly appropriated the forms of antimoral comedy for its own moral ends, the joylessness of the finale is evidence that its appropriating power does, in fact, have limits.[84]

---

[81] Leach (1969b: 295–96), Ketterer (1986a: 113).

[82] Leach (1969b: 273–74): "Even if ultimate justice prevails, there is no answer, no palliative, for the injustices committed in ignorance."

[83] As noted above, the function of Stalagmus as a double scapegoat avoids just such a moral distinction between the tricksters and the *senex*.

[84] Another possible explanation for the joylessness of the ending lies in Tyndarus' unusual enactment of the role of the heroine. We are so used to seeing the identities of women flexible enough to change from being *meretrices* to being brides in a matter of moments, that the

These similarities to and differences from the *Rudens* also give us a foundation for understanding the importance of irony and other "tragic" elements in the *Captivi*.[85] Again, by choosing to include a deception trick within what is essentially a comedy of mistaken identity, the playwright has here put himself in the difficult position of reconciling two very different views of human knowledge and agency, and these views produce two very different kinds of theater. Because the more farcical plays, centered on deception, seek to foreground their own artifice (often through the conceit of an "inner playwright"), they make no use of the type of irony that suffuses the *Captivi*, where the audience is in a position of knowledge superior to that of all the characters. The metatheatrical stance of some of Plautus' other comedies does not allow for this division between the world of the audience and that of the characters and instead continually seeks to unite the two worlds. The type of irony in the *Captivi* is of a piece with its naturalism and its acknowledgment of the superhuman power of the gods and of Tyche. However, just as the comparison with the *Rudens* showed that the *Captivi*'s attempt to absorb farce within its moralizing world strains that play's emotional harmony by introducing an element of hostility between deceivers and deceived, so too the *Captivi*'s admission that human knowledge and agency interact with Tyche's control of events strains the play's naivete and makes it rely all the more on irony to smooth out the tensions.

Irony is equally important in the philosophical and social levels of the play as in its literary level. The attitude of the audience—its pleasure in the juicy ironies of the situation—distracts them from the strictly logical considerations of the propositions at hand. Both for the philosophical issue of the stability of identity and for the ideological issues surrounding slavery, the atmosphere of irony contributes to their suspension, an illogical satisfaction with included middles. Irony may be excited by the intellectual contemplation of a situation, but it has the effect of deflecting the problem into an emotional contemplation and away from a definitive solution. Our response—"isn't it ironic?"—is, after all, not an answer or an analysis but a question that substitutes for these. Like the effect of *agnoia* in obscuring

---

incorporation of their pimp into the final feast is less shocking. When this part is played by a man, however, whose identity is throughout the corpus assumed to be much more fixed, and any change much more problematic, we cannot let his enslaver off so easily.

[85] Petrone's (1983: 56–63) discussion of the play, and of the element of deception in the corpus as a whole, relies a great deal on the distinction between comic and tragic modes. Although many of her observations are useful, I think that her terminology is fundamentally misleading. If we simply associate qualities like naturalism and moralism with tragedy and qualities like metatheatricalism and amoralism with comedy, we are left with a system that has no satisfying place for either (much of) the comedy of Menander or (some of) the tragedy of Euripides, for example.

the role of opposed interests in creating the hostile situation, irony softens our judgments without explicitly arguing in defense of any character or position.

The ironic nature of the *Captivi* also makes itself felt in the emphatic way it combines the most characteristic elements of tragedy and comedy. This play seems to parade its skill at fusing these two diametrically opposed literary modes. Like the ideological effect of irony noted above (that it allows us to feel deeply a problem without coming to a solution), this generic irony also creates a suspended perspective. The suspension between these two literary modes embodies a suspension of the essential question asked by this play: are slaves ultimately the same as masters or ultimately different? The tragic mode, in which Tyndarus courts death at his father's hands for his noble defense of the master fate has given him, would emphasize the fundamental hazard of human life. The comic mode, in which our hero is freed from captivity through a series of tricks and disguises, would extol the virtue of cleverness and argue that any slave who is not witty enough to work his way out deserves to be a slave. Thus the ironic suspension of a decision between these two modes echoes the mechanisms of mastery itself, which must see the slave as both same and different.

Conclusion

THE SLAVE'S IMAGE IN THE MASTER'S MIND

IN HIS DESCRIPTION of blackface minstrel shows, the folklorist Roger D. Abrahams quotes a nineteenth-century commentator, "And thus it came to pass, that while James Crow and Scipio Coon were quietly at work on their masters' plantations, all unconscious of their fame, the whole civilized world was resounding with their names."[1] The same paradox applies to the real slaves in real Roman households in the mid-Republic. While they lived in obscurity and servitude, the whole city was resounding with the names of Pseudolus, Epidicus, and Tranio. In both slave societies, fictive slaves captured the imagination and attention of the public in a way that real slaves never could.

In minstrel shows, as in Roman comedy, we have a window into the ways that communities use play time to reinforce a sense of security and order. Because each community is not homogeneous and is separated by great disparities in power, certain members (men, citizens, masters) have more control over shaping the game than other members (women, aliens, slaves). But these more powerful members of the community are not independent of the institutions that grant them their power. It is part of the ideology of masters to pretend that slavery only affects slaves; that it degrades, infan-tilizes, and dehumanizes slaves but leaves masters unscathed except, per-haps, by pity. The truth that I hope to have shown in these chapters is that slavery affects masters, that it puts them in the position of having constantly to create, defend, and shore up the illogical bases of their domination. The presence of real women, aliens, and slaves and the constant reminder that they do not willingly participate in the institutions that constrain them create a pressure that profoundly influences the fantasies painted by the more powerful members of the community. Furthermore, masters are never just masters, but in a variety of other relations they may be almost as subject to others' wills as their slaves are subject to theirs. Thus, they are themselves in need of fantasies of rebellion.

A comparison of blackface minstrel shows and Plautine comedy, in their broadest outlines, will underscore the descriptions offered in the chapters above, of the fantasies fictive slaves enacted for masters. Like the four plays examined in this study, these minstrel shows fulfilled the opposing demands

[1] J.K. Kinnard, Jr. in *The Knickerbocker Magazine* (October, 1845), as quoted in Abrahams (1992: 145).

of reinforcing their mastery and allowing them a release from the perceived burdens of both mastery and the need to resist their own potential subordination to others.

First, and most obviously, both kinds of entertainments provided the soothing spectacle of slaves who were content in their servitude. The singing and dancing that dominated the purported scenes of plantation life gave the impression of slaves who lived in a dream world of peace and security.[2] The corollary of this image of contentment, sometimes made explicit, is that slaves were so debased that these creature comforts and simple pleasures meant more to them than their freedom.[3] At first glance, this heavy-handed racism seems worlds away from the portrait of the astute scheming slave of Roman comedy. But the lack of interest that clever slaves show in manumission underscores their essential collusion in their servitude. True, the pleasures that keep the Plautine clever slave content with his bondage may seem more elevated, but the characterization of the slave in both types of performance is fundamentally childlike. The pleasure that these fictive slaves take in singing, dancing, disguise tricks, and jokes pleases masters precisely because it reinforces their own idea that slaves are incapable of or uninterested in taking life seriously.

The second function of such entertainments grows out of masters' enjoyment of this childlike quality with which they have endowed fictive slaves. The attribution to slaves of a view of life that is simple, playful, joyous has a double edge in the fictions of a slave society. It offers apologists a reason why these childlike creatures are better off under the paternalistic protection of a master. But this view of life also embodies, for each culture, some of the aspects that are at once desired and rejected. For Romans, the scheming of the slave expresses the pleasures of playfulness (*otium*) and rebellion against authority.[4] In the antebellum South, the docility and cheerfulness attributed to slaves aligned them with Christian virtues that nostalgia associated with simpler, less commercial times. Thus, for each culture, the fictional representations of slaves push to the extreme values

---

[2] Van Deburg (1984: 43–46).

[3] Van Deburg (1984: 43) quotes a minstrel song "Once I say to massa, whar de cane brake grow, / I pay you for my freedom if you let me go, / And he tell dis nigga dat it neber can be, / 'Case dat no sum ob money worth so much as me. / Den I jump up an holler, even dis ting I hear, / And I stretch my red mouf across from ear to ear," and comments, "To the minstrel show songwriter, and to those in the audience who would believe the sentiments expressed in these verses, black slaves were so obtuse as to exchange the hope of freedom for a few deceptively kind and flattering words."

[4] This can be seen as adding a level of complexity to Segal's (1987: 15–41 and *passim*) argument about the satisfactions provided by comedy. Comedy does have an element of wish fulfillment, but we should acknowledge that the master's wishes are often fulfilled through the persona of the fictive slave.

that the master class longs for and yet acknowledges as impractical.[5] The vision of slaves' lives as playful and joyous (and unconscious of the day-to-day cares so obvious to masters in their own lives) both glossed over the unnerving realities of slaves' lives and gave masters, by association, a feeling of release from the grinding cares imposed on them by their civil, economic, and political freedom. Masters invent carefree slaves and then are jealous of the qualities with which they have endowed these fictions, without acknowledging how deeply they depend on the respect accorded to them as free people. This observation leads directly to the economy of Plautine comedy, as argued for in this study, in which fictive slaves are imagined to be completely opposite to all the values of the culture, but then the fictive authority of these slaves is desired by and appropriated by masters.

It should be clear from the description of these functions that the representation of slaves in fiction expresses simultaneously the master's disdain for the slave and the master's desire for the idealized simplicity with which the fictive slave is endowed. These contradictory effects echo the contradiction of mastery itself, that masters' desire to see slaves as carefree (and thus mask the compulsion required to maintain the system) serves as a contrast to their own experience of the hard work involved in keeping up their mastery. The creation of the carefree slave justifies their mastery and is also a reaction to the tiring labor of that mastery. The frantic quality of mastery, the huge expenditure of energy it entails, comes precisely from the constant need to maintain this cognitive dissonance and to act on it.[6] The picking, grinning, scheming, charming, deceptive fictive slave was the master's ally in this never-ending labor.

---

[5] The idea of the members of the master class enjoying these qualities by their *possession* of members of the class was conceivable even by abolitionists and even after emancipation. A tract of 1864, advocating not miscegenation but a cultural amalgamation with the freed slaves, envisioned the black race as an instrument in the bettering of the white race: "We want them, that our harsh and grasping spirit, as a race, may be tempered by the sight of their more simple-hearted and forgiving natures. We want them, that our anxious and never-resting lust for gain may be shamed and softened by their more joyous and holiday feeling." (I. N. Tarbox, *The Curse: Or the Position in the World's History Occupied by the Race of Ham* [Boston, 1864], as quoted in Fredrickson [1971: 123]).

[6] Patterson (1982: 336–37), expanding on the sociologist Anatol Rapoport's analysis of human parasitism: "Parasitism is most rewarding for the parasite when both he and the parasitized party minimize laziness. . . . Effective parasitism is hard work! The southern U.S. slaveholders were basically right in always insisting on this in their defense of the system of slavery, though they did not, of course, express their views in these terms. Where they were completely wrong was in their equally vehement claim that their hard-working parasitism was in the best interest of their parasitized slaves and of all non-slaveholding freemen."

WORKS CITED

Abel, K.-H. 1955. *Die Plautusprologe*. Dissertation, University of Frankfurt.

Abrahams, R. D. 1992 *Singing the Master: The Emergence of African-American Culture in the Plantation South*. New York: Penguin Books.

Anderson, W. S. (1983) "Chalinus *armiger* in Plautus' *Casina*." *Illinois Classical Studies* 8: 11–21.

———. (1993) *Barbarian Play: Plautus' Roman Comedy*. Toronto: University of Toronto Press.

Averna, D. (1983) "Spettatore-attore in Plauto?" *Dioniso* 54: 205–9.

Bakhtin, M. (1981) *The Dialogic Imagination*, trans. Caryl Emerson and Michael Holquist. Austin: University of Texas Press.

Barton, C. (1993) *The Sorrows of the Ancient Romans: The Gladiator and the Monster*. Princeton: Princeton University Press.

Beacham, R. (1995) "A Funny Thing Happened on the Way to the Wedding." In *Plautus: The Comedies*, vol. 1 ed. David R. Slavitt and Palmer Bovie, 251–318. Baltimore: Johns Hopkins University Press.

Bettini, M. (1977) "Il parasito Saturio, una riforma legislativa e un testo variamente tormentato." *Studi Classici e Orientali* 26: 83–104.

———. (1982) "Verso un' antropologia dell' intreccio: Le strutture semplice della trama nelle commedie di Plauto." *Materiali e Discussioni per l'analisi dei testi classici* 7: 39–101.

———. (1985) "La poesia romana arcaica 'al lavoro' (con una apologia della medesima)." *Materiali e Discussioni per l'analisi dei testi classici* 14: 13–43.

———, ed. (1991) *Plauto: Mostellaria e Persa*, 3rd edition Milan: Mondadori.

Bourdieu, P. (1990) *The Logic of Practice*, trans. R. Nice, Stanford: Stanford University Press.

Bradley, K. R. (1987) *Slaves and Masters in the Roman Empire: A Study in Social Control*. Oxford: Oxford University Press.

———. (1994) *Slavery and Society at Rome*. Cambridge: Cambridge University Press.

Chiarini, G. (1978) "*Casina* o della metamorfosi." *Latomus* 37: 105–20.

———. (1979) *La Recita: Plauto, La Farsa, La Festa*. Bologna: Patron.

Clover, C. (1987) "Her Body, Himself: Gender in the Slasher Film." *Representations* 20: 187–228.

Cody, J. M. (1976) "The *senex amator* in Plautus' *Casina*." *Hermes* 104: 453–76.

Conte, G. B. (1994) *Latin Literature: A History*. Baltimore: Johns Hopkins University Press.

Cooper, F. (1977) *Plantation Slavery on the East Coast of Africa*. New Haven: Yale University Press.

Danese, R. (1985) "La poesia plautina: forma linguistica di creazione." *Materiali e Discussioni per l'analisi dei testi classici* 14: 79–99.

Dessen, C. (1977) "Plautus' Satiric Comedy: The *Truculentus.*" *Philological Quarterly* 56: 145–68.

Dingel, J. (1981) "Herren und Sklaven bei Plautus." *Gymnasium* 88: 489–504.

Duckworth, G. (1938) "The Unnamed Characters in the Plays of Plautus." *Classical Philology* 33: 267–82.

———, ed. (1940) *Epidicus.* Princeton: Princeton University Press.

Dumézil, G. (1977) "L'esclave romain et le *genius.*" In *Mélanges Offerts à Leopold Sedar Senghor,* 121–30. Dakar: Les Nouvelles Éditions Africaines.

Dumont, J. (1966) "La strategie de l'esclave plautinien." *Revue des Études Latures* 44: 182–203.

———. (1984) "Guerre, paix et servitude dans les *Captifs.*" *Latomus* 33: 505–22.

Fantham, E. (1968) "Act IV of the *Menaechmi*: Plautus and His Original." *Classical Philology* 63: 173–83.

Feeney, D. (1998) *Literature and Religion at Rome.* Cambridge: Cambridge University Press.

Finley, M. I. (1980) *Ancient Slavery and Modern Ideology.* New York: Penguin Books.

Fitzgerald, W. (2000) *Slavery and Roman Literature.* Cambridge: Cambridge University Press.

Flury, P. (1968) *Liebe und Liebesprache bei Menander, Plautus und Terenz.* Heidelberg: C. Winter.

Forehand, W. (1973) "Plautus' *Casina*: An Explication." *Arethusa* 6: 233–56.

Fraenkel, E. (1922) *Plautinisches im Plautus.* Berlin: Weidmann.

———. (1960) *Elementi Plautini in Plauto,* trans. F. Munari, with addenda by the author. Florence: La Nuova Italia.

Fredrickson, G. (1971) *The Black Image in the White Mind: The Debate on Afro-American Character and Destiny, 1817–1914.* New York: Harper and Row.

Frye, N. (1957) *The Anatomy of Criticism.* Princeton: Princeton University Press.

———. (1965) *A Natural Perspective: The Development of Shakespearean Comedy and Romance.* New York: Harcourt Brace Jovanovich.

Galinsky, K. (1996) *Augustan Culture: An Interpretive Introduction.* Princeton: Princeton University Press.

Gosling, A. (1983) "A Rather Unusual Old Man: Hegio in the *Captivi.*" *Acta Classica* 26: 53–59.

Gratwick, A. (1982) "Drama 2: Light Drama." In *Cambridge History of Classical Literature,* vol. 2, *Latin Literature,* ed. E. J. Kenney and W. Clausen. Cambridge: Cambridge University Press.

Grimal, P. (1975) "Jeu et vérité dans les comédies de Plaute." *Dioniso* 46: 137–52.

Grote, D. (1983) *The End of Comedy: The Sitcom and the Comedic Tradition.* Hamden, CT: Archon Books.

Gruen, E. S. (1990) *Studies in Greek Culture and Roman Policy.* Leiden: E.J. Brill.

———. (1992) *Culture and National Identity in Republican Rome.* Ithaca: Cornell University Press.

Halporn, J. (1993) "Roman Comedy and Greek Models." In *Theater and Society in the Classical World,* ed. R. Scodel, 191–213. Ann Arbor: University of Michigan Press.

Hopkins, K. (1993) "Novel Evidence for Roman Slavery." *Past and Present* 138: 3–27.

Hough, J. N. (1942) "The Reverse Comic Foil in Plautus." *Transactions of the American Philological Association* 73: 108–18.

Hunter, R. L. (1985) *The New Comedy of Greece and Rome.* Cambridge: Cambridge University Press.

Jachmann, G. (1931) *Plautinisches und Attisches.* Berlin: Weidmann.

Jekels, L. (1952) "On the Psychology of Comedy." In *Selected Papers,* 97–104. New York: International Universities Press.

Jones, G. (1992) *Honey I'm Home! Sitcoms: Selling the American Dream.* New York: Grove Weidenfeld.

Ketterer, R. C. (1986a) "Stage Properties in Plautine Comedy, II." *Semiotica* 59: 93–135.

———. (1986b) "Stage Properties in Plautine Comedy, III." *Semiotica* 60: 29–72.

Konstan, D. (1983) *Roman Comedy.* Ithaca: Cornell University Press.

Leach, E. (1969a) "*Meam quom formam noscito*: Language and Characterization in the *Menaechmi.*" *Arethusa* 2: 30–45.

———. (1969b) "Ergasilus and the Ironies of the *Captivi.*" *Classica et Mediaevalia* 30: 263–96.

———. (1969c) "*De exemplo meo ipse aedificato*: An Organizing Idea in the *Mostellaria.*" *Hermes* 97: 318–32.

Lefèvre, E. (1979) "Plautus Studien III. Von der Tyche-Herrschaft in Diphilos' *Kleroumenoi* zum Triummatronat der *Casina.*" *Hermes* 107: 311–39.

Leo, F. (1912) *Plautinische Forschungen,* 2nd edition. Berlin: Weidmann.

———. (1913) *Geschichte der römischer Literatur,* vol. 1. Berlin: Weidmann.

Lilja, S. (1982) "Homosexuality in Plautus' Plays." *Arctos* 14: 57–64.

Lindsay, W. (1900) *Plautus:* Captivi. London: Methuen & Co.

Lott, E. (1995) *Love and Theft: Blackface Minstrelsy and the American Working Class.* Oxford: Oxford University Press.

Lowe, J. C. B. (1989a) "Plautus' Parasites and the Atellana." In *Studien zur vorliterarischen Periode in frühen Rom,* ed. G. Vogt-Spira (*ScriptOralia,* no. 12), 161–70. Tübingen: Gunter Narr.

———. (1989b) "The Virgo Callida of Plautus' *Persa.*" *Classical Quarterly* 39: 390–99.

———. (1991) "Prisoners, Guards, and Chains in Plautus' *Captivi.*" *American Journal of Philology* 112: 29–44.

MacCary, W. T. (1973) "The Comic Tradition and Comic Structure in Diphilos' *Kleroumenoi.*" *Hermes* 101: 194–208.

———. (1974) "Patterns of Myth, Ritual and Comedy in Plautus' *Casina.*" *Texas Studies in Language and Literature* 15: 881–88.

MacCary, W. T., and M. M. Willcock. (1976) *Plautus: Casina.* Cambridge: Cambridge University Press.

Middleton, R. (1983) "Play It Again, Sam: Some Notes on the Productivity of Repetition in Popular Music." *Popular Music* 3: 235–70.

Middleton, R. (1986) "In the Groove, or Blowing Your Mind? The Pleasures of Musical Repetition." In *Popular Culture and Social Relations,* ed. T. Bennett et al., 159–75. Philadelphia: Open University Press.

Moore, T. J. (1995) "Seats and Social Status in the Plautine Theatre." *Classical Journal* 90: 113–23.

Morson, G., and C. Emerson (1990) *Mikhail Bakhtin: Creation of a Prosaics*. Stanford: Stanford University Press..

Mumford, L.S. (1995) *Love and Ideology in the Afternoon: Soap Opera, Women and Television Genre*. Bloomington: University of Indiana Press.

Nicolet, C. (1980) *The World of the Citizen in Republican Rome*, trans. P. S. Falla. Berkeley: University of California Press.

Nixon, P. (1934) *Plautus*, vol. 5. Loeb Classical Library. Cambridge, MA: Harvard University Press.

Norwood, G. (1932) *Plautus and Terence*. New York: Longmans, Green and Co.

O'Bryhim, S. (1989) "The Originality of Plautus' *Casina*." *American Journal of Philology* 110: 81–103.

Parker, H. (1989) "Crucially Funny or Tranio on the Couch: The *Servus Callidus* and Jokes about Torture." *Transactions of the American Philological Association* 119: 233–46.

Pasquali, G. (1927) "Un Monologo dei *Captivi*." *Rivista di Filologica e di Instruzione Classica* 5: 24–30.

Patterson, O. (1982) *Slavery and Social Death: A Comparative Study*. Cambridge, MA: Harvard University Press.

Petrone, G. (1977) *Morale e antimorale nelle commedie di Plauto*. Palermo: Palumbo.

———. (1983) *Teatro antico e inganno: Finzione plautine*. Palermo: Palumbo.

———. (1988) "Ridere in silenzio: tradizione misogina e trionfo dell' intelligenza femminile nelle commedia plautina." In *La donna nel mondo antico*, vol. 2, ed. Renato Uglione, 87–103. Torino: Regione Piemonte, Assessorato alla Cultura.

Prescott, H. W. (1916) "The Interpretation of Roman Comedy." *Classical Philology* 11: 125–47.

———. (1920) "Inorganic Roles in Roman Comedy." *Classical Philology* 15: 245–81.

Preston, K. (1916) *Studies in the "Sermo Amatorius" of Roman Comedy*. Dissertation, University of Chicago.

Rei, A. (1998) "Villians, Wives and Slaves in the Comedies of Plautus." In *Women and Slaves in Greco-Roman Culture*, ed. Sandra Joshel and Sheila Murnaghan, 92–108. London and New York: Routledge.

Saller, R. P. (1994) *Patriarchy, Property and Death in the Roman Family*. Cambridge: Cambridge University Press.

Schuhmann, E. (1977) "Der Typ der *uxor dotata* in den Komoedien des Plautus." *Philologus* 121: 45–65.

Scodel, R. 1993. "Tragic Sacrifice and Menandrian Cooking." In *Theater and Society in the Classical World*, ed. R. Scodel, 161–76. Ann Arbor: University of Michigan Press.

Scott, J. (1990) *Domination and the Arts of Resistance: Hidden Transcripts*. New Haven: Yale University Press.

Segal, E. (1969) "The *Menaechmi*: A Roman Comedy of Errors." *Yale Classical Studies* 21: 75–93.

———. (1974) "The Business of Roman Comedy." In *Perspectives of Roman Poetry*, ed. K. Galinsky, 93–103. Austin: University of Texas Press.

————. (1987) *Roman Laughter: The Comedy of Plautus*, 2nd edition. Oxford: Oxford University Press.

Sharrock, A.R. (1996) "The Art of Deceit: Pseudolus and the Nature of Reading." *Classical Quarterly* 46: 152–74.

Slater, N. (1985) *Plautus in Performance: The Theatre of the Mind*. Princeton: Princeton University Press.

————. (1992) "Plautine Negotiations: the *Poenulus* Prologue Unpacked." *Yale Classical Studies* 29: 131–46.

Spranger, P. (1984) *Historische Untersuchungen zu den Sklavenfiguren des Plautus und Terenz*, 2nd edition. Stuttgart: F. Steiner.

Stace, C. (1968) "The Slaves of Plautus." *Greece and Rome* 15: 64–77.

Stallybrass, P. and A. White. (1986) *The Politics and Poetics of Transgression*. Ithaca: Cornell University Press.

Tatum, J. (1983) *Plautus: The Darker Comedies*. Baltimore: Johns Hopkins University Press.

Taylor, E. (1989) *Prime Time Families: Television Culture in Post-War America*. Berkeley: University of California Press.

Taylor, L. R. (1937) "The Opportunities for Dramatic Performances in the Time of Plautus and Terence." *Transactions of American Philological Association* 68: 284–304.

————. (1966) *Roman Voting Assemblies*. Ann Arbor: University of Michigan Press.

Thalmann, W. G. (1996) "Versions of Slavery in the *Captivi* of Plautus," *Ramus* 25: 112–45.

Tobias, J. B. (1979) "Bacchaic Women and Iambic Slaves in Plautus," *Classical World* 73: 9–18.

Van Deburg, W. (1984) *Slavery and Race in American Popular Culture*. Madison: University of Wisconsin Press.

Viljoen, G. van N. (1963) "The Plot of the *Captivi*." *Acta Classica* 6: 38–63.

Way, M. (1998) "Ars Cladis": *Violence and the Construction of Society in Plautus*. Dissertation, University of California, Berkeley.

Webster, T. B. L. (1953) *Studies in Later Greek Comedy*. Manchester: Manchester University Press.

————. (1960) *Studies in Menander*, 2nd edition. Manchester: Manchester University Press.

————. (1974) *An Introduction to Menander*. Manchester: Manchester University Press.

Wilamowitz, U. (1894) *De Tribus Carminibus Latinis Commentatio*. Göttingen.

Wiles, D. (1991) *The Masks of Menander*. Cambridge: Cambridge University Press.

Williams, G. (1982) "The Genesis of Poetry in Rome." In *Cambridge History of Classical Literature*, vol II, *Latin Literature*, edd. by E. J. Kenney and W. V. Clausen, 53–59. Cambridge: Cambridge University Press.

Wilner, O. (1930) "Contrast and Repetition as Devices in the Technique of Character Portrayal in Roman Comedy." *Classical Philology* 25: 56–71.

————. (1931) "The Character Treatment of Inorganic Roles." Classical Philology 26: 264–83.

Wilner, O. (1938) "The Technical Device of Direct Description of Character in Roman Comedy." *CP* 33: 20–36.

Woytek, E. (1982) *T. Maccius Plautus, "Persa": Einleitung, Text und Kommentar*. Vienna: Verlag der Osterreichischen Akademie der Wissenschaften.

Wright, J. (1974) *Dancing in Chains: The Stylistic Unity of the* Comoedia Palliata, vol. 25. Rome: Papers and Monographs of the American Academy in Rome.

INDEX OF PLAUTINE PASSAGES

All other texts will be found in the general index under the author's name.

Amphitruo, 87n.18, 99–100, 115–17, 130
    16: 133n.25
    151: 133n.25
    254: 117n.82
    I.1 (341–462): 194, 87n.18
    463–98: 52n.30
    515: 134n.30
    565: 138n.45
    633–53: 90–91
    664–67: 117n.82
    861–81: 52n.30
    874: 58n.46
    984–1108: 52n.30
    993: 134n.30
    999: 58n.46
Asinaria, 44n.15, 65n.62, 81, 118n.83,
    154, 179, 202; as example of *senex amator*
    comedy, 39n.5, 56n.41, 68–69, 91, 115;
    shift in plot-type, 16n.25, 176
    72: 133n.28
    I.2 (111–52): 91n.27
    312–20: 142
    351: 141n.53
    416: 138n.45
    III.1 (504–44): 142n.54
    547: 164n.101
    III.3 (591–745): 141–42, 196
    650–52: 141
    673: 133n.28
    712–13: 58n.47
    V.2 (851–942): 56n.41
    871–72: 54n.37
    914: 95n.37
    933: 112n.75
    935–36: 107n.66
Aulularia, 78n.4, 110, 175, 178, 187
    167–69: 119n.84
    193: 132n.23
    218: 143n.55
    401: 156n.91
    III.5 (475–536): 119n.84
    478–95: 134n.31
    587–91: 131n.20

Bacchides, 5, 11n.16, 65n.63, 105, 107,
    126nn.6, 9, 157, 160, 172, 194n.57
    93–100: 64n.59
    II.3 (235–367): 129n.14
    532: 113n.77
    564: 149n.75
    573–83: 52n.30
    640: 58n.47
    649–50: 147n.70
    IV.6 (770–98): 195n.60
    829: 138n.45
    913–15: 131n.19
    962: 58n.46
    1067–71: 153
    1087–88: 154n.87
    1125–28: 190n.47

Captivi, 11n.16, 12n.19, 13n.20, 30, 33, 34,
    38, 48n.22, 49n.23, 70n.73, 118, 122,
    154, 155, 161, 165, 167–209
    1–2: 186n.39
    27–28: 175, 189
    55–58: 176n.21
    I.1 (69–109): 42n.9, 62–63, 182–83,
      202n.72
    69–70: 134n.29
    77: 134n.30, 183
    98–101: 175, 189
    103: 185
    I.2 (110–94): 183–85, 205
    116–18: 43n.12, 184
    129–91: 135n.34
    142–43: 168
    Act II (195–460): 186–90
    II.1 (195–250): 186–88
    195–209: 169
    224: 58n.46
    232–36: 168
    II.2 (251–360): 188–89
    255–56: 176–77, 188
    261–62: 186n.40
    266–69: 190n.47
    274–76: 190n.47
    284: 190n.47

Captivi (continued)
  313–15: 206
  324–28: 177, 189
  II.3 (361–460): 176, 189–90
  432–41: 168n.3
  III.1 (461–97): 42n.9, 52n.30, 182,
    190–91, 204
  484: 204
  489: 204
  III.2 (498–515): 177, 191–92
  III.3 (516–32): 192–93
  III.4 (533–658): 193–95
  543–44: 193
  551: 138n.45
  629: 173
  657–59: 184n.36
  III. 5 (659–767): 194–95
  682–743: 169
  715–20: 171
  751–65: 176
  759–63: 200
  Act IV (768–921): 195–98
  768–80: 52n.30
  778: 203
  781–87: 177
  939–48: 199
  951: 138n.45
  954: 171
  985–96: 168, 172
  992: 200
Casina, 11n.16, 16n.25, 30, 32–33, 39n.5,
  55n.38, 74, 77–121, 122–23, 125n.5, 127,
  130, 159n.95, 165–66, 177n.22, 190
  36–38: 77n.2
  64–66: 77n.2
  67–74: 116
  I.1 (89–143): 87–89
  124–25: 101n.50
  132–40: 88, 101, 112
  II.1 (144–64): 89
  II.2 (144–216): 89–90, 102, 121n.87
  II.3 (217–78): 90–94, 107, 191n.51
  227–28: 102
  229–35: 102
  230: 94n.34
  234: 102
  251: 95
  II.4 (279–308): 94–95
  297–98: 96n.40
  307–8: 93, 96n.40
  II.5 (309–52): 95–96
  344: 93, 96n.40

  352: 93, 96n.40
  II.6 (353–423): 96–98
  404–11: 93, 97
  419–22: 64n.59
  424–36: 101
  II.8 (437–514): 101–3, 106, 112
  504–6: 95n.35
  III.1 (515–30): 103
  III.2, III.3 (531–90): 104
  531–33: 89n.23
  532: 107n.63
  552: 117
  554–56: 104
  563–73: 54
  585–86: 104
  588: 107n.63
  III.4 (591–620): 103
  III.5 (621–719): 104–5, 197
  618: 107n.63
  685–88: 147n.70
  III.6 (720–58): 105–7, 141, 196n.64
  IV.1, IV.2 (759–97): 107
  775–79: 111, 117
  IV.3 (798–814): 108
  IV.4 (815–54): 108–9
  V.1 (855–74): 111
  855–61: 147n.70
  860–61: 82
  V.2 (875–936): 112
  V.3 (937–62): 113, 130
  V.4 (963–1018): 113–14, 130
  1013–14: 77n.2, 114
Cistellaria, 16n.25, 63n.54, 65n.62, 154, 178
  I.1 (1–119): 142n.54
  22–41: 63n.54
  133–42: 170n.6
  II.1 (203–28): 91n.27
  203–8: 90–91
Curculio, 9, 48n.22, 65n.62, 130, 176, 202
  16: 135n.33
  145: 149n.76
  167: 96n.40
  II.2 (280–370): 197
  317–25: 135n.34
  322: 135n.33
  366–70: 135n.34
  371–83: 191n.50
  490–91: 170n.6
  614: 138n.45
  698: 200n.69
  700: 200n.69

Epidicus, 26, 48n.22, 87n.18, 126n.6,
  154n.86, 158n.94, 160n.97, 175, 179, 199
    1–80: 87n.18, 130
    81–103: 192
    82: 54n.34
    96: 54n.34
    I.2 (104–65): 91n.27
    107–8: 170n.6
    161: 54n.34
    194: 54n.34
    410–24: 191n.51
    410: 141n.53
    V.2 (665–731): 195n.60

Menaechmi, 26, 30, 31–32, 35–76, 81,
  86n.16, 94, 95, 99n.48, 105, 118n.83,
  120–21, 122–23, 160, 161, 172, 182, 187,
  190, 202, 205
    I.1 (77–109): 41–43, 135n.34, 191n.49,
      202n.72
    77–78: 134n.29
    97: 42, 136n.38
    104–6: 72
    I.2 (110–81): 43–46
    110–24: 43, 66
    113–16: 66
    120–22: 44, 50n.24
    121: 156n.91
    124: 66
    130: 66
    132: 147n.69
    137–39: 45, 136
    152–55: 49n.23
    156–57: 42
    I.3 (182–218): 46, 62, 63
    189: 67n.67
    193–95: 46, 56n.40
    205–6: 64
    207: 46, 63, 65n.60
    210–12: 72
    I.4 (219–25): 64
    II.1 (226–72): 49–51, 70
    249–52: 49, 50n.24, 144
    II.2 (273–350): 51–52
    II.3 (351–445): 51–52, 66
    III.1 (446–65): 52–53, 135n.32, 191n.49
    451–54: 183n.32
    III.2 (466–523): 53–54
    492: 49n.23
    513–15: 46n.19
    III.3 (524–58): 54, 64
    IV.1 (559–70): 54, 62

    562: 55n.39
    569: 95n.38
    IV.2 (571–674): 55–56, 66–67, 194
    IV.3 (675–700): 64, 66–67
    677: 65n.60
    708: 112n.75
    713: 112n.75
    714–18: 95n.38
    V.2 (753–875): 55, 56–58, 194
    765: 95n.37
    784: 95n.37
    787–806: 90
    795–97: 46n.19, 57
    853: 71
    882–88: 57n.43
    889–93: 59
    V.5 (899–965): 55, 58–59
    V.6 (966–89): 59–60, 71–72, 131n.20
    V.7 (990–1049): 60n.50, 184n.36
    V.9 (1060–1162): 59–61
Mercator, 39n.5, 68–69, 91, 115, 118n.83,
  126n.6
    16–39: 63n.54
    65–68: 88n.20
    111–19: 196
    189: 138n.45
    262–67: 92
    II.2 (272–354): 103n.54
    408: 149n.76
    535: 149n.75
    III.3 (562–87): 103n.54
    601–2: 96n.40
    690: 116
    714–40: 56n.41
    IV.4 (741–802): 194
    817–29: 68n.69
    823–29: 134n.31
    956: 116
    959: 95n.39
    983: 112n.75
    1015–26: 67–68, 114n.78, 134n.31
Miles Gloriosus, 11n.16, 26, 28, 65n.63, 75,
  107, 124, 154, 179
    189a: 164n.101
    II.3 (272–353): 87n.18
    348: 134n.30
    465: 164n.101
    476: 156n.91
    494: 138n.45
    685–700: 119n.84
    709: 135n.33
    767: 147n.69

Miles Gloriosus (continued)
    768: 190n.47
    941: 164n.101
    961–63: 150n.77
    967: 150n.77
    IV.2 (991–1093): 150n.79
    IV.4 (1137–99): 150n.79
    1163: 58n.46
    1374–77: 191n.51
    1434: 138n.45
Mostellaria, 3–4, 26, 76n.78, 105, 126n.9,
    175, 179, 187; as example of comedy
    centered on clever slave, 28, 158n.94,
    160, 172
    I.1 (1–83): 4, 87n.18, 88n.20, 130
    38: 164n.101
    15–24: 88n.20
    35–37: 88n.20
    84–156: 3–4, 90–91
    348–62: 192
    II.2 (431–531): 129n.14
    699: 95n.39
    IV.1 (858–84): 73, 131n.20
    885–903: 161n.98
    V.1 (1041–1121): 73, 195n.60
    1041–61: 73
    1068: 54n.34
    1149–51: 147n.70
    1173: 156n.91
    1178–79: 4, 94n.33

Persa, 11n.14, 28n.48, 30, 33–34,
    86n.16, 105, 111, 122–66, 179, 201, 202;
    influence of *leno* on structure, 65n.62,
    76, 176
    I.1 (1–54): 130–33, 141n.52
    1–2: 128
    22: 145n.64
    39: 164n.102
    I.2 (53–80): 42n.9, 62–63, 134–35,
        191n.49, 202n.72
    53: 134, 144n.62, 183
    58: 183
    60: 182n.28
    62–74: 52n.31, 134–35
    65–67: 135, 143
    75–76: 143
    I.3 (81–167): 135–37
    82: 157
    152: 151n.82
    II.1 (168–82): 137–38
    168: 144n.62

    175–76: 151n.82
    176: 144n.62
    II.2 (183–250): 137–40
    183–87: 151n.82
    191: 144
    193–94: 163–64
    230–32: 164n.103
    243–44: 163–64
    II.3 (251–71): 140–41, 195
    251–56: 153, 195n.61
    261: 146n.65
    273: 141n.51, 157
    280a: 159
    284–86: 164
    286: 161
    292: 137n.39
    294: 137n.39
    II.5 (302–28): 141–42
    304: 150n.78
    305: 144n.62, 151n.82
    308: 141n.53
    III.1 (329–99): 142–44, 160
    357–58: 163
    379–81: 151n.82
    382: 159n.96
    383–84: 162
    390–92: 136n.37
    392: 203n.74
    392–96: 42n.10
    399: 152, 157
    III.3 (405–48): 144–47, 148n.72
    420: 145n.64, 156
    IV.1 (449–61): 146–47
    449: 148
    451: 148
    456: 164n.102
    462–66: 147
    IV.3 (470–548): 147–48
    470–79: 191
    474–75: 157
    483: 150
    484: 157
    491: 157
    518: 150
    539: 150
    548: 150
    IV.4 (549–682): 148–51, 176
    591–603: 162
    624–26: 163n.100
    649: 183n.29
    683–700: 151
    693: 163

700: 163n.100
702–5: 152
737: 157
745–52: 152
749: 129
V.1 (753–76a): 153–55, 195
753–62: 195n.61
757–62: 153–54, 195
V.2 (777–858): 155–58, 195n.60
829: 190n.47
833–37: 154
845: 129, 158
Poenulus, 48n.22, 76, 124, 130, 154n.86,
161, 176
17–35: 19n.28
157–58: 145n.64
210–32: 90–91
313: 117n.82
325: 117n.82
367: 117n.82
581: 147n.70
825–26: 145n.64
901: 147n.69
1035–36: 156n.91
1221: 200n.69
Pseudolus, 7n.6, 11n.16, 65n.62, 126n.6,
130, 157, 176, 179, 202; as example of
comedy centered on clever slave, 26, 28,
126n.9, 158n.94, 160, 172; as example of
metatheater, 34
87: 133n.28
109–10: 58n.47
360–68: 144–45
394–414: 192
394: 54n.34
401–8: 147n.70
446: 138n.45
453: 54n.34
458: 133n.25
460–61: 194
519: 141n.53
574–93: 192
700: 141n.53
713: 132n.23
III.1 (767–89): 161n.98
775–78: 129n.15
905–7: 195
911: 138n.45

946: 147n.69
1103–13: 131n.20
1205: 138n.45
V.2 (1285–1334): 195n.60
1333: 79n.5

Rudens, 11n.16, 65n.62, 75, 111, 154,
167n.1, 178, 184n.35, 205–8
9–30: 206
35–38: 127n.10, 206
106: 170n.6
431: 133n.25
651–53: 145n.64
III.5 (780–838): 184n.36
1398–99: 156n.91

Stichus, 111
155–233: 42n.9, 62–63, 202n.72
168–70: 183
171–73: 183
174–77: 134n.29
221–25: 42n.10
274–87: 196n.64
III.2 (454–504): 203n.74
454: 164n.101
632: 54n.34
637: 134n.30

Trinummus, 12n.19, 48n.22, 126n.6, 167n.1,
205n.78
217–21: 134n.31
II.1 (222–75): 91n.27
500: 143n.55
572: 143n.55
1024: 141n.53
1056: 133n.28
Truculentus, 65, 65n.63, 105, 107, 119, 179
154–56: 119
II.2 (252–321): 87n.18
372: 96n.40
390: 58n.46
II.5 (448–64): 90–91, 129n.14
464: 58n.46
472: 58n.46
II.6 (482–550): 119
II.7 (551–630): 119
621: 138n.45
964: 147n.69

acting, in relation to metatheater, 57–58
(esp. n.46), 97, 105, 140, 144, 162n.99

adulescens, 20n.31, 45, 63n.54, 74–76, 126,
158n.94, 178–79, 189–90; language of,
92, 96n.40, 128, 141–42; *senex amator* assimilated to, 69, 91–93, 96n.40, 105–6,
109; *servus callidus* assimilated to, in *Persa*,
122–23, 128, 130–33, 141–42

agnoia (misunderstanding, mistaken identity): relation to insanity theme, 51, 194–
95; relation to naturalistic mode, 41, 48,
55, 125, 189, 206–9

amicitia. *See* friendship

anagnorisis. *See* recognition

Anderson, W. S., 14n.21, 126n.6

animal imagery, 88, 183

Aristotle, *Politics* 1253b: 22n.35; 1254b16–
1255b15: 170n.5

asides, character's relation to audience
through, 45, 46, 94n.32, 102, 135,
190n.47

audience: contemporary Roman 6, 17–21,
25, 29; metatheater and, 101, 103, 112.
See also asides; monologues

Aulus Gellius 10.3.19: 184n.36

authority: farcical authority (of rebels, tricksters), 16, 38, 73, 112, 116, 163, 197; —,
ludificatio and, 156; —, metatheater and,
57, 161; naturalistic authority (of fathers,
masters), 110, 116; —, religion and, 57,
96–99 passim, 107; —, as used in rebellion, 32, 96, 98–99, 109; relation of different forms of, to each other, 32, 74–75,
83, 97, 100, 120, 161, 190, 195; resistance
to, and metatheater, 85–86, 101; in
Roman society, 22–25, 27, 29; romantic
authority (of *adulescentes*), 74–75, 97, 120,
161

Bakhtin, M. M., 6, 8n.9, 17n.26, 27, 164–
65. *See also* dialogism

Barton, C., 29n.49

Bettini, M., 9n.10, 16, 124n.2, 131n.19,
134n.31, 175n.19

blocking characters, 39–40, 43, 86–87, 89,

112, 118, 135, 176–78, 184; comedy of
humors and, 111, 177–78; father vs. *leno*
as, 16n.24, 76, 123–24, 132, 180; legal
idiom of, 57, 58n.46; metatheater and,
113–14; money as motivation for, 147–
48, 177, 189, 204–5; relation to motif of
Saturnalia, 107; relation to resolution, 61,
180; relation to romantic comedy, 82;
uxores dotatae as, 39–40, 68–69, 99, 116.
See also under punishment

Bourdieu, P., 23n.37

Bradley, K. R., 18n.27, 24, 26n.42

character types, 61–76, 91, 102, 104–5; functions of, 81–82, 98, 116, 175–80; mixed
types, 122–23, 126–27, 127–30. *See also*
adulescens, lena, leno, meretrix, parasite,
*pseudomeretrix, puer delicatus, senex, servus
bonus, servus callidus, uxor*

Chiarini, G., 11n.14, 14n.21, 72n.74,
92n.28, 102, 137, 138, 140, 148, 155n.89,
162n.99, 165n.104

Cicero, *In Verrem* I.121: 136n.36; *Pro Caecina* 51–52: 23n.36

city and country, imagery of, 87–88,
101n.50, 107

civic values (citizen identity, civic ideology),
33–34, 122–23, 129, 134–35, 137; gender
and citizen identity, 161–62; punishment
of *leno* and, 136–37, 148–49, 153, 158,
165–66; relation to naturalistic and romantic comedy, 123–27, 161–62, 166

clientela. *See* patron/client relationship

Clover, C., 21n.32, 28n.47, 29n.49

comedy, sub-genres. *See* comedy of humors;
farce; naturalism/ naturalistic comedy; romantic comedy

comedy of humors, 13, 110–11, 175–80
passim

comic conventions, 15–16, 31, 57n.43, 91,
102, 104–5; comic 'decorum', 43n.14; relation to parasites, 62–63, 202–3. *See also*
character types; metatheater; plot types;
resolution

deception. *See* trickery
dialogism, 7–17 passim, 26, 29–31, 33,
    37–38, 55, 78–79, 158–66 passim, 167,
    173–75, 181, 198, 201–7. *See also* Bakhtin
Diphilus, 77n.2
Dumézil, G., 129n.15, 170n.7
Dumont, J., 180n.25

eavesdropping, 88, 101–3 passim, 135
economic life (money), 60–61, 86, 120–21,
    177, 189, 201–5; marriage and, 44–45,
    66–67; mastery/household authority and,
    36–37, 41–47, 60–61, 71–73; money as
    motivation for blocking characters, 147–
    48, 177, 189, 204–5; women and, 64–67,
    69–70, 89–90, 121n.87

farce (farcical mode), 12–13, 14–15, 164–66,
    202–3; in the *Casina*, romantic comedy
    and, 32, 77–79, 88; clever slave in, 14, 16,
    29; ideological effect of, 25–26, 38, 79,
    110, 158; metatheater and, 159–65 pas-
    sim; moral perspective of, 14–15, 167;
    non-teleological aesthetic of, 32, 33, 78,
    100, 107, 127, 137–38, 158–66; rebellion
    in, 37–38, 79–80, 109–10; relation to nat-
    uralistic comedy (*see* dialogism); resolu-
    tions typical of, 76, 109–10; slavery and,
    79, 169; temporal structure of, 79. *See
    also under* authority; *malitia*; metatheater;
    rebellion; *servus callidus*; trickery
father-son relationships. *See* parent-child re-
    lationships
fides, 129, 139–40, 147–48, 150, 162–64
Finley, M. 21n.34
Fitzgerald, W., 19n.28, 21n.33, 72n.74,
    80n.9
food, 64, 71–73, 85–86, 92n.28, 103, 111;
    banquet as finale, 107, 111, 118, 129,
    153–55, 197–98, 207; role of, in house-
    hold authority, 42, 86, 88, 185, 195–97,
    205; sex and, 54n.38, 106n.61, 107, 108,
    117–18; women and, 117–19. *See also* eco-
    nomic life; parasite
Forehand, W., 77n.1, 86n.15, 114n.78, 117
Fraenkel, E., 9–10, 18n.27, 54, 131n.19,
    138n.44, 153
friendship, as motif in naturalizing comedy,
    125–26, 129, 132–33, 140–41, 150, 154,
    158–59
Frye, N., 4n.1, 13, 57, 68n.70

Galinsky, K., 22
gender, 21n.32, 80, 105n.57, 107, 111, 179,
    207n.84. *See also under* civic values; eco-
    nomic life; food; *meretrix*; *pseudomeretrix*;
    trickery; *uxor*
Greek comedy, 5, 10–11, 57n.43, 183n.33;
    'Middle' comedy, 123n.1. *See also* Diphi-
    lus; Menander; Philemon
Grimal, P., 12n.18

Halporn, J., 42n.9
hodie (as marker of festive inversion). *See* Sat-
    urnalia
Hopkins, K., 18n.27
Horace, *Epistles* 2.1.175–76: 202n.73

imagery. *See* animal imagery; city and coun-
    try; legal language; religious language
internal playwright, 82–84, 111, 129, 150,
    151, 208; parasites as, 203n.74; *senex ama-
    tor* as, 92n.28, 94; *servus callidus* as, 13, 14;
    uxor dotata as, 100, 103–4, 109–10. *See
    also* metatheater
inversion. *See* Saturnalia
irony, 176, 186, 188, 189n.45, 192–93, 200,
    208–9

Juno: absence of, from *Am*, 116; *uxor dotata*
    as, 97
Jupiter: *adulescens* as, 96n.40; in *Am*, 99–
    100, 115–17; *senex amator* as, 83, 85, 93–
    97 passim

Ketterer, R. C., 47n.20, 65n.61, 186n.41,
    200n.68
Konstan, D., 16n.25, 44n.15, 65, 68n.70,
    171n.8, 175, 176, 193n.54, 199n.67, 200

Leach, E. W., 4n.1, 35, 43n.13, 48n.21,
    58n.46, 70, 184n.34, 189n.45, 190n.48,
    195, 197–98
Lefèvre, E., 100n.49, 117, 125n.5
legal language, 136, 152; blocking charac-
    ters and, 57, 58–59; comic legislative pro-
    posals, 52n.31, 67–68, 134–35, 191;
    uxores dotatae and, 94n.33, 95
lena, 63n.54, 65
leno, 16n.24, 65, 76, 144–45, 175, 176–78
    passim, 179n.24, 205; as blocking charac-
    ter, 123–24, 132, 180; as threat to commu-
    nity, 34, 136–37, 148–49, 151, 153, 158,
    165–66

lorarius, 184–85

Lott, E., 17, 18, 28n.47

Lowe, J. C. B., 42n.10, 183n.33

ludificatio, 154–58

ludi scaenici. See production conditions

Machiavelli, Niccolò: *Clizia*, 78n.2, 88n.20

malitia, 4, 14n.21, 38, 48–49, 110–11, 116, 159n.96, 165, 204; *ludificatio* and, 157; metatheater and, 138, 140–41

manumission, 24–25, 60–61, 71, 94–95, 160–61, 164, 199

marriage, representation of, in comedy, 39–40, 64–65, 110–11, 114n.78, 115–17; analogous to slavery, 79–81, 100–103, 106, 108–9, 111; economics and, 36–37, 44–45, 64–65, 66–67, 69–70, 89–90; as resolution in romantic comedy, 12, 75, 78–79, 114, 166, 178, 180

mastery. *See* slavery: ideology of

matrona. See *uxor*

Menander, 10n.13, 11n.17, 12n.18, 59n.48, 125, 208n.85; *Aspis*, 125n.5; *Dis Exapaton*, 5; *Dyskolos*, 5, 78n.4, 110; *Epitrepontes*, 119n.85; *Heros*, 9

meretrix, 40, 63–68, 70, 91, 138n.43, 149n.77, 161, 179, 182–83, 203; compared to *uxores/matronae*, 44–45, 64–65, 66–67, 69–70, 118–19

metatheater, 100, 113–14, 133n.25, 147, 208; as common 'past' of characters, 62n.52, 102, 164; as image for control, 82–84, 85, 92–94; *malitia* and, 138, 140–41; parasites and, 62–63, 136n.37; relation to authority, 82–84, 96–97, 98, 100; relation to dialogism, 34, 123, 125, 129, 159–61, 165. *See also* acting

military language, 43, 87–88, 93, 96n.40, 107, 132, 150, 153, 185n.38

minstrelsy (blackface), 11n.15, 18, 211–13

misanthrope plot-type. *See* comedy of humors

money. *See* economic life

monologues: of parasites, 41–43, 52n.30, 62–63, 134–35, 174, 182–83, 202n.72; relation of speaker to audience in, 45n.18, 64, 190; relation of speaker to other characters in, 182, 190–91

naturalism/naturalistic comedy, 11–12, 13–14, 47–49, 74–76, 123; family reconciliation in, 37–38, 59, 124; ideological effect of, 26; moral perspective of, 13–14, 39; rebellion in, 13, 55, 58; relation to farce (*see* dialogism); resolutions typical of, 76, 79, 175; trickery in, 48–49, 51–52, 53–54, 73, 173, 178–79, 188–89, 194–95. *See also* romantic comedy

opening scene types, 62–63, 130, 174, 182–83

parasite, 42, 54n.38, 62–63, 151, 155, 174, 190–91, 195–98, 201–3; animal imagery for, 183; as blocking character, 40; compared to Greek *sycophantês*, 134n.31; compared to *meretrix*, 182, 203; compared to *servus callidus*, 195–96, 202; as emblem of farcical mode, 34, 174, 198; as father, in *Persa*, 143, 159; monologues of, 41–43, 52–53, 134–35, 174, 182–83, 202n.72; nicknames of, 63, 134n.29, 182–83, 203; relation to *uxor dotata*, 118n.83

pardon: of non-slave trickster, 109–10, 112–13; of slave by master, 86, 113n.76, 126, 199, 207

parent-child relationships: compared to master-slave relationships, 79, 144, 150–51; father-son, in romantic comedy, 74–76, 79, 91, 99, 123, 173, 178; parasite as father, in *Persa*, 143, 159

Parker, H., 20n.31

parody, 58n.46, 104–5, 108, 130–31, 133n.25, 140

Pasquali, G., 192n.52

patron/client relationship, 45, 54, 135, 183, 185–86, 191, 197–98, 205

Petrone, G., 14n.21, 90n.25, 192n.52, 208n.85

Philemon, 126n.6

philia. See friendship

Pliny, *Letters* III.14: 25n.41

plot types, 16, 103, 175–80; shift in, within play, 142, 176

production conditions, 6, 17

pseudomeretrix, 124n.3, 161–62, 179; male characters in function of, 38, 75, 161–62, 175, 200

puer delicatus, 138nn.43, 45, 155, 157, 161

punishment: of blocking characters, 69, 125, 127, 129, 147, 148–49, 165; language and attitude towards, of *servi callidi*, 26–27, 113, 140–41, 192; relation to civic ideology, 151, 153–58; of rival, 88,

punishment: (continued)
101; of tricksters, 71, 72, 73, 88, 109–10,
177, 187, 194, 199, 207

rebellion, 20, 82, 89, 109–11, 212–23; of authority figures, esp. paterfamilias, 28–29,
30–31, 35, 38–40, 46, 81, 85, 93–96,
98–99, 114–15, 116; of characters subordinated to rebels, 159–64; filial, in relation
to romantic comedy, 32, 74–75, 79, 123,
126; in naturalistic mode, 13, 55, 58–59;
relation to farce and naturalism, 13, 26,
28, 35, 38; of uxor, 80, 109–10, 119
recognition (anagnorisis), 34, 60, 114–15,
137, 170, 200–201, 207; relation to
civic ideology, 124–25, 129, 162, 166;
relation to naturalistic comedy, 12, 14,
30, 37–38, 77
Rei, A., 110n.73, 179n.23
religious language, 51, 57, 58, 94n.34, 143;
image of divinity for trickster, 58n.47,
96n.40, 100; prayers, 140, 153, 195n.61;
religious imagery, in Casina, 85, 93, 95,
98. See also Juno; Jupiter
resolution, 31, 60–61, 65, 78–80, 88, 111,
117, 175–76; associated with senex amator,
112, 113n.76; in farce, 13, 32, 86, 109,
114; ludificatio vs. reconciliation, 154,
156, 207–9; in naturalistic/romantic comedy, 12, 75, 114, 124, 126, 180, 198–201;
relation to blocking character, 16n.24, 76,
124; relation to dialogism, 32, 109–11,
120–21, 166; servus bonus in, 73; servus callidus in, 109–10, 113n.76. See also ludificatio; pardon; punishment; See also under
marriage
ritual, used in deception schemes, 96–97,
108. See also religious language
romantic comedy, 74–76, 81–82, 117, 128,
131–32, 137, 146, 175–80 passim, 198,
200; civic identity theme of, 123–27,
161–62, 166; 'oedipal' theme of, 32, 68,
79, 123, 132, 166; relation to comedy of
humors, 110–11; relation to farce, in
Casina, 77–79, 88, 89; temporal structure
of, 78–79. See also under authority; marriage
running-slave scene, 105n.57, 195–97

safety-valve theory of comedy, 20–21
Saturnalia, (hodie/cras, today/tomorrow,
temporary inversion), 40, 43, 46, 79, 94,
107, 156

Scodel, R., 59n.48
Scott, J., 18, 21n.32, 23n.38, 25n.40
Segal, E., 5n.1, 20n.31, 35, 39–40, 43n.13,
48n.21, 58n.47, 72n.74, 79, 117, 167n.2,
172n.15, 212n.4
senex, 16n.24, 40, 176–78, 185–86,
204–5, 206; senex amator, 54, 75, 82, 94,
114–15, 115–17, 201–2; —, as assimilated
to adulescens, 91–93, 105–6 —, Jupiter in
Am as, 115–17; —, plot-type associated
with, 103–4; —, as rebel, 37, 39, 46, 86–
87, 91–93, 96, 98–100; —, relation to
uxor dotata, 67–70, 94, 115–17,
118n.83; —, resolution associated with,
112, 113n.76; senex iratus, 44n.15, 155
servus bonus, 70–73, 160, 172, 184–85; distinguished from callidus, 60, 82, 87–88, 187;
ideological force of, 26–27; language of,
131n.20, 146–47; relation to naturalistic
mode, 29
servus callidus, 42n.9, 43n.14, 46, 127–30,
130–33, 141–42, 164, 189–90, 211–13; adulescens and, in Persa, 33–34, 122–27,
127–28; contrasted to parasite, 195–96,
202–3; contrasted to servus bonus, 26–28,
60, 71–73, 82, 87–88, 187; ideological
force of, 19–21, 26–28, 158–61, 172–73;
lack of interest in manumission, 95n.35,
119, 124n.2, 160–61, 190, 212; language
of, 130–31, 138–39, 141n.53, 192–93;
—, used by other characters, 43, 54,
96n.40, 113, 150, 160; metatheatrical
style of, 83–84, 103, 105, 129; as notional
template of farcical rebel/trickster, 38, 94,
108, 111, 113, 194–95; relation to farcical
mode, 14, 16, 29; role in resolutions, 76,
109–10, 113n.76
sexuality, 88, 108, 120–21; between masters
and slaves, 80, 100–102, 106, 108n.68,
139, 161; food and, 54n.38, 117–19; homosexuality and heterosexuality, 45–46,
106, 180n.25; parasites and, 151, 183;
used as punishment, 88, 155–57; of
women, 70, 117–18, 161–62
Shakespeare, William, 57, 76; Comedy of Errors, 75n.77; Two Gentlemen of Verona,
117n.82
Sharrock, A., 7n.6
Situation comedy (sit-coms, TV), 8n.7,
79n.7
Slater, N., 14n.23, 42n.9, 53n.33, 78n.4,
92n.29, 135n.35, 137, 156

slavery: analogous to marriage, 79–81, 100–103, 106, 108–9, 111; comparison of Rome to other slave societies, 19n.30; by condition/by nature, 169–70, 186n.41, 193; ideology of (mastery), 17n.27, 19–28, 36–37, 42–43, 49–50, 59–60, 70, 123–24, 157, 163–64, 169–73, 187–88, 209, 211–13; loyalty, 171, 188; relation to dialogism, 29–30; relation to farce, 79, 103; resistance, 24–25, 27, 36, 94–95, 138–39, 158; *See also under* authority; economic life; parent-child relationships; *servus bonus*; *servus callidus*; sexuality

Spranger, P., 14n.23, 26nn.42, 43

Stace, C., 26n.42

Stallybrass, P., and A. White, 29n.49

stylization: stylized language, 7–9, 127, 130–31, 139–40, 177, 185, 188, 192

Tacitus, *Annals* XIV.42–45: 25n.41

Terence, 9n.10, 183n.33

Thalmann, W. G., 172n.13

trickery: authority figure as trickster, 28, 30–31, 43, 93, 98, 115–16; blocking character, as target of, 123, 135; as an end in itself, 82, 160, 172–73, 203; language of divinity for tricksters, 58n.47; in naturalistic mode, 31, 48–49, 51–54, 73, 188–89,

190, 193–95; relation to dialogism, 26, 73, 125, 136–37, 173–74, 188–89, 208; relation to farcical mode, 12–13, 14, 30, 38, 138; relation to teleology of plot, 16n.24, 78, 109–10; resistance to, within farce, 160–61; style of, in relation to household authority, 83–84, 85–86, 93, 96–97, 100; *uxor dotata* as trickster, 80, 100, 103–4, 110–12; women and, 107, 179. *See also under* authority; farce; *servus callidus*

Tyche (Chance), 37, 125, 154, 162, 167, 170, 188, 196, 201, 206, 208–9

uxor, 118–19; *uxor dotata*, 67–70, 82, 89–90, 94, 95, 102, 117, 118n.83, 121n.87, 159n.95, 201–2; —, as compared to *meretrix*, 44–45, 64–65, 66–67, 69–70, 118–19; —, legal language and, 94n.33, 95; —, parasites and, 118n.83; —, as trickster/rebel/internal playwright, 100, 103–4, 109–10, 110–12, 117, 119

Varro, *de Re Rustica* I.17.1: 22n.35

Wiles, D., 11n.17, 12n.18

Woytek, E., 123n.1, 131nn.21, 22, 133n.25

Wright, J., 7, 9, 14n.23, 15, 18n.27